# CROPPING AND FARMING SYSTEMS

# CROPPING AND FARMING SYSTEMS

*By*

**Dr. Renuka Sharma**

**DISCOVERY PUBLISHING HOUSE PVT. LTD.**
**NEW DELHI-110 002**

*Published by:*
**Tilak Wasan**

**DISCOVERY PUBLISHING HOUSE PVT. LTD.**
4383/4B, Ansari Road, Darya Ganj
New Delhi-110 002 (India)
*Phone* : +91-11-23279245, 43596064-65
*Fax* : +91-11-23253475
*E-mail* : discoverypublishinghouse@gmail.com
sales@discoverypublishinggroup.com
parul.wasan@gmail.com
*web* : www.discoverypublishinggroup.com

*Reprinted:* 2019
***First Edition:* 2014**

**ISBN: 978-93-5056-371-7**

**Cropping and Farming Systems**



*Printed at:*
Dynamic Printers
Delhi

# Preface

Cropping systems vary among farms depending on the available resources and constraints; geography and climate of the farm; government policy; economic, social and political pressures; and the philosophy and culture of the farmers. In tropical environments, all of these cropping systems are practiced. In subtropical and arid environments, the timing and extent of agriculture may be limited by rainfall, either not allowing multiple annual crops in a year, or requiring irrigation. Altering crops through breeding practices changes the genetic make-up of a plant to develop crops with more beneficial characteristics for humans, for example, larger fruits or seeds, drought-tolerance, or resistance to pests.

In modern times, this struggle takes the form of multiple cropping, intensive cultivation of high yielding varieties, integrated farming and mixed cropping with a view to keeping land, labour, capital and other resources occupied for the maximum period during the year, maintaining their productive efficiency at the highest level and thereby, attaining the highest yields in terms of agricultural production as well as return on the resources employed.

—*Author*

# Contents

1

# Introduction

## CROPPING SYSTEM

A cropping system may be defined as a community of plants which is managed by a farm unit to achieve various human goals. The latter include food, fibre and other raw materials, wealth and satisfaction. Conway encompassed these multiple goals in the phrase 'increased social value'. Farmers are part of the system. They are able to set, or modify, their own goals, so two farms with identical climates and soils may be managed with different aims to achieve a different mix of outputs.

**Table 1.1. Properties of Agro-ecosystems and Their Assessment**

| Property | Measure |
|---|---|
| Effectiveness | Opinion, or econometric measure of satisfaction |
| Production | Output of system (*e.g.*, yield of grain per household) |
| Productivity | Output per unit land (*e.g.*, yield of grain per hectare) or per unit of labour, capital or any technological input |
| Stability | Coefficient of variation, across region or time |
| Sustainability | • Resource change: rate of decrease or increase in key indicators or resources, *e.g.*, soil pH<br>• Forcing: level of inputs (*e.g.*, fertilizer) necessary to maintain characteristic resource and production levels |

(*Contd...*)

| | |
|---|---|
| | • Inertia: level of perturbation (*e.g.*, rainfall event) that can be accommodated without system change<br>• Elasticity: recovery time to return to trend line after perturbation (*e.g.*, number of years after drought)<br>• Amplitude: maximum displaced attribute level (*e.g.*, productivity, say in tonnes per hectare per annum) from which recovery is possible |
| Equitability | Income ranking of population |

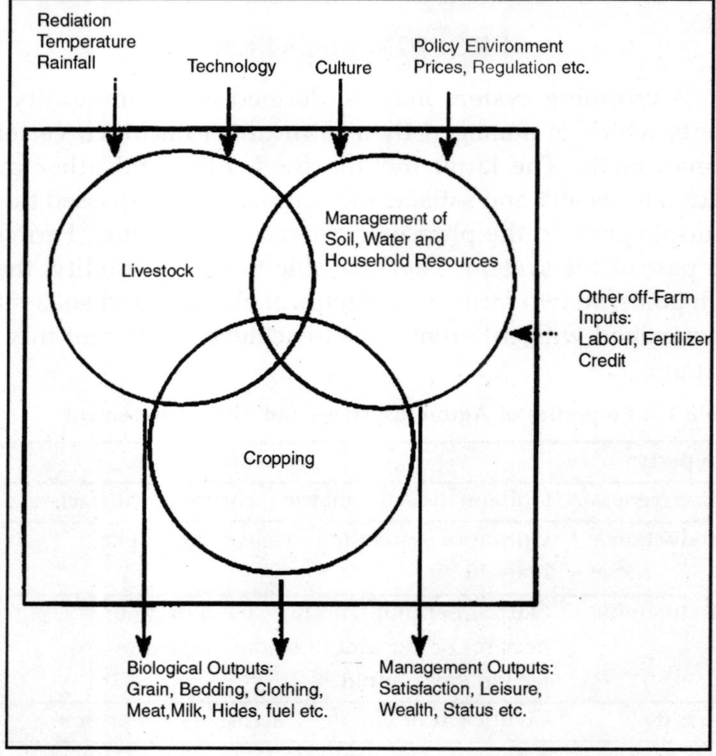


**Fig 1.1. A Farming System or Farm-household System**

IRRI gives a more detailed definition of a cropping system: '.the crop production activity of a farm. It comprises all cropping patterns grown on the farm and their interaction with farm resources, other household enterprises and the physical, biological, technological and sociological factors or environments". This is illustrated in Figure in which the cropping system is one of three sub-systems likely to be present within a broader farming system.

Food security is the most basic output from a cropping system. For a subsistence household, all other outputs are secondary. For corporate agriculture, under a sophisticated cash economy, food security is established and other goals, such as profit, predominate. Thus, the first property of a cropping system is its effectiveness; that is its ability to meet the needs of the goal-setter (the farmer or corporate manager, etc.).

The effectiveness of a system is a subjective attribute which should be assessed by the goal-setters and their society. It can be estimated or quantified through surveys using ranking techniques or by econometrical devices such as shadow pricing and opportunity costing (Table).

To illustrate the importance of assessing the effectiveness of a cropping system, consider Figure. Here, in a survey, 270 Indonesian households were classed into six types (*e.g.*, aiming to be self-sufficient in food, wage-earning or in commercial agriculture) and, depending on their diet and the possibility of their diet being inadequate at some times of year, they were assigned to four classes of 'food insecurity'. Households managing cropping systems for self-sufficiency occur in all categories of food insecurity.

A successful household whose cropping system supports them in a 'food secure' state, will have different opinions on the effectiveness of their cropping system from a neighbouring 'food insecure' household that also aims at self sufficiency. Furthermore, it is likely that their attitudes to risk-taking and change are likely to be quite different. This is in part because of the difference in effectiveness of the two systems. One family may be open to innovation and the other perhaps caught in a spiral of conservative thinking and poverty.

Production is a most obvious output and measure of the activity of a cropping system. It can be measured as the biological or economic output from the system, for example as the grain or cash generated. It is implicitly an output from the activity of one or more management units (*e.g.*, families). It is also a measure of the efficiency of the management of the cropping system and can be related to productivity-measured as output per unit of input (land, labour, capital, energy) (Table).

Conway (1985) defines other ecosystem properties as sustainability, stability and equitability (Figure). Of these, sustainability, the subject of this *Bulletin,* is the most difficult to define and estimate. FAO (1989b) states that the goal of sustainable agriculture is to 'maintain production at levels necessary to meet the increasing aspirations of an expanding world population without degrading the environment', and that sustainability 'implies concern for the generation of income, the promotion of appropriate policies, and the conservation of natural resources'.

Similarly, sustainable agriculture and rural development are defined as 'the management and conservation of the natural resource base, and the orientation of technological and institutional change in such a manner as to ensure the attainment and continued satisfaction of human needs for present and future generations'.

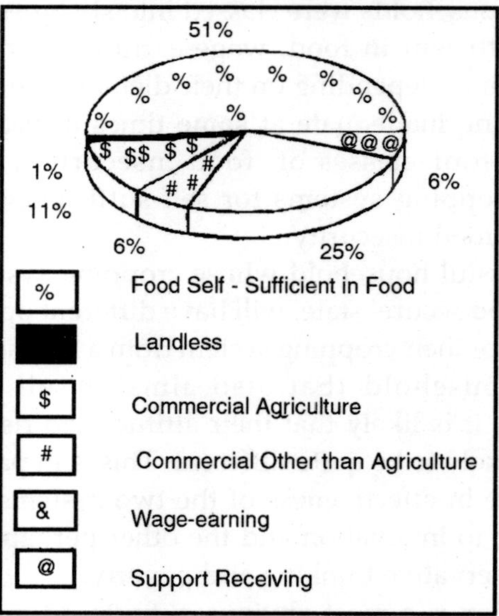


**Fig 1.2. Four Classes of Food Insecurity, Based on Diet and Possible Seasonal food Shortage Among Indonesian Households.**

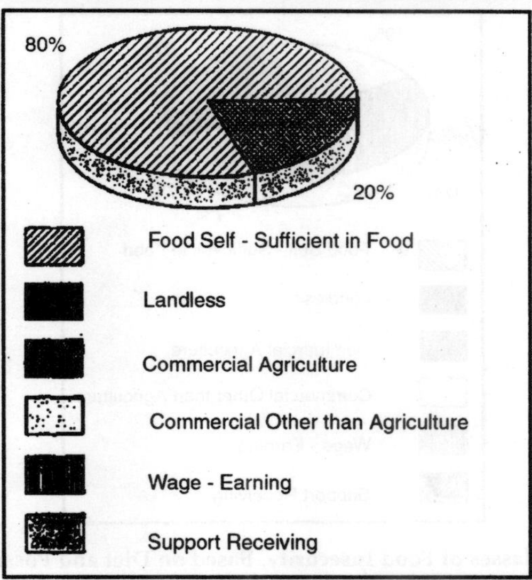


**Fig 1.3. Four Classes of Food Insecurity, Based on Diet and Possible Seasonal food Shortage Among Indonesian Households**

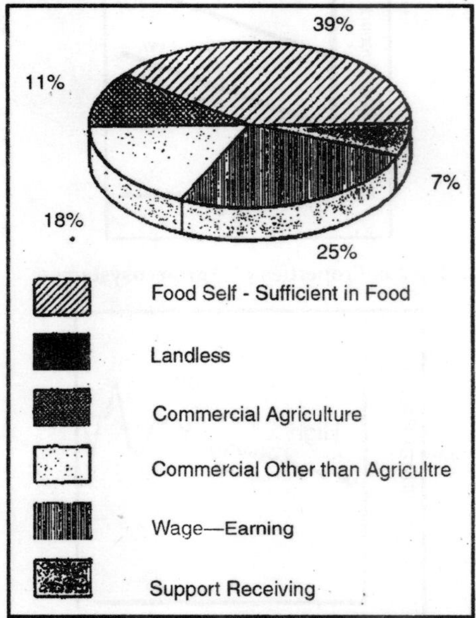


**Fig 1.4. Four Classes of Food Insecurity, Based on Diet and Possible Seasonal food Shortage Among Indonesian Households**

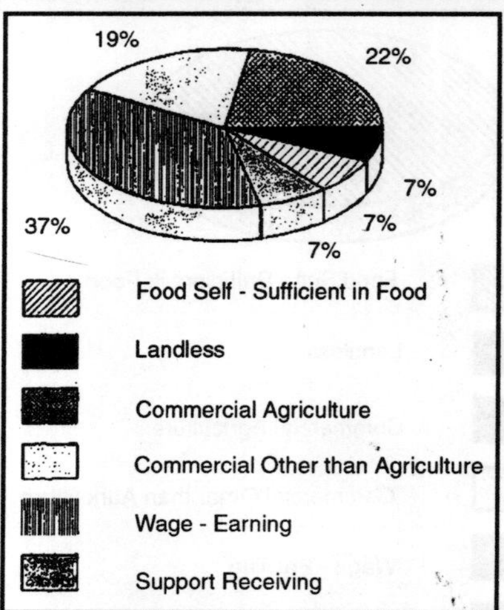


**Fig 1.5. Four Classes of Food Insecurity, Based on Diet and Possible Seasonal Food Shortage Among Indonesian Households**

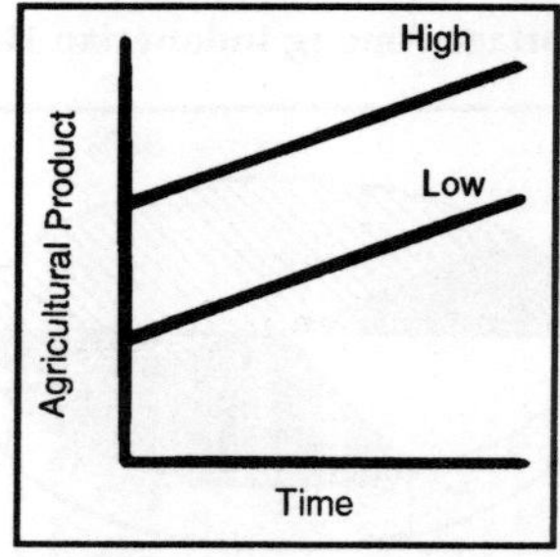


**Fig 1.6. Properties of Agro-ecosystems**

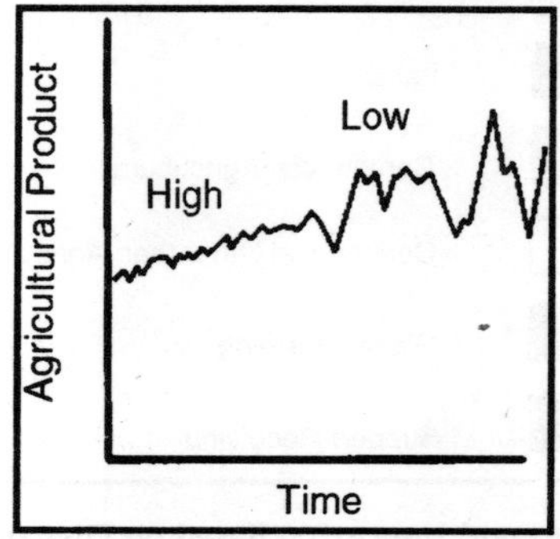


**Fig 1.7. Properties of Agro-ecosystems**

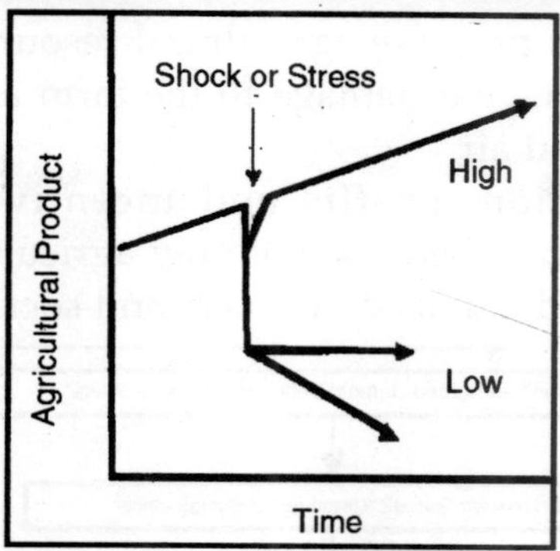


**Fig 1.8. Properties of Agro-ecosystems**

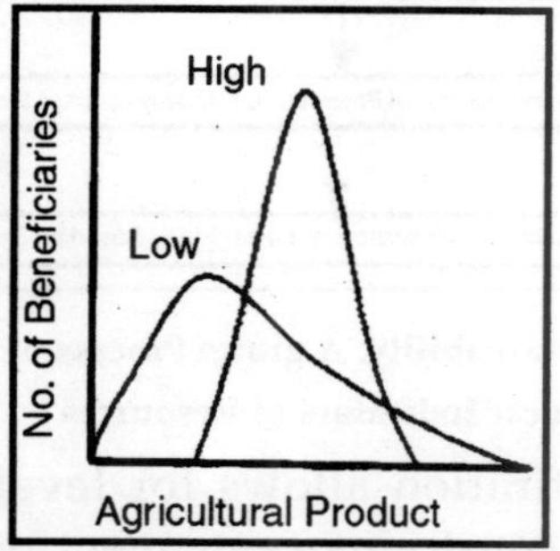


**Fig 1.9. Properties of Agro-ecosystems**

Conway defines sustainability as the ability of an ecosystem to maintain productivity when subjected to a major disturbing force. He is thus forced to draw a continuum between stability (in the face of minor, expected forces) and sustainability (in response to major forces). He also indicates that to assess sustainability, one needs a measure 'of the effectiveness of internal adjustments that agro-ecosystems make in response to stresses and shocks'. A more pragmatic definition of sustainability, with which most agronomists would agree, is that 'a sustainable cropping system... is one which maintains resources, such as soil and water, while providing an adequate and economic level of production, both now and for generations to come'.

Similarly, a sustainable system is one in which:

- Resources are kept in balance with their use through conservation, recycling or renewal.

- Practices preserve agricultural resources and prevent environmental damage to the farm and off-site land, water and air.
- Production, profits and incentives retain their importance, because not only agriculture needs to be sustained, but so do farmers and society.

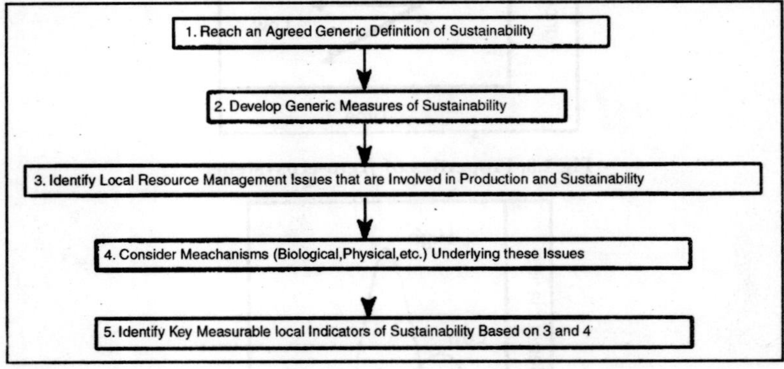


**Fig 1.10. Measuring Sustainability: A group Process of Identification of Generic and Local Indicators of Resources**

Conway's definition allows for levels, or degrees, of sustainability but constrains assessment of sustainability to measurements after shock. Hoare and others define a sustainable system in terms easy to relate to, but often do not accommodate degrees of sustainability, which is unhelpful for management and policy development. Here, Conway's concept is accepted that it is useful to consider the possibility of various degrees of sustainability, and the widespread, but rarely developed, implication that sustainability should be measurable in either biological or economic terms (just as in measuring productivity). It follows that a biologically sustainable system may not be economically sustainable. This is witnessed by land in various parts of Europe and elsewhere that has gone in and out of cropping on several occasions during historic times depending on economic conditions.

Here, sustainability is defined consistent with FAO, as the ability of a cropping system to maintain productivity over a long term. Since, this definition implies also maintenance of resources such as soil, it requires that all participants (farmers, researchers, extension specialists and policy-makers) agree upon appropriate measures by which the sustainability of particular cropping systems are assessed.

An operational schema is given in Figure. Generic measures of sustainability were proposed by Conway and others, Here, forcing, inertia, elasticity and amplitude are offered as functional measures (Table).

**Table 1.2. Indicators of Key Natural Resources in Rainfed Cropping and Animal Production Systems**

| | |
|---|---|
| Nutrient balance | Organic matter-rate of change<br>Nitrogen cycling-especially when using grain legumes in rotation with cereals<br>Monitoring phosphorus, sulphur and potassium<br>Micro-nutrients |
| Erosion | Vegetation cover-includes trees as well as stubble<br>Soil surface cover-stubble retained (30 per cent sufficient to prevent wind and water erosion)<br>Stream bank<br>Sheet and gully erosion |
| Productivity, yield and quality | Water use/efficiency-*i.e.*, actual *versus* potential (in some areas the potential is much less than the actual) (biomass/ grain yield/US dollars), recharge (dryland salinity and nutrient leaching)<br>Pasture composition-legume and perennial content<br>Matched animal versus pasture production-appropriate enterprise selection/capability<br>Maintenance of genetic base/ improvement |
| Soil structure | Infiltration<br>Permeability/water storage |

(*Contd...*)

| | |
|---|---|
| | Stability<br>Waterlogging<br>Compaction |
| pH | Change<br>Toxicity-deficiency<br>Indicator plants |
| Energy efficiency | Input *versus* output of the whole agricultural system |
| Biological factors | Soil macro/micro flora and fauna<br>Animal health<br>Plant health (root growth and other)<br>Pests (animals and plants) |
| Farm management skills | Understanding-a good indicator would be the understanding the farmers have of their own technical system |

**Table 1.3. Key Measurements of Sustainability in Rainfed Cropping and Animal Production Systems**

| Indicator | Why | Process/measurement |
|---|---|---|
| Water use efficiency | Easy to relate production to rainfall; usable for both crops and pastures | Yield (kg/mm/ha); at scales of farm, shire and region to detect trends in time and between areas |
| Soil health | A direct expression of sustainability of system | Soil analysis of pH (trends), nutrient balance, direct measurement of worm counts, surveys of microflora |
| Farm management skills | Understanding is needed before change occurs; good level required for financial survival | Farm records and farm surveys; units of cash flow, debt equity, whole-farm planning |

It is important that everyone involved in an assessment of the sustainability of a cropping system should agree on an inventory of resources which encapsulates its essential features. From this, the most critical attributes and, in some cases, those most easy to estimate, can be identified (Figure ). Table illustrates the type of resource inventory that might be agreed necessary to define the sustainability of a semi-arid cropping system. Defined critical resources will differ for other systems. After defining the critical resources, it is necessary to identify those indices of sustainability that are easily and relatively-cheaply measured. Some measurements emerging from consideration of Tables.

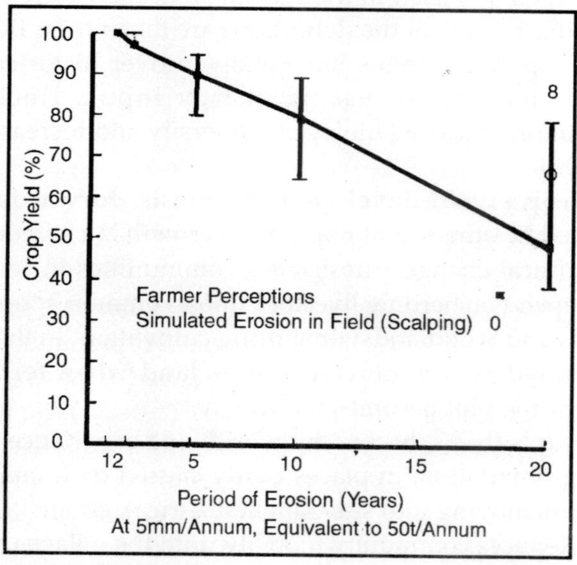


**Fig 1.11. Crop Yield Declines with Continuing Soil Degradation and Erosion.-In this Study, farmers' Perceptions of the Rate of Decline in Crop Yield Related Well to Soil Loss through Simulated Erosion**

If a system is not sustainable, remedial action depends on agreement on the extent of non-sustainability and the changes in inputs to make it sustainable. Some research is encouraging here: for example, Rickson *et al.* find reasonable agreement between farmers' perceptions of the impact of continued soil loss on sustainability, as estimated by the extent of decline in wheat yields.

Stability (or variability) is the constancy of productivity in the face of small disturbances such as seasonal or year-to-year fluctuations in weather. It is a measure of the spatial- or year-to-year robustness of a farming practice and reflects not only variations in crop response to weather and soil type, but also variations in prices of inputs (such as labour and pesticides) and of the product. Last, but not least, equitability is the property that reflects how the resources and outcomes of the cropping systems are shared among the population.

## EVOLUTION OF FIELD CROP ECOSYSTEMS

Various terms used in the sections that follow are defined in Appendix 1. Most of the definitions are taken from IRRI and ICRAF. Cropping systems have evolved over historical time along a catena of increasing energy inputs (including mechanisation), reduced biological diversity and increased risk or instability.

Boserup (1965) developed the thesis, forwarded and embellished by others, that population growth is a precondition for agricultural change. Subsistence communities in semi-arid regions depend on herding livestock (most common in semi-arid grasslands and woodlands) or shifting cultivation. In the latter, the cultivated plot is moved to new land when fertility is depleted or the plot becomes too weedy.

Boserup's thesis, backed by worldwide experience, is that increasing population, in places partly caused by immigration (*e.g.*, settlers moving into sub-Sahelian Africa), either:

- Reduces community mobility until the villages become static and maintain permanent fields;
- Already semi-permanent villages are so deprived of hunting/foraging grounds that they too need to develop permanent cropping systems. As the fallow period between crops is shortened and the fields become more permanent, two strategies are available;
- Extensification and/or increased mechanisation. For example, use of draught animals or tractors;
- Intensification including use of shorter fallows, perhaps coupled with use of unused poorer land. This

is accompanied by increased complexity of cropping, *e.g.*, household gardens, and environmental modification, *e.g.*, irrigation.

Okigbo comprehensively described these changes in cropping systems, and their implications for sustainability.

## EXTENSIFICATION

Extensification of cropping requires livestock for draught, or mechanisation. Extensification may encourage supplementary pasture systems outside, as well as part of, the cropping systems themselves. It is also possible to develop extensive cropping without livestock. Agriculture in northeast Argentina and parts of Brazil, for example, has shifted directly from uncultivated grasing land or unused bush to extensive, mechanised cropping. Where cropping and livestock farming develop together, there are options as to their integration. In semi-arid Australia, mechanised extensification of 60 million ha of arable land has seen little (long term) change in the ratio of crop to pasture. Pasture land has increased in area since, about 1930 to stabilise at about 28 million ha in 1970.

Though livestock are not used for draught, this extensification has maintained a close link between crops and pasture in an integrated ley farming system. In contrast, in the semi-arid Near East, extensive cropping has been developed by private landholders without livestock. Here pasturage remains largely in the public domain with nomadic herds and common grasing land. Thus, though Australia and the Near East both have crop and livestock subsystems, in Australia they are integrated and managed by one family or corporation but in the Near East they may be separate and owned by distinct social groups.

## INTENSIFICATION

Intensification involves biological or environmental modification. Biological modification occurs by increasing the complexity of a local cropping system by the development of multi-storied household gardens, relay cropping or mixed cropping. It is done by individual households. It increases labour inputs, diversifies crop management (though not necessarily crop diversity which may be greatest in hunter-gatherer systems), and usually increases the range of livestock (chickens, ducks, goats, fish and sometimes cattle are common in Javanese household gardens). It may reduce insect herbivores. Importantly, it creates food and income stability. Biological intensification can also be carried out on a larger, usually corporate scale. Multi-story plantation crops, such as beans under coffee, alley cropping and agroforestry, seek high outputs per unit area and stability in ways analogous to complex household gardens. Such intensification appreciably modifies the micro-environment as a secondary outcome. For example, tree legumes were planted along fence-lines in semi-arid Ethiopia in the late 1980s to provide quality forage for cattle and income from the sale of seeds. The trees provided shade and habitats for birds, which became more prized by villagers than the forage.

**Fig 1.12. An agro-climatic classification of world climates into 10 Regions (Listed in Figure) and 34 Classes**

**Table 1.4. System Properties of the home Garden when Compared with a Rice Field**

| | Home Garden | Rice Field |
|---|---|---|
| 1 | 2 | 3 |
| Productivity | Higher standing biomass<br>Higher net income | Higher gross income |

*(Contd...)*

| 1 | 2 | 3 |
|---|---|---|
| | (low inputs)<br>Greater variety of production (food, medicines, fuelwood) | |
| Stability | Year-round production ('living granary')<br>More stable from year to year | Seasonal production<br>Vulnerable to climatic and disease variation |
| Sustainability | Maintenance of soil fertility<br>Protection from soil erosion | Heavy pest and disease attack |
| Equitability | Home gardens in most households<br>Barter of products | Product to land owners |

Intensification can also be carried out by deliberate modification of the environment, most obviously through irrigation.

Intensification, whether by biological or environmental modification, generally gives:

- Greater diversity of land use.
- Some intensively-used cropping land, usually in areas with favourable hydrology, fertility or social attributes (*e.g.*, prior settlement, easy transport).
- Some under-used or unused land. Cropping systems in Mediterranean lands often show these features, though there under-used land sometimes reflects lack of population pressure.

It is notable that extensification of cropping systems can create relative uniformity but intensification creates diversity. Neither, however, has a predictable social or environmental outcome. Extensification, often using monocultures, can be inherently stable and sustainable, or not. The social distribution of its benefits may be egalitarian (giving either uniform prosperity, or uneconomic, socially-deprived family farms), or it may be hierarchical with economically-strong landowners and a landless class of labourers and farmhands. Intensification at the household level benefits the family directly; intensification through village cooperatives or corporations may be advantageous or create negative social and environmental outcomes. Table illustrates this for a home garden and a rice field.

## DRYLANDS

FAO (1987) uses the term 'drylands' to describe climates with fewer than 120 days growing season. These are divided into 'arid drylands' with less than 75 days growing season, and 'semi-arid' areas which have from 75 to 119 days growing season (Table). Seasonal changes in indices of crop growth in tropical drylands, classed by Hutchinson *et al, as* having climate types I (hot, seasonally wet/dry: uppermost row) or E (warm, seasonally wet/ dry: middle row), and in temperate drylands (lowermost row). Growth index () is a dimensionless index from zero (no growth) to 1 (maximum growth).

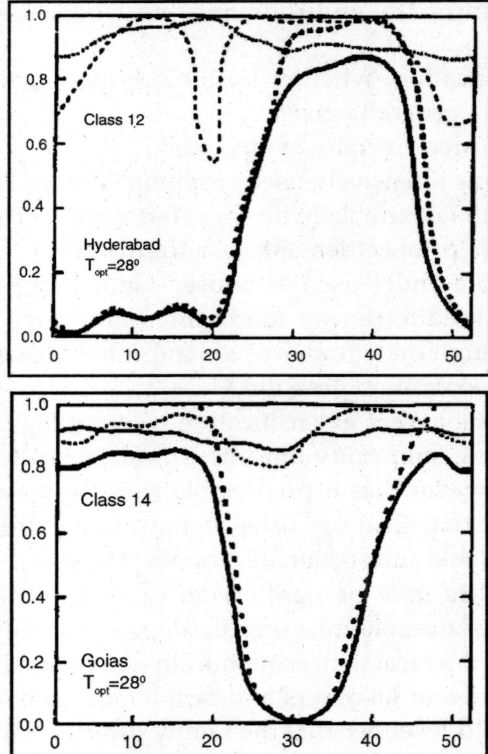

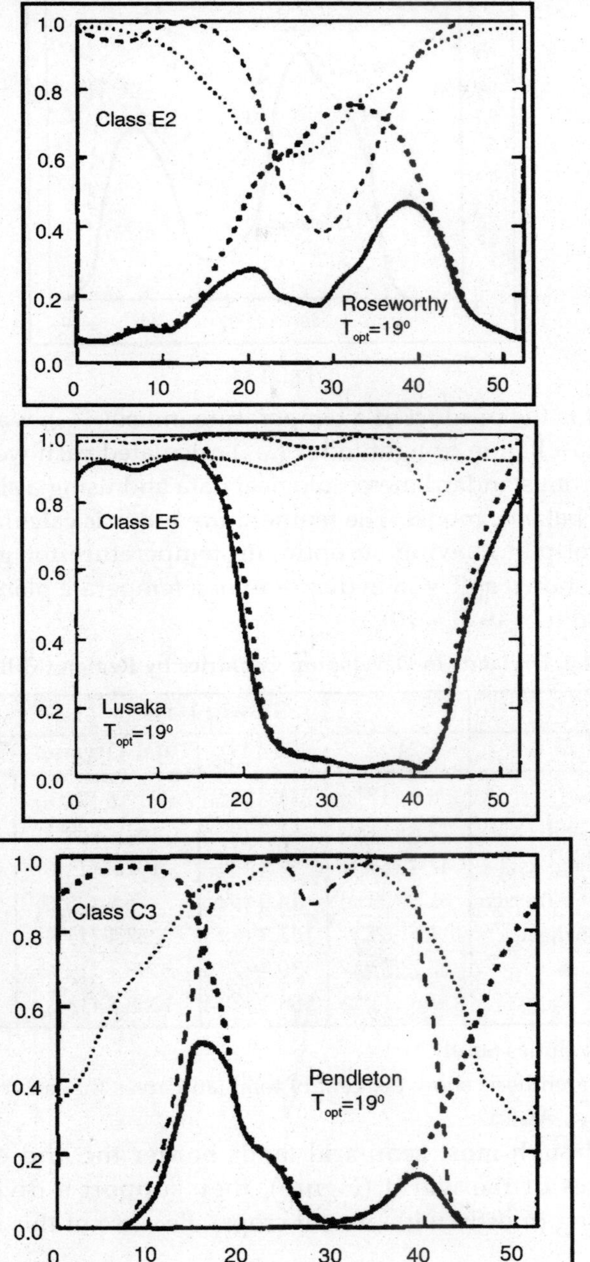
1.0
0.8
0.6
0.4
0.2
0.0
0
10
20
30
40
50
Class E2
Roseworthy
$T_{opt}$=19°
Class E5
Lusaka
$T_{opt}$=19°
Class C3
Pendleton
$T_{opt}$=19°

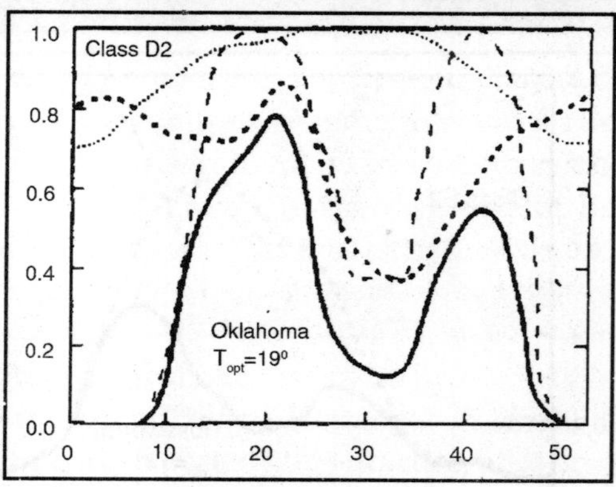


Fig. 1.13

It is the product of a temperature index (--- -), water index () and radiation or light index (.....) calculated each week of the year from standard meteorological data and using a simple soil water balance model. The temperature index is calculated for a tropical plant having an optimum temperature for growth of 28°C (shown as T = 28 in diagram) or a temperate plant with an optimum of 19 (T = 19).

**Table 1.5. Drylands in Developing Countries by Region (Million ha)**

| | Growth Days | | | |
|---|---|---|---|---|
| | <74 | 75-119 | Total Drylands | Total Area |
| Africa | 488.0 (17%) | 231.8 (8%) | 719.8 (25%) | 2878.1 |
| Southwest Asia | 72.6 (11%) | 61.8 (9%) | 134.4 (20%) | 677.4 |
| Southeast Asia | 47.4 (5%) | 54.9 (6%) | 102.3 (11%) | 897.6 |
| Central America | 62.3 (23%) | 14.5 (5%) | 76.8 (28%) | 271.6 |
| South America | 114.6 (6%) | 142.8 (8%) | 257.4 (14%) | 1770.2 |
| East Asia | 27.7 (3%) | 70.4 (7%) | 98.1 (10%) | 954.6 |
| Total | 812.6 (11%) | 586.2 (7%) | 1388.8 (18%) | 7449.5 |

*Note*: Excludes South Africa.

Parenthesis show per cent of total land areas for each region, *e.g.*, Africa.

Though most semi-arid lands border the arid or desert climates of the world (Figure), they support a diversity of cropping (mostly with annual crops). Because of this diversity their climate should be quantified and any variations within them delineated. Such drylands have either one or two wet seasons. Bimodal rainfall regimes are characteristically found in latitudes between the wet tropics and the unimodal more temperate, semi-arid zones. Their distribution, however, is governed more by pressure systems and land masses. For example, bimodal patterns are rarely found in east Asia. In the tropics, the wet season(s) coincide with a high solar angle except for a relatively small area in east Brazil. The tropical drylands are commonly called monsoon (in Asia) or savannah (in Africa) although there is confusion over these terms. Koppen uses 'monsoon' in a restricted sense, as a climate with a dry season but able to support rainforest. In temperate areas, there is usually a single wet season that coincides with a low solar angle (winter). These wet-and-dry climates are generally called Mediterranean and, on the drier margins, semi-arid.

The tropical drylands (to use FAO's term) are categorised I and E by Hutchinson *et al.*, (1992); and the temperate drylands as E, D and C on the basis of seasonably of available water and temperature. This delineation of climates is based on calculations of the relative constraints of soil water, temperature and solar radiation on growth of temperate and tropical crops. Each of the indices ranges from zero (no growth) to 1 (climate optimal for growth). The water, temperature and radiation indices are multiplied together to calculate a growth index, which is an estimate of the overall suitability of the location for crop growth in a particular week or month of the year. Hutchinson's climate classification, unlike more traditional, geographically-oriented classifications, reflects seasonal fluctuations of environmental factors related quantitatively to crop growth. Examples relevant to the tropical drylands and climatically-similar wet-and-dry temperate areas, are shown in Figure.

Tropical drylands that support cropping have mean annual water indices as low as 0.29, but have a growth index (the product of the water, temperature and radiation indices) during the highest quarter (three-month period) greater than 0.3 (commonly 0.3-0.8). This is sufficient to support good growth of a single crop. Zone I coincides with parts of the Aw, Bsh and Cwa types of Koppen (1900) and Trewartha and corresponds with the 1.3, 1.4, 1.5, 1.7 and 1.9 zones of Papadakis. Hutchinson's E zone, which is not as hot coincides with parts of Koppen's Cfa, Cwa and Bsh types and Papadakis' zones 1.7, 2, 4.2 and 5 in the tropics.

**Table 1.6. Classification of Climates: Critical Characteristics which Hutchinson et al. use to Define 34 Agro-climatic zones. $TI_{19}$ and $TI_{28}$ are the Thermal Indices for Temperate crops (having an Optimum Temperature for growth of 19°C) and tropical crops (28°C), MI is Water Index and GI is the growth index derived from Multiplying the Monthly Water, Temperature and Radiation Indices.**

| Group | Annual Mean $TI_{19}$ | Highest Quarter $GI_{19}$ | Annual Mean $TI_{28}$ | Highest Quarter $GI_{28}$ | Annual Mean MI |
|---|---|---|---|---|---|
| 1 | 2 | 3 | 4 | 5 | 6 |
| Very Cold | | | | | |
| A | 0.09 | 0.16 | 0.00 | 0.00 | 0.82 |
| Cold | | | | | |
| B1 | 0.27 | 0.57 | 0.04 | 0.10 | 0.90 |
| B2 | 0.42 | 0.72 | 0.05 | 0.13 | 0.94 |
| Cool, Dry | | | | | |
| C1 | 0.49 | 0.13 | 0.25 | 0.06 | 0.23 |
| C2 | 0.39 | 0.28 | 0.14 | 0.11 | 0.45 |
| C3 | 0.56 | 0.31 | 0.27 | 0.10 | 0.45 |
| C4 | 0.49 | 0.41 | 0.27 | 0.32 | 0.32 |
| Cool, Wet | | | | | |
| D1 | 0.38 | 0.64 | 0.17 | 0.40 | 0.59 |
| D2 | 0.49 | 0.57 | 0.38 | 0.61 | 0.53 |
| 03 | 0.43 | 0.78 | 0.13 | 0.33 | 0.91 |
| 04 | 0.50 | 0.79 | 0.26 | 0.56 | 0.88 |
| 05 | 0.63 | 0.66 | 0.17 | 0.18 | 0.76 |
| Warm, Seasonally Wet/Dry | | | | | |
| E1 | 0.81 | 0.65 | 0.35 | 0.13 | 0.55 |

*(Contd...)*

| 1 | 2 | 3 | 4 | 5 | 6 |
|---|---|---|---|---|---|
| E2 | 0.79 | 0.37 | 0.37 | 0.09 | 0.37 |
| E3 | 0.75 | 0.46 | 0.36 | 0.30 | 0.45 |
| E4 | 0.79 | 0.30 | 0.56 | 0.34 | 0.32 |
| E5 | 0.97 | 0.85 | 0.51 | 0.51 | 0.57 |
| E6 | 0.80 | 0.19 | 0.47 | 0.12 | 0.17 |
| E7 | 0.89 | 0.69 | 0.54 | 0.62 | 0.62 |
| E8 | 0.90 | 0.51 | 0.60 | 0.47 | 0.29 |
| **Warm, Wet** | | | | | |
| F1 | 0.57 | 0.78 | 0.43 | 0.81 | 0.91 |
| F2 | 0.74 | 0.77 | 0.66 | 0.86 | 0.89 |
| F3 | 0.84 | 0.81 | 0.35 | 0.51 | 0.78 |
| F4 | 0.94 | 0.85 | 0.50 | 0.66 | 0.87 |
| F5 | 0.98 | 0.89 | 0.63 | 0.66 | 0.96 |
| **Warm to Hot, very Dry** | | | | | |
| G | 0.63 | 0.10 | 0.64 | 0.12 | 0.10 |
| **Hot, Dry** | | | | | |
| H | 0.56 | 0.19 | 0.89 | 0.44 | 0.20 |
| **Hot, Seasonally Wet/Dry** | | | | | |
| 11 | 0.51 | 0.48 | 0.96 | 0.87 | 0.52 |
| 12 | 0.53 | 0.40 | 0.81 | 0.82 | 0.38 |
| 13 | 0.62 | 0.60 | 0.78 | 0.87 | 0.64 |
| 14 | 0.90 | 0.80 | 0.82 | 0.78 | 0.65 |
| **Hot, wet** | | | | | |
| J1 | 0.65 | 0.66 | 0.94 | 0.84 | 0.66 |
| J2 | 0.59 | 0.62 | 0.96 | 0.88 | 0.82 |
| J3 | 0.68 | 0.67 | 0.94 | 0.88 | 0.97 |

The tropical drylands have close affinities with temperate semi-arid climates where annual cropping is practised. In the latter areas, the growing season exceeds the FAO limit of 119 days, and is often as much as 150-190 days because the cropping period coincides with the season of low temperature and evaporation. The C climates of Hutchinson *et al.*, (1992) are cool and dry while their cropping systems overlap with the dry margin of their D climates, which are cool but wetter (Table).

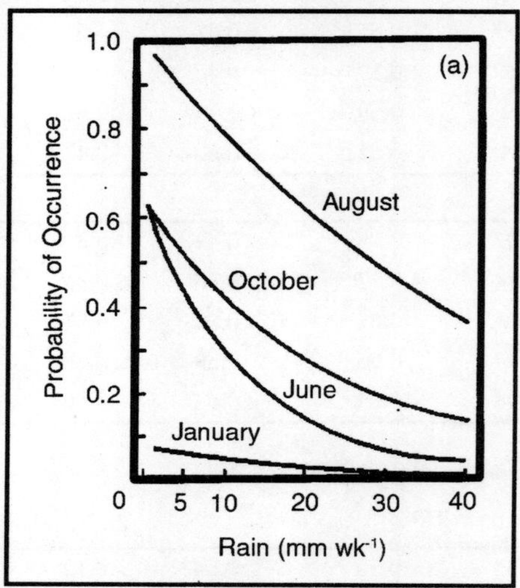


**Fig. 1.14. Probability of Occurrence of a Given Rainfall Intensity for three Soil types at Hyderabad, India (mm/week)**

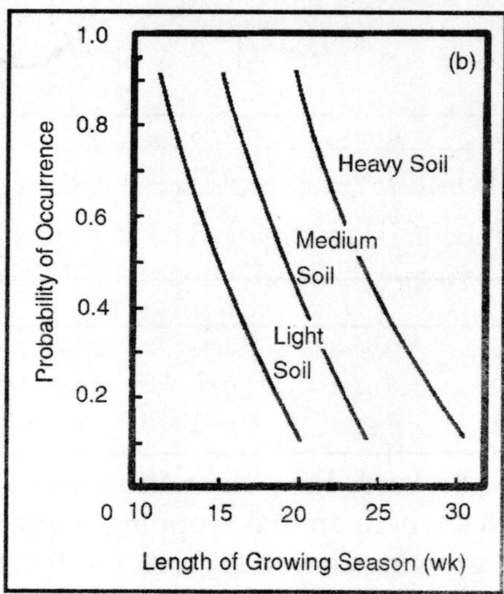


**Fig. 1.15. Probability of Occurrence of a given Length of Growing Season (weeks) for three Soil types at Hyderabad, India**

## SOILS

Figure shows the global distribution of the main soil patterns. The predominant soils of the semi-arid croplands are Luvisols and Calcisols in Africa and Australia, Mollisols and Luvisols in temperate areas of the Americas, Ferralsols in wet-and-dry tropical America, Luvisols and Chernozems in temperate Eurasia and Calcisols and some Acrisols in wet-and-dry tropical Eurasia.

The climatic distribution, area and chief limitations of the main major soil orders are shown in Figure. All these soils occur in seasonally wet-and-dry climates, although the Acrisols are not extensive in drylands (Figure). Lixisols, most widespread in potential cropping areas within seasonally wet-and-dry climates, have poor water-holding capacity, hard-setting surface horizons with a risk of crusting, run-off and erosion.

The topsoil texture varies from loamy sand to loam and clay, but the hard-setting properties and relatively poor infiltration and drainage (compared with, say, Acrisols) mean that crop growth is frequently limited by water availability. Figure shows a delay in sowing of about two weeks on Luvisols compared with adjacent Vertisols. Lixisols often have low levels of organic matter and generally low effective cation exchange capacity (ECEC). They are commonly deficient in phosphorus.

Calcisols are extensive, particularly in north and west Africa but, lying on the dry margin of cropland, they contribute less than Luvisols to crop production in semi-arid regions. They are high in bases, in places saline, and low in organic matter. Chemozems are relatively well structured and fertile with high levels of base saturation. Their topsoil does not harden on drying, as is common in Luvisols and Lixisols. Ferralsols and Acrisols are acid, highly weathered and more common on the wetter margins than in strictly semi-arid regions. Being highly weathered, they have low fertility and ECEC though they often have high levels of exchangeable aluminium. Applied fertilizer may be leached, because of the low ECEC, or made unavailable. They have high water infiltration capacity but a relatively low water-holding capacity and are susceptible to compaction.

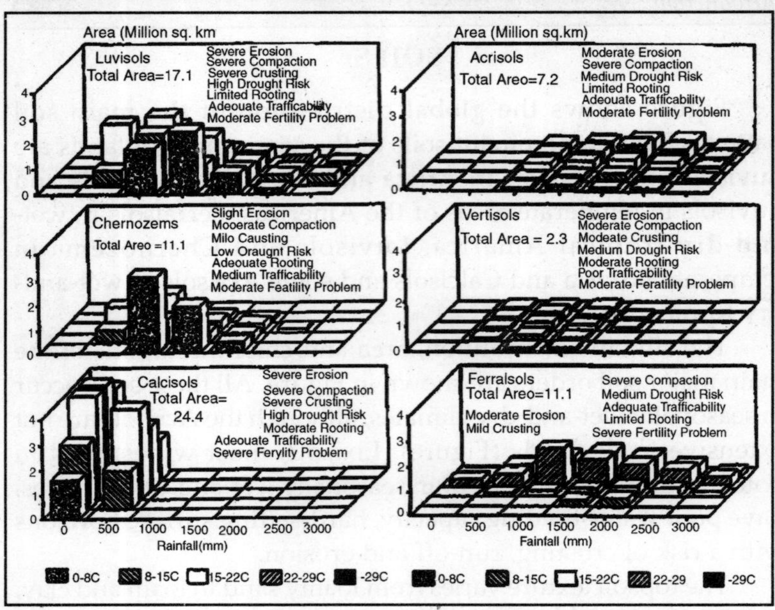


**Fig.1.17. Approximate Climatic Distribution, area and Chief Constraints of Selected Soil Orders**

Vertisols, dark-coloured cracking clays, though not extensive in all continents, are important in some seasonally wet-and-dry cropping systems. They have a high ECEC and base status and are often naturally fertile, though sometimes low in nitrogen, phosphorus and zinc. They have a large water-holding capacity. Their surface does not crust; they self-mulch as surface clods break down naturally on drying to small aggregates forming a good tilth.

The soil cracks deeply on drying, but as it re-wets the cracks close reducing infiltration and lateral movement of water. When wet the soils are so plastic and sticky that, in Australia, Vertisols were not cropped until tractors replaced horses thus enabling them to be ploughed quickly during the short period when soil moisture is optimum.

It is useful to draw attention to the major soil types and broad climate and soil groupings, as above. For example, the extensive cereal-fallow-pasture system, covering 60 million ha of temperate semi-arid Australia, is found on four broad types of soil and differences in crop rotations largely reflect regional soil differences. However, the more common situation is that soils are linked through topography and moisture regime to landscape, as illustrated in West Africa.

# 2

# Physical Aspects of Crop Productivity

## INTRODUCTION

The soil resources in this table fall into three broad groups, reflecting their underlying interrelationships: those related to soil structure (water use, structure, erosion) are dealt within this Chapter, those related to nutrition or biological factors are discussed later.

As this *Bulletin* deals with dryland crops, water availability is the major constraint on crop performance. Table suggests that water use efficiency (WUE) is a key measurement of performance. WUE reflects water availability (seasonably of rainfall) but also, importantly for management, it integrates the influences of factors such as the volume of soil exploitable by roots.

Long-term trends with time in WUE and trends between areas provide estimates of the relative sustainability of specific cropping systems. This is illustrated in Figure crops below the theoretical WUE line are less efficient or effective than they should be. One reason for such ineffectiveness is poor management during the growing season, for example weediness and nutrient deficiency. This is correctable, as shown by the vertical lines on Figure 2.1, where WUE was increased during experimental treatments. Other reasons for poor WUE are related more to fundamental issues associated with soils.

## INTERRELATIONSHIPS OF SOIL RESOURCES AND CROPPING SYSTEMS

A traditional view of the influence of soil is that it provides an opportunity, or a constraint on the type of cropping system that can be implemented and its productivity. A more responsible view is that 'the soil' combines various properties which interrelate and are directly influenced by the procedures of cropping. Figure 2.2 attempts to illustrate this for a non-sustainable cropping system, in which soil resources are declining through changes in surface properties, subsoil compaction, loss of organic matter and reduced biological activity. It shows that each of these properties may affect the others and that all can directly and indirectly reduce plant performance, as well as affecting other aspects including erosion, salinisation and acidification. Some of the mechanisms underlying these interconnections are described below.

## SOIL PORES AND WATER CHARACTERISTICS

Soils are made up of three parts: mineral materials, organic matter and space (called pore-or void-volume). The relative importance of these varies with soil type but pore space can occupy about half the volume of a medium-textured soil. At optimum water content for plant growth, approximately half the pore space is filled with water and half with air. The proportions of water and air can change rapidly depending on weather, evapotranspiration and other factors.

The dimensions (size, shape and arrangement) and number of pore spaces are most important in determining soil water and soil structure.

Porosity is the volume of soil voids (*pore* space). It is expressed in relation to the bulk volume of the soil. The water holding capacity of a soil depends on its porosity, and the size distribution of its pores. Small pores retain water at greater suctions than larger pores. The moisture (or water) potential is the amount of energy required to remove water from a soil; field capacity is the water-holding capacity after a free-draining soil has been allowed to drain.

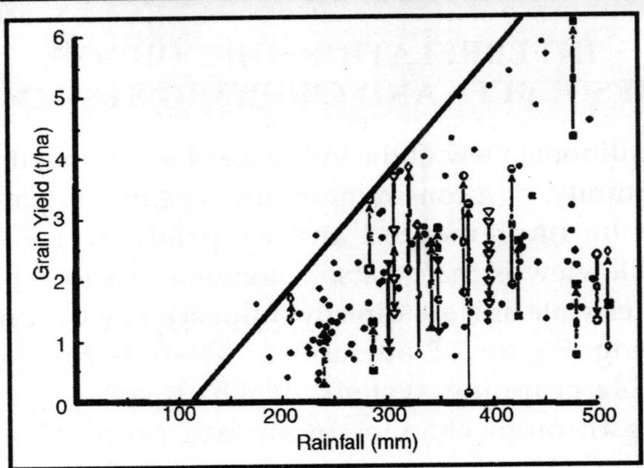


**Fig. 2.1. Relationship between Grain Yield of wheat and April-October Rainfall for Experimental Sites and Farmers' Paddocks in Southern Australia**

The suction corresponding to this state has variously been defined as 0.33, 0.1 and 0.05 bar and so the convention used should always be checked. Wilting point, beyond which plants cannot exert sufficient suction to remove water from a soil, is generally considered to correspond to a suction of 15 bar.

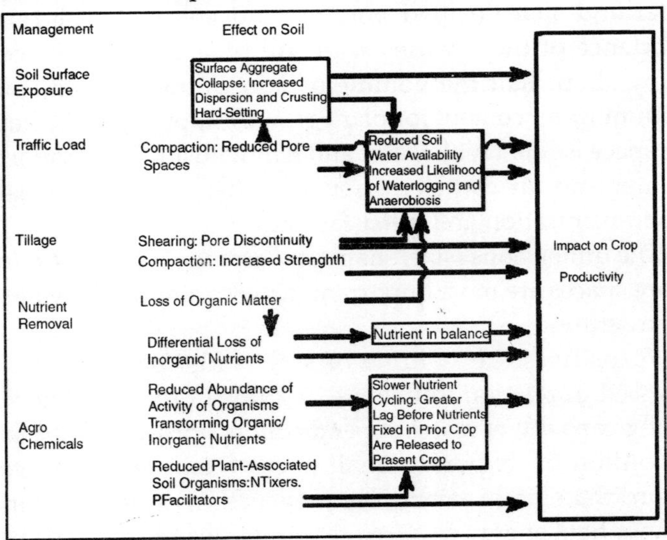


**Fig. 2.2. Interrelationships between Management and Soil as they Impact on Crop Productivity**

**Table. 2.1. Generalised view of Pore Size Groups and Functions**

| Pore Diameter (mm) | Function | Equivalent Particle or Aggregate Size[1] | Biological Cause (if not Due to Natural Particle Arrangement) | Equivalent Soil Water[2] Tension (kPa) |
|---|---|---|---|---|
| >0.5 | Aeration and Water Transmission | >1.6 (mostly Gravel Size, Some Coarse sand Size) | Ants, Worms | <0.6 |
| 0.50-0.05 | Water Transmission (Infiltration, Permeability) | 0.16-1.6 (mostly Coarse Sand Size, some Fine Sand Size) | Roots | 0.6-6.0 |
| 0.0005-0.05 | Water Storage | 0.0016-0.16 (Mostly Silt and Fine sand Size, some Clay Size) | Lateral Roots, Root Hairs | 6.0-600 |
| < 0.0005 | Residual (bound) Water, Unavailable to Plants | <0.0016 (Mostly Clay Size) | Fungal Hyphae and Bacteria | >600 |

*Note*: 1 Equivalent particle size = 3.2 × pore size (assuming spherical, uniform size particles).

2 Based on equation: Pore diameter (mm) = 0.30/soil water tension (kPa).

**Table. 2.2. Typical Values of Water-holding Capacity of Soils**

| International Textural Class | Field Capacity (10 kPa) (Gravimetric) | Wilting Point (Gravimetric) per cent | Available mm Water/m Soil |
|---|---|---|---|
| Coarse sand | 8 | 4 | 80 |
| Sand | 14 | 4 | 150 |
| Loamy sand | 18 | 7 | 160 |
| Sandy loam | 26 | 9 | 180 |
| Loam | 30 | 13 | 180 |
| Silty loam | 34 | 16 | 200 |
| Sandy clay loam | 26 | 15 | 150 |
| Clay loam | 34 | 18 | 180 |
| Silty clay loam | 43 | 20 | 190 |
| Sandy clay | 29 | 19 | 140 |
| Clay | 42 | 25 | 180 |

**Table. 2.3. Typical Values of Saturated Hydraulic Conductivity based on Texture and Degree of Structure**

| Texture | Structure | Infiltration | Permeability (mm/h) |
|---|---|---|---|
| Sand | Apedal | Very rapid | >120 can be measured >250 |
| Sandy loam | Weakly pedal<br>Apedal | Very rapid<br>Rapid | >120<br>60-120 |
| Loam | Peds evident<br>Weakly pedal<br>Apedal | Rapid<br>Mod. rapid<br>Mod. rapid | 60-120<br>20-60<br>20-60 |
| Clay loam | Peds evident<br>Weakly pedal<br>Apedal | Mod. rapid<br>Moderate<br>Slow | 20-60<br>5-20<br>2.5-5 |
| Light clay | Highly pedal<br>Peds evident<br>Weakly pedal | Moderate<br>Slow<br>Very slow | 5-20<br>2.5-5<br><2.5 |
| Medium to heavy clay | Highly pedal<br>Peds evident<br>Weakly pedal | Slow<br>Very slow<br>Very slow | 2.5-20[1]<br><2.5<br><2.5 |
| Clay | Sodic and saline<br>Sodic<br>Highly sodic | Moderate<br>Very slow<br>Extreme | 8.0<br><2.5<br><1.0 |

*Note*: [1] Strongly structured polyhedral subsoils, e.g. Krasnozem.

Available soil water (ASW) is the amount of water which is available for uptake by plants, namely that held at suctions between wilting point and field capacity. It varies with soil type and can be correlated with the clay content and structural arrangement of the soil. It varies also with soil treatment because the size and distribution of pores in the topsoil reflects surface exposure, normal seasonal wetting and drying, and management. Williams *et al.* (1983), studying the water content of 244 soil samples, found that the ASW of well-structured soils was one-third to twice as large as that in comparable (similarly-textured) poorly structured or degraded soils. Bearing in mind that ASW varies with natural weathering and management, Table 2.3 gives typical values of ASW for various soil texture classes.

Hydraulic conductivity (K) of a soil is its conductivity to movement of water down a pressure gradient. High values of K are associated with well-structured soil and contiguous pores; they allow high infiltration rates and rapid drainage. Earthworm channels, which can have populations of 500 $m^{-2}$ in Mediterranean climates (Barley 1959), and continuous deep voids left by dead roots (5-10 000 $m^{-2}$) contribute greatly to hydraulic conductivity. Hydraulic conductivity varies with soil type and management (Table). K values below 10 mm/h are low and likely to cause run-off following rainfall or problems with irrigation, given that steady rain falls at about 10 mm/h. K values of 10 to 20 mm/h can give intermittent run-off (a downpour falls at about 50 mm/h) while values up to 120 mm/h are associated with occasional, increasingly rare run-off. Values above 120 mm/h may facilitate regular drainage to the groundwater, causing potential problems for heavily-fertilised soils, and those treated with effluent, herbicides or pesticides.

Both soil water content and saturated hydraulic conductivity generally relate to the number and continuity of pores, particularly the larger macro-pores. It is, however, difficult to measure these soil attributes and they are highly location-specific, so that variability is great and they sometimes have little interpretive value. Moran *et al.*, (1988), however, in a study of a soil in a wet-and-dry environment, show that a soil treated with minimum tillage had more pores, identified directly by image analysis, and higher hydraulic conductivity, measured in the field, than did a similar soil traditionally cultivated (*see fig. 2.3 a,b on page 31 and 32*). Figure also illustrates the impact of management on soil pore soil water characteristics; this is discussed further in the section below.

Surface sealing and crusting are common in wet-and-dry climates. Sealing increases run-off and seriously reduces the amount of water infiltrating into the soil thus reducing the water held in the soil. Sealing can also increase ponding at the surface and thereby evaporation.

Infiltration rates are often reduced 1000-fold by crusting. The crust can have a skin with a conductivity of only about 0.1

mm/h, able only to accommodate the lightest rate of precipitation (fine mist) and commonly overlies a layer of poorly-aggregated material which also has a conductivity substantially lower than that of the underlying soil. Chase and Boudouresque (1989) and Chase *et al.*, (1989) illustrate the impact of crusting in the Sahel on increased run-off from soils. They show how run-off may be reduced, and the depth of wetting increased, by covering the soil surface with mulch.

## SOIL FABRIC, DENSITY AND STRENGTH

The solid soil material is arbitrarily divided into fractions, the proportions of which determine the texture of the soil.

The fractions in the International Method of particle-size analysis are:

- *Sand*: Grains, which feel gritty and are large enough to be seen and felt individually; coarse sand has particle sizes between 2 and 0.2 mm and fine sand 0.2 and 0.05 mm.
- *Silt*: Imparts a smooth, soapy or silky and only slightly sticky feeling, silt grains cannot be individually detected; their particle sizes range from 0.05 to 0.002 mm.
- *Clay*: Gives a sticky feel to the soil. Clay particles are less than 0.002 mm diameter.

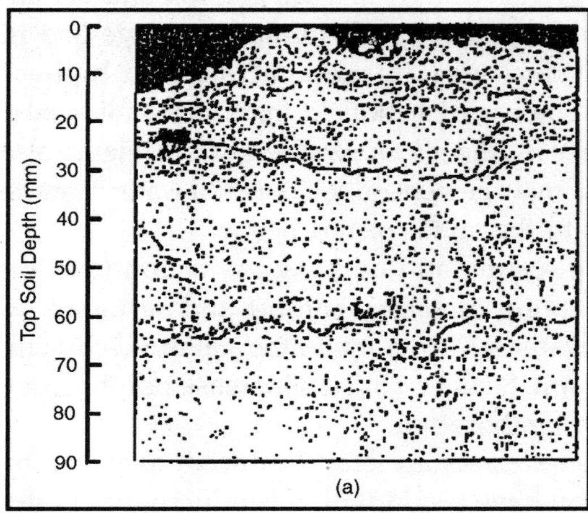

(a)

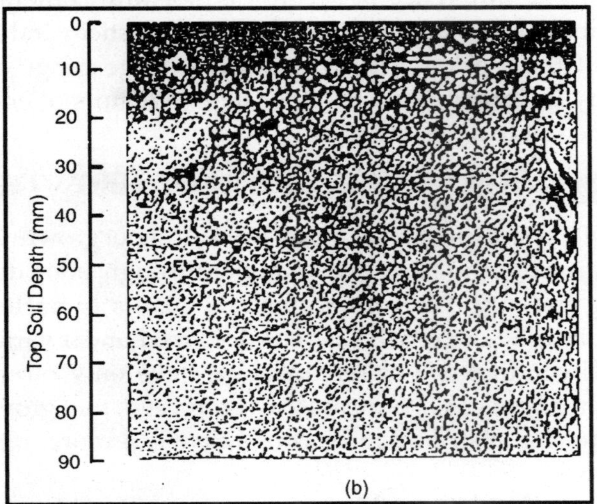


**Fig. 2.3. Photographic Images of Vertical Slices of Soils: The Vertical Faces of soil were taken from a Direct Drill (DD) Treatment *(a)* and a Conventionally Tilled soil *(b)* at the same Location. Hydraulic Conductivities were 42.5 and 5.0 mm/h Respectively**

These solid fractions contribute to the consistence and strength of the soil, and their packing determines bulk density.

*Bulk density* is a measure of the packing or compression of the three constituents of soil. Just as the inherent bulk density of a soil will vary by 30 per cent according to its constituents, so the limiting values of bulk density for root penetration will range from about 1.4 g $cm^3$ in a soil of clay texture to 1.8 g $cm^3$ in a sandy one.

*Soil strength* is the resistance of soil to shearing or structural failure. This reflects the friction which is built up between the soil and an implement, and depends on the density, and the roughness and shape of the soil particles. The shear strength of an individual clod decreases with wetting but, more importantly, the strength of the bulk soil increases with increasing moisture to about the lower plastic limit (known to field operators as the 'sticky point'), at which each particle is surrounded by a film of water which acts as a lubricant. Soil strength drops sharply from that point to the upper plastic limit, where the soil becomes viscous. The difference between the moisture content at the upper and lower plastic limits, termed the plasticity index, is an index of the workability of the soil. A large range or high plasticity index implies a need for large amounts of energy to work the soil to a desired tilth.

## SOIL STRUCTURE AND CROP GROWTH

Soil physical properties affect root and shoot growth directly and indirectly, the latter for example through poor drainage causing pores to fill with water and plants to suffer from anaerobiosis. Root growth has been described under various soil physical conditions, but relationships have only rarely been established between features such as crop yield, root growth and soil pore size distribution or conductivity, a more aggregate measure.

The difficulty in establishing simple relationships does not mean that soil has little influence upon root growth; rather it points to the complexity of the interactions (*see fig. 2.4 on page 36*) and the internal homeostasis which plants maintain. Roots both elongate and proliferate and spread laterally as they grow and age. Concomitantly some roots die and others become suberised and function as conduits, but not as absorbers, of water and nutrients. Roots can elongate downwards as fast as 8 cm/d, as for example, soybean growing in a silt loam in a rhizotron. Deep-rootedness and maximum rooting depth reflect soil properties (for example, roots will not grow through pores that they cannot deform to a larger diameter than the root).

However, relationships are not often reported. Maximum rooting depth varies with species and soil type. For example, wheat roots penetrated to 0.8 m in heavy-textured soils and to 1.2 m in a loamy sand but it is often found that a variety will have a consistent rooting depth across similar soil types in a particular year or in one soil across several years. Angus *et al.* found that rice and six dryland crops (mung bean, cowpea, soybean, groundnut, Maize and sorghum) extracted different amounts of stored soil water (ranging from 100 mm for rice to 250 mm for groundnut) and that extraction was, in part, related to rooting depth.

The spread of roots with age can be related to the growth (increase in weight) of the whole plant, and to accumulated temperature or growing day-degrees (GDD) (*see fig. 2.5 on next page*); indeed, there is some evidence that temperature influences the direction of newly-appeared roots as well as the rate of appearance and extent of growth. Clearly, however, there are factors other than plant size, temperature and soil which influence root proliferation. Otherwise the plants sown at three different times of year in the same soil in Figure would align their root growth along a single growth-GDD relationship. These other factors, of which day length is probably particularly important, tend to mask underlying relationships between growth and soil structure.

Figure 2.6 shows that tillage can affect root length, though in this case its effects took three years to develop. (*see on page 37*) Measurable differences in soil porosity developed under two tillage treatments: in the first year both root growth and water infiltration (K approximately 5 mm/h) were the same under minimum tillage and conventional tillage. By the third year, when differences were measured between roots, infiltration rates were 84 mm/h in minimum tillage and 0.2 mm/h under conventional tillage. Despite the differences in root growth there were no substantial differences in grain yield, reflecting the overall constraint of climate in the semi-arid environment.

One of the clearer associations between soil porosity and plant growth is described by Tisdall and Cockroft and Tisdall. Soil was ameliorated by deep ploughing, inserting gypsum at depth, and incorporation of straw and green manure in the topsoil. This treatment gave 10-fold increases in the number of earthworms and a 4-fold increase in soil pores. Infiltration rates also increased 10-fold relative to untreated soil. Root growth was not measured, but fruit yields from peach trees increased from 18 to 75 t/ha.

Lateral spread of roots in three sowings of 1987, 1988 and 1989; the ratio $r_L/R_L$ (mean of minimum and conventional tillage) increased with Days After Sowing (DAS) according to $r_L/R_L = 1 - 2.33 \times 0.97^t$ (r = 0.96) where t is DAS. are means od both cultivars and tillage treetments for 1st, 2nd and 3rd sowings (O, □, Δ, respectively) of 1987 (open), 1988 (closed and the 1989 sowing (♦).

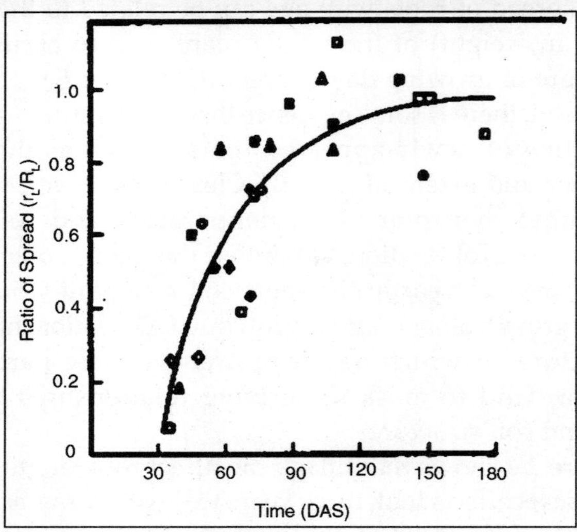


**Fig. 2.4.**

Relationships between root length at each sowing and growing day-degrees (°Cd).

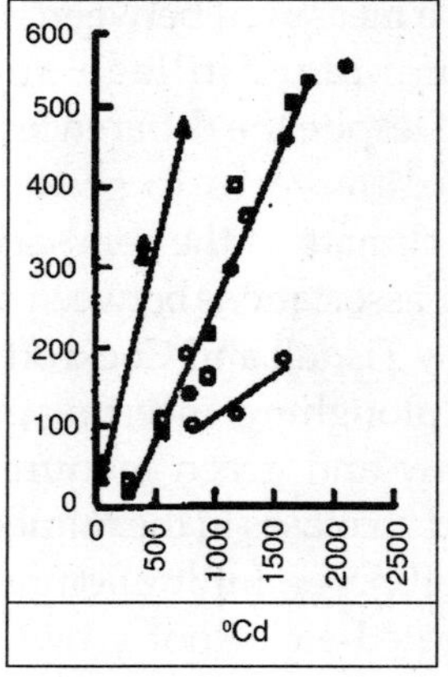


**Fig. 2.5.**

Comparison of total root length per plant in each tillage treetment (minimum tillage/conventional tillage ratio) indicated that root length were lower under minimum tillage than conventional tillage during early growth in 1987, similar in 1988 and higher under minimum than following conventional tillage in tillage in 1989; vertical bars are SE.

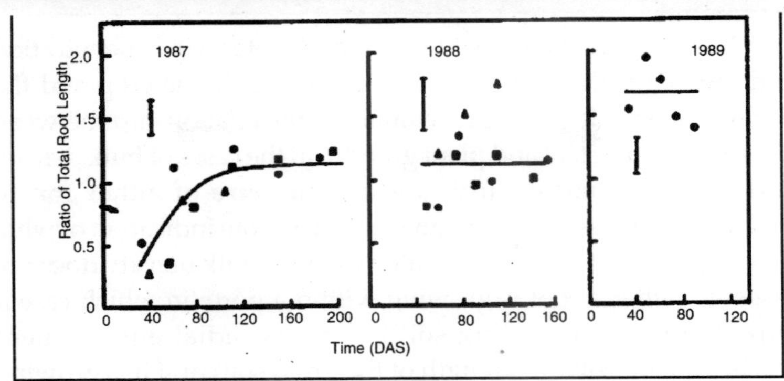


**Fig. 2.6. Spread of Wheat Roots with Age, and Effects on Root Growth of Minimum or Direct Drilling Compared with Conventional Tillage**

**Table. 2.4. Values of Air-filled Porosity (Per Cent) and Bulk Density(g cm$^3$) which are Critical and which Limit Root Growth for Various Soils**

| Texture class | Non-limiting | Critical[1] | Limiting |
|---|---|---|---|
| **Air-filled porosity** | | | |
| Fine loamy | 20 | 10 | 5 |
| Coarse silty | 20 | 10 | 5 |
| Fine silty | 20 | 10 | 5 |
| Clay: | | | |
| 35-45 | 15 | 10 | 5 |
| >45 | 15 | 10 | 5 |
| **Bulk density** | | | |
| Sandy | 1.60 | 1.69 | 1.85 |
| Coarse loamy | 1.50 | 1.63 | 1.80 |
| Fine loamy | 1.46 | 1.67 | 1.78 |
| Coarse silty | 1.43 | 1.67 | 1.79 |
| Fine silty | 1.34 | 1.54 | 1.65 |
| Clayey: | | | |
| 35-45 per cent | 1.40 | 1.49 | 1.58 |
| 45 per cent | 1.30 | 1.39 | 1.47 |

*Note*: [1] 'Critical' is defined as causing <20 per cent reduction in root growth; 'limiting' is about the value at which root growth ceases.

Increases in soil density or strength retard root penetration and thus limit the volume of soil exploited by the crop and the water available. It is difficult to quantify the relationships between these soil parameters and plant growth. In the cases of bulk density and strength, particularly, a gross measure of either for an undisturbed mass of soil can give only a remote indication of what a root encounters. A determination of gross bulk density does not assess whether a root is growing within a pore (in which case it may deform surrounding soil before its radial environment reaches the density or strength of the gross soil) or if it is growing within the soil material, in which case it has already exerted a radial force equivalent to that measured for the gross soil.

This problem of scale-what is measured in a gross estimate cannot assess the micro-environment of the root, to which it (and through hormonal signals, the plant top) responds—does not invalidate some general hypotheses about plant behaviour in response to soil compaction and structural arrangement. Roots stop growing when they are unable to deform their micro-environment. This probably occurs at suctions about 60 kPa when they cannot generate adequate internal turgor. It is thought that root elongation declines curvilinearly with increasing either bulk density or shear strength. In the case of bulk density, little effect is noted until a 'critical value' and root elongation ceases within a further 10 per cent increase in bulk density (*see table 2.4*). As explained earlier, these values vary with soil type. Root elongation declines asymptotically with increasing soil strength (*see fig. 2.7*) though the actual critical values would be expected to vary with soil type, water content and the method of measurement (those in Figure 2.7 were measured with a penetrometer).

Studies of the effect of bulk density or strength on other plant processes, particularly germination and shoot elongation, also suffer from the same technical problem of scale. Shoots are able to explore macropores without being subject to the gross values of the soil they are in. The actual local values which inhibit shoot elongation appear to be quite small, for example, 0.76 kPa. These values from controlled situations contrast sharply with gross field values and with the large number of inconsistent correlations which arise from attempting to correlate crop performance with grossly-measured soil structure. Perhaps, most encouragingly, studies of genetic variation in the sensitivity of crops to soil strength suggest that there is appreciable range in plant sensitivity. The relative ranking of genotypes is, however, the same when under near-critical stress as when growing with virtually no mechanical stress. Genotypes suited to stressful situations may be selected, therefore, by screening at a single soil strength.

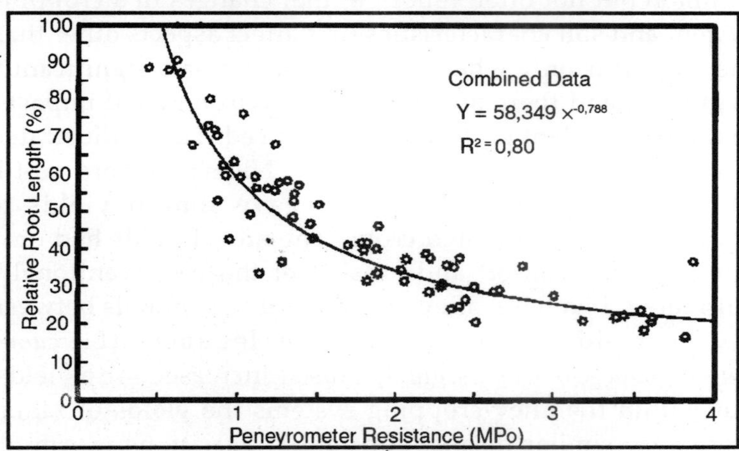


**Fig. 2.7. Relative Root Length with Penetrometer Resistance for Combined Maize, Wheat, Cotton and Groundnut Data**

**Table. 2.5. Grain and Stover Yield (t/ha) of Maize and Seasonal water Run-off and Soil Loss under Maize grown with and without Alley Cropping, with two tree Legumes, and Tillage in Nigeria**

| Treatment | Maize | | Runoff[1] (mm [% of rainfall]) | Soil Loss (t/ha) |
|---|---|---|---|---|
| | Grain | Stover | | |
| **Without Alley Cropping** | | | | |
| Tilled control | 2.3 | 3.1 | 66.0 (9.4) | 6.18 |
| No-tillage | 2.4 | 3.2 | 5.6 (0.8) | 0.43 |
| **Alley-cropped** | | | | |
| 2 m Gliricidia | 3.2 | 4.6 | 4.8 (0.7) | 0.57 |
| 4 m Gliricidia | 2.8 | 4.2 | 23.1 (3.3) | 1.44 |
| 2 m Leucaena | 3.4 | 4.9 | 2.6 (0.4) | 9.17 |
| 4 m Leucaena | 3.1 | 3.9 | 10.7 (1.5) | 0.82 |

*Note*: [1] Seasonal rainfall (March-July 1988) = 704.2 mm.

The above comments relate to the direct effects of soil physical properties on crop growth. Two further points may be made. First, changing soil properties may not cause, or at least not immediately cause, measurable differences in plant performance (*see fig. 2.8 on page 42*). This neither invalidates an association between the soil and the plant, nor the need to remain concerned about changes in soil properties. It is common but not often reported, that changes in a cropping system and soil characteristics first affect aspects other than the crop. It is only when a system has become significantly degraded, and there are associated environmental impacts, that reduced plant performance is noticed. This is illustrated (*see table. 2.6*) in a study at Ibadan, Nigeria, where no-till Maize in rotation with cowpea gave similar yields to conventionally cultivated crops. The no-till fields had only one-tenth the run-off and erosion of those conventionally cultivated. Likewise, alley-cropping of the annuals between six year-old hedgerows of tree legumes (*Leucaena leucocephala, Gliricidia sepium*) caused increased crop yields, but within the alley-cropping systems the yields of Maize were very similar despite substantial variations in run-off and soil loss.

**Table. 2.6. Desirable Crop Attributes that Sustain Soil Productivity**

| Attribute | Contributing Characteristic |
|---|---|
| Rapid establishment | (Relatively) large seed for establishment and seedling vigour; abundant seed for propagation |
| Groundcover to reduce soil exposure, suppress weeds | Early branching; perhaps rhizomes or stolons; horizontal leaves (high canopy-extraction coefficient) |
| Low requirements for nutrients | • Colonisation by associative bacteria (*e.g., Brachyrhizobiun*), micorrhizae (*e.g., Glomus*) and free-living organisms (*e.g., Azospirillum*)<br>• Low P, K, etc., requirement per |

(*Contd...*)

| | unit dry matter, *e.g.*, high 'phosphate efficiency' |
|---|---|
| Efficient water use | Short growth duration (to utilise residual moisture after crop); high water use efficiency |
| Deep rooting to reduce water table (salinity) and recover nutrients at depth and increase macropores | Vertical root distribution; roots penetrate high impedence soils |
| Useful products | High leaf/stem ratio; edible seeds; easily digestible; no nutritional compounds in material for livestock; leaf retention on stems for cut and carrying to livestock |
| Non-host for diseases and pests of main crop (to break disease cycle) or decoy (to attract diseases from concurrent crops) | Botanically unrelated to main food crop(s) |
| Suppress other species | Allelopathy (leachates, exudates which suppress or kill other plant species); also physical attributes (as above) |

The second point about soil-crop relations is that the crop also affects the soil through ground-cover, depth of rooting and other properties. The crop attributes that most influence soil physical properties are speed of establishment and development of foliage cover. Rapid establishment and growth minimizes topsoil structural decline and soil erosion by wind and water. Thereafter, deep-rooting directly affects soil structure, particularly if deep-rooted crops, such as safflower, are grown in rotation as a 'biological plough' to create macropores and these are minimally disturbed before the next crop is sown. A general list of desirable crop characteristics is given in Table. Not all these are universally applicable (nor indeed, accepted by all scientists) because some attributes such as stolons and rhizomes, on the one hand, can provide advantageous ground cover and bind the soil, but they are undesirable if the species presents weeding or other problems.

The list includes both herbaceous and tree species. Ezenwa considers the attributes important for the choice of trees in Sahelian areas as the ability to:

- Enrich a microsite by depositing litter;
- Fix nitrogen and not be allelopathic;
- Avoid competition;
- Withstand stress, either water or wind;
- Provide alternative produce such as fodder, fuel or fruit.

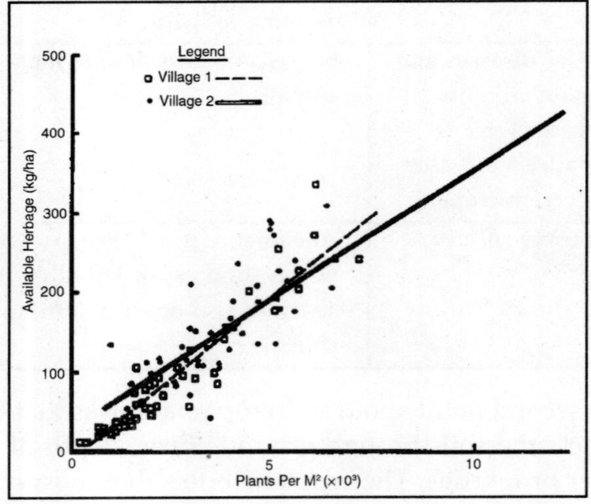


**Fig. 2.8. Relationship between Herbage Yield and Plant Numbers on Marginal land Near two Villages in Syria where Rainfall is about 270 mm**

## HOW MANAGEMENT DIRECTLY AFFECTS SOIL STRUCTURE

The three management practices which most affect soil physical properties (and consequent *in-situ* degradation and erosion) are groundcover, tillage and traffic load. Additionally, water harvesting techniques (FAO 1991) can be used to increase the amount of water stored within the soil and in surface catchments, though this does not necessarily affect soil structure.

Ground cover is crucial for the maintenance of soil structure in wet-and-dry climates. In marginal cropping areas in particular, plant populations (of weeds or pasture in non-crop periods) range widely and affect crop productivity. Their effects in semi-arid Syria are shown in Figure 2.8.

On resource-poor farms near the dry margins of the wet-and-dry croplands, populations of crop and weedy species tend to be small and variable during the cropping period. The effects of such sparse cover are clear, erosivity is directly related to the area exposed.

In practice, during the crop phase there is a five-fold range in erosive risk associated with the area covered by living plants, consistent with the crop factor (C) values which are used in the Universal Soil Loss Equation (Table 2.7).

**Table. 2.7. Effect of Crop Cover on Crop Management Factor C in the Universal Soil Loss Equation**

| Crop cover | C[1] |
|---|---|
| No cover | 1.0 |
| Maize, sorghum | 0.3-0.9 |
| Groundnut | 0.4-0.8 |
| Cassava | 0.2-0.8 |
| Cotton, tobacco | 0.5 |
| Oil palm, coffee, cacao with cover crops | 0.1-0.3 |
| Rice | 0.1-0.2 |
| Rapidly growing cover crop | 0.1 |
| Savannah or pasture (without grasing) | 0.01 |
| Forest or crop with thick layer of mulch | 0.001 |

*Note:* [1] C values range from almost zero, when the vegetation stops loss of soil directly related to rain, to 1 when the soil is fully exposed to rain.

The very low value for forests in Table has encouraged advisers to advocate planting of trees as part of mixed crop systems. Young points out, however, that trees are usually part of spatially-heterogeneous systems, such as hedgerows.

Thus the tree canopy is usually not extensive and does not cover and protect the cropped land. He believes that such tree canopies are not likely to reduce erosion and may indeed increase it. Under agroforestry systems, however, the use of cut leaves and litter as groundcover may directly or indirectly improve protection by providing barriers to lateral water flow and wind.

Mineral ions are lost during lateral surface erosion. Eroded sediment commonly contains a higher proportion of organic matter and nutrients than the topsoil from which it is derived. This enrichment, frequently 1.5-4-fold, but sometimes as high as 10-fold, is because the eroded soil comes from the uppermost layer with the more organic matter than the soil below and because water differentially removes light particles and soluble nutrients. Loss of plant cover also increases downward movement of ions and fine soil particles. The loss of mineral ions to groundwater is illustrated in Table 2.8. Such losses contribute to the negative nutrient balance of cropping systems and may also pollute groundwater.

Under bare soil, downward translocation of silt and clay particles may fill subsoil pores and thus reduce infiltration. Vertical loss of organic material and fine particles may create a less-well-structured surface layer with less water-holding capacity, poorer infiltration and a tendency to crust.

The best ground covers are living crops and pastures. Soil stability declines in the order: living mulch; dead mulch on surface and incorporated dead mulch; and lastly, no mulch. The benefits of mulch incorporation depend on slope, soil erodibility, and on the type of organic matter. These and the type of tillage used determine whether the dead mulch will remain on the surface.

Costs and availability of both mulch and labour (human, animal or tractor) are also important. Though farmers may appreciate the benefits of surface mulching, it is unlikely that it will become practice in those tropical and temperate wet-and-dry climates where there is a shortage of feed for livestock in the dry period(s).

**Table. 2.8. Influence of Plant Cover of Catchments on Ion Leaching**

| Type of catchment | Catchment | Percent of area | | | Outflow of elements during 2 years (g m$^2$) | | | | |
|---|---|---|---|---|---|---|---|---|---|
| | | Arable | Forests | Grass-lands | N-N0$_3$ | P-PO$_4^3$ | $K^+$ | $Ca^{2+}$ | $Mg^{2+}$ |
| Larger contribution of cultivated fields | 1 | 53 | 12 | 35 | 1.63 | 0.03 | 3.32 | 37.66 | 2.82 |
| | 2 | 62 | 8 | 28 | 1.43 | 0.04 | 2.99 | 35.42 | 3.30 |
| | 3 | 53 | 32 | 13 | 1.13 | 0.04 | 2.57 | 30.95 | 2.28 |
| | 4 | 51 | 21 | 27 | 0.71 | 0.02 | 2.91 | 32.40 | 2.70 |
| **Mean** | | 55 | 18 | 26 | 1.22 | 0.03 | 2.36 | 34.13 | 2.78 |
| Smaller contribution of cultivated fields | 1 | 38 | 44 | 17 | 0.60 | 0.02 | 1.58 | 23.33 | 1.80 |
| | 2 | 29 | 45 | 26 | 0.48 | 0.01 | 1.00 | 25.63 | 1.44 |
| | 3 | 21 | 65 | 14 | 0.39 | 0.01 | 0.91 | 22.54 | 1.56 |
| | 4 | 32 | 47 | 21 | 0.44 | 0.01 | 0.91 | 15.26 | 1.20 |
| **Mean** | | 30 | 50 | 19 | 0.48 | 0.01 | 1.10 | 21.69 | 1.50 |

**Table. 2.9. Objectives, Advantages and Disadvantages of Soil Tillage in Crop Production**

| Objective<br>1 | Type of Tillage<br>2 | Advantage<br>3 | Disadvantage<br>4 |
|---|---|---|---|
| Soil conditioning | Cutting, loosening, granulating | Weed control, water conservation, structure improvement, seedbed preparation, better drying of wet soils | Greater erosion potential, high energy input[1], increased evaporation |
| Eradication or control of plants or plant materials | Cutting, inverting, mixing | Weed control, volunteer plant control, water conservation, establish desirable plant populations, pest control[2], better drying of wet soils, mineralization of soil nutrients | Greater erosion potential, may cause compaction, high energy input, decreased soil organic matter, increased evaporation |
| Establishing soil boundaries and surface configurations | Cutting as with coulters to improve ploughing, operation, land forming | Weed control, soil conservation, water conservation, residue incorporation, seedbed preparation, better drying of wet soils, warmer soil temperatures | Greater erosion potential, may cause compaction, high energy input, increased evaporation |

| | | | |
|---|---|---|---|
| Incorporating, covering, or handling foreign materials | Cutting, inverting, mixing | Weed control, residue incorporation, mineralization of soil nutrients, fertilizer and pesticide incorporation, pest control, better drying of wet soils, warmer soil temperatures | Greater erosion potential, may cause compaction, high energy input, decreased soil organic matter, increased evaporation |
| Segregation | Move soil materials from one layer to another | Wind erosion control, better drying of wet soils | High energy input, increased evaporation |
| Mixing | Mixing | Better drying of wet soils, improved soil amendment distribution, fertilizer and pesticide incorporation, soil texture improvement (mixing of two or more layers), soil structure improvement, mineralization of soil nutrients | Great erosion potential, high energy input, decreased soil organic matter, increased evaporation |
| Compaction or firming | Rolling or pressing | Improved seed-soil contact | May cause compaction |

*Note*: [1] High energy input: may include fuel for tractors, feed for animals, labour and equipment inventories or usage.

[2] Pests controlled may be insects, diseases, rodents, etc.

The objectives, advantages and disadvantages of tillage are summarised in Table. Had this been written 8-10 years ago, tillage would have been emphasised. Currently, tillage is seen as appropriate for some objectives, for example to break impervious layers of subsoil and to incorporate organic matter topsoil, but generalisations about the value of tillage or the 'best' type of tillage are not regarded as transportable from one system to another. Tillage may be defined as the mechanical manipulation of soil to enhance the outcomes from a cropping system. So, given the broad range of system outcomes, it is likely that tillage will continue for reasons such as tradition and satisfaction long after its beneficial benefits on soil structure and weed control have been discounted.

When advocating particular tillage methods, or interpreting experimental results and their transferability to other environments, it should be noted that tillage is usually affected by the type of ground cover. The variables of tillage are the degree of contact with the soil, the type of manipulation, and the number of implement passes through the soil. Thus, minimum tillage (one-pass) and conventional tillage (perhaps 3-5 passes, in the Australian farming system), might have the same effects on the soil, differing only in degree.

Conservation tillage, which uses different implements and ground covers, is defined as 'any tillage or cultivation system that maintains at least 30 per cent of the soil surface covered by residue after planting to reduce soil erosion by water; or where soil erosion by wind is the primary concern, maintains at least 450 kg/ha of flattened small grain residue equivalent on the surface during critical erosion periods'.

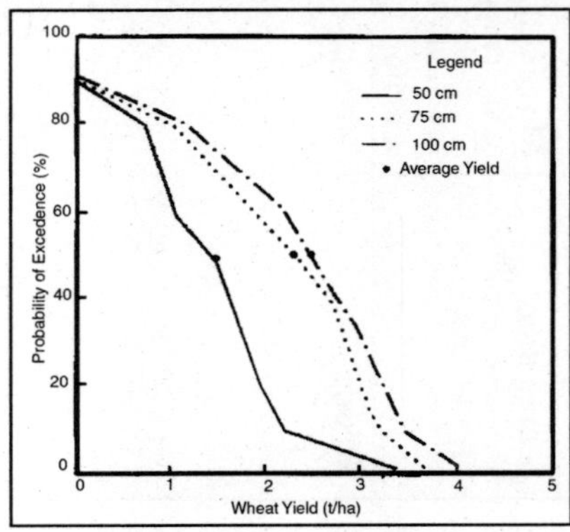


**Fig. 2.9. Variation in Crop Yield for Different Soil Depths of a Vertisol in the Central Highlands of Queensland, Australia**

In seasonally wet-and-dry climates, the most apparent benefits from tillage are weed control and reduced evapotranspiration from weeds preceding the crop. This increases the water available at the beginning of the crop period and the volume of soil into which roots may penetrate (and thus, the available soil water). The impact of tillage on soil volume is modelled in Figure. This shows that rooting depth (or soil depth in this example) has a marked effect on the probability of achieving certain crop yields. Thus, exploitation of larger soil volumes may both increase yield and increase the likelihood of attaining a particular yield, that is, reduce the year-to-year risk.

The variable effects of type of tillage on crop growth (Figure) are interpreted by recognising that some effects of tillage, such as increasing the potential root volume, occur within the season of tillage, while other effects are longer term. Tillage will, over several years, reduce the outer permeability of clods, restricting water-holding capacity and increasing the power required for further effective tillage.

In some soils it dis-aggregates clods, causes downward movement of silt and clay which fills soil pores and reduces infiltration. It can also accelerate the breakdown of organic matter. Some of these effects on plant growth are discussed in the previous section and Unger (1984) presents further data on the impact of different types of tillage implement on soil and erosion.

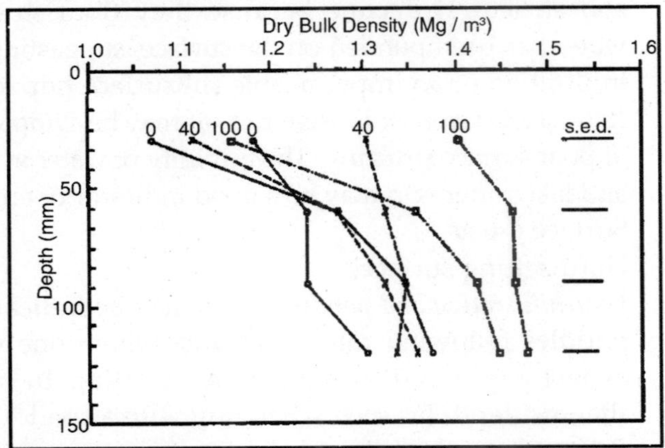


**Fig. 2.10. Bulk Density Profiles for each Treatment for 1987 and 1990**

Compaction by machinery or by treading by livestock is common and is reviewed elsewhere. The ultimate example of soil degradation through tillage and compaction is *the* formation of impermeable beds for rice production.

Figure 2.10 illustrates the effects of compaction and plant activity on bulk density. Three levels of compaction were created (0, 40 and 100 kPa) under grassland. At depths below 15 cm the porosity and pore length reflected these pressures. In some places the volume of pores was halved by the heaviest compaction treatment. The subsoil bulk densities also reflect the deleterious effect of pressure. From 1987 to 1990, however, all bulk densities near the surface decreased. Grass roots were apparently able to offset the effects of machinery pressure.

## FIELD INDICATORS OF PHYSICAL PROBLEMS

General field indicators of poor soil physical conditions include:

1. *Patchiness or absence of vegetation*: This can be an obvious sign of degraded structure or other factors. When structural, it may reflect surface structure degradation (see previous sections) or non-wetting characteristics which give rise to poor infiltration, or subsoil impermeability.
2. *Weedy vegetation*: *Cyperaceae* or *Juncaceae* may indicate soil structural decline because they flourish where water has been ponded on the surface, suggesting poor infiltration or an impermeable subsurface horizon.
3. *Rill and sheet erosion*: Erosive run-off may be symptomatic of poor surface structure. The turbidity of water in ponds and lakes after rain may be a good indicator of erosion.
4. Surface crusts.
5. Hard-setting surfaces.
6. *Poor infiltration and ponding*: This may be indicated by puddles following rain in an area where one would expect rapid infiltration, or by wetting to only a shallow depth (as seen when dug with a spade).
7. *Pale surface soil colour and absence of organic matter*: The surface of degraded soils may be brittle and pale,

lacking organic matter and having lost clay either through eluviation (differential movement downwards) or by water or wind erosion.

8. *Cloddiness*: This may be apparent if after a single cultivation, large, tough clods are formed requiring further cultivation to form a reasonable seedbed.
9. *Restricted root growth*: This can be seen by digging with a narrow-faced spade and washing the roots free of soil. The root mass can be restricted to the upper soil or be constricted in particular places such as a less pervious layer, above and below which the roots may proliferate.

When assessing soil degradation on a large scale as for a catchment, Hamblin (1991a) argues that most precise (scientific) measurements are time-consuming and complex, and that robust surrogate assessments amenable to remote sensing are appropriate.

Vegetation cover is one useful surrogate. Ranges in groundcover (often easier to estimate than plant densities) provide a direct index of soil productivity and they usually, although not necessarily, correlate closely with underlying problems of soil structure or fertility. Sparse groundcover might also, of course, reflect inappropriate management of non-degraded soil.

This could suggest inefficient management which will lead to loss of sustainability though there are no current problems with soil structure. The surrogate features Hamblin appears to favour are turbidity of water, transient ponding and waterlogging.

Transient ponding is particularly attractive as it can be sensed remotely, relates directly to the field being measured, and reflects several important physical aspects. These latter include surface degradation, continuity of vertical macropores, and subsurface compaction, none of which can currently be satisfactorily measured directly to give cheap meaningful data.

At farm level, attuned observers and local farmers will probably identify, often subconsciously, more indicators than those in the above list. Farmers are often good observers of their fields and can recognise soil degradation.

For example, interviews with 55 farmers in Mindanao, Philippines, found that 90 per cent reported yield declines associated with soil erosion: 'Many farmers said their soils initially had been dark on top and reddish underneath but over time the top layer had eroded away. The infertile, red subsoils were exposed. Farmers estimated that erosion reduced the depth of the darker soil from 50 cm in 1976 to 10 cm in 1986. Table illustrates their insights to declining soil productivity. Many farmers recognise changes in soil structure (*e.g.*, compaction) through the increased power needed during tillage, or by the formation of brick-like clods rather than a fine crumby tilth. These observations, however, are made at the beginning of the growing season, when there is little opportunity for soil amelioration.

Farmers should be encouraged to dig small inspection holes to examine roots during the life of the crop. This supplements observations described above. Live roots are easily exposed and reflect many soil structural factors. Such examinations allow the farmer to consider soil amelioration, using stubble and crop residues, prior to the next crop. Figure illustrates clear differences in root patterns revealed by digging in three tillage systems in India.

**Table. 2.10. Examples of Farmer Concepts/Statements Concerning Aspects of Sustainable Crop Production**

*Crops and soil nutrients*

"Cassava adds soil acidity."

"Cassava gobbles up soil nutrients."

"Rice is more tolerant of acidic soils than is Maize."

"Rice is more vigourous on an area previously planted in tomato."

"Intercropping is good only if there are complete chemicals."

*Nutrient depletion*

"Soil fertility has been used up."

"The soil is weak."

"Fertility is spotty."

*(Contd...)*

"Soils are overtrained."

"The soils are getting older."

"Poor, but not used up, in the sense of the hardest part within a log."

*Fallows*

"The decomposing leaves of the weeds help to enrich the soil."

"The land is resting so the soil can store some nutrients."

"Rich because it is rested."

"Fertility is added and the soil is made cool."

"The soil is slightly enriched if left a short time."

*Weeds*

"Rice was harmed by *cogon* (*I. cylindrical*) roots."

"Poor soil if *cogon* dominates."

"*D. longiflora* and *cogon* consume soil nutrients and destroy soil quality."

"Acidity increases where *cogon* dominates."

"Weeds are thin on infertile soils."

"*R. cochinchinensis* rapidly produces seed; thus, easily soars in population; if not weeded, it exceeds the height of rice or corn."

"Fertility is added and the soil is made cool" (re. *Calapogonium* spp.).

"Soil is good where there are weeds/grasses with nodules."

*Soil erosion*

"Soil slides down and floats away."

"Nutrients are drawn down."

"Plants are eroded along with soil."

"Soil was drawn down and fertility was washed out."

"The land was shaven and eroded after trees were removed."

"Fertilizer is collected (on lower plots) due to rain."

*Erosion control*

"Banana and coconut are better because they hold the soil."

"Contour plowing reduces downslope erosion.loss

"Weedy strips can decrease erosion effects."

"Trees planted above and below fields can decrease erosion effects."

(*Contd...*)

"Banana planted above and below fields can decrease erosion effects."

It is important too that farmers, whether resource-poor or advanced, understand the conditions under which soil degradation is most likely to be severe. Broadly, human-induced structural damage occurs during tilling, when heavily trampled by livestock, and by poor management of soil cover.

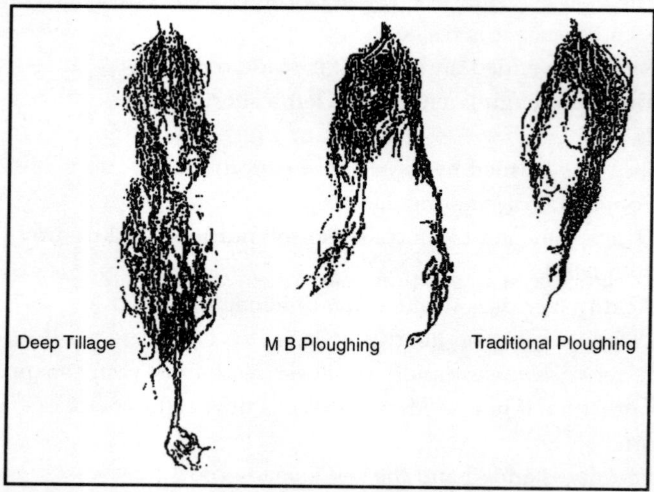


**Fig. 2.11. Roots of Sorghum Plants Grown on a Luvisol under three Tillage Systems**

Weather-induced damage is episodic rather than continuous. Virmani (1990) explains wind and water erosion as follows:

*Wind erosion* is a serious problem in the arid and semi-arid tropics on sandy, loamy sand or sandy loam surface soils low in organic matter with weak topsoil structure in areas with high winds (>20 km/h). In tropical areas where wind erosion occurs the annual rainfall is generally less than 600 mm and is seasonal. The rest of the year is dry. In the tropics, 80-90 per cent of the annual wind erosion losses occurs in the hot and dry period preceding the short rainy season.

During this period the daily maximum temperature usually exceeds 35-40°C, the wind speeds exceed 20 km/h, and open pan evaporation exceeds 8 mm/d. As a rule of thumb, on uncultivated bare sandy soils, the soil displaced by wind erosion is around 1 t/ha/WED, where WED is the sum of the number of days during which the wind speed exceeds 20 km/h, the day temperature exceeds 35 °C and the wind fetch is more than 60 km. For freshly cultivated soils the amount of soil eroded may be as large as 50 t/ha/WED.

*Water erosion* is serious in areas with an average annual rainfall of 600-1100 mm. Using the concept of a rain erosion month (REM), that is a month in which rainfall exceeds pan evaporation, Virmani states that water-induced erosion at rates of approximately 1 t/ha/REM occurs on cropped Vertisols in areas where the rain/pan evaporation ratio ranges between 1 and 2 and where improved soil and water conservation practices have been applied. He records rates of 4 to 8 t/ha/REM where practices are not improved.

## MANAGEMENT FOR MAINTENANCE OF SOIL PHYSICAL PROPERTIES

'In the struggle against aridisation and desertification, dry-farming is no less important or urgent than revegetation and irrigation'.

Maintenance or improvement of soil structure requires:

- Recognition of the interrelated nature of soil attributes and their interaction with cropping.
- The ability to recognise the symptoms indicating physical problems or their likely existence.
- Action.

The interrelated nature of soil and plant attributes, and measures of degradation, are discussed above. The size of the problem, regionally and internationally, is also well recognised. Likewise, the magnitude of local soil losses is established: for example, values as high as 200 t/ha/y in Niamey and measured losses of 282 t/ha/y in the highlands of Ethiopia. Lastly, and significantly, it is becoming recognised that soil physical characteristics may be less robust than chemical attributes. In Australia, the rates of degradation of structure and compaction are faster, on the same soil types, than the degradation of chemical attributes (*see table 2.11*).

The issue now is to reflect in a general way, as is possible only in a bulletin like this, on appropriate action.

There are many regionally-based assessments of land degradation and various studies on how management may improve, or reduce the rate of deterioration in, soil physical structure. Regional identification of the size of the problems, and general prescriptive strategies to ameliorate them, are appropriate for planning and allocation of resources. An example from Africa (FAO 1986) is outlined in the extensive quotation that follows:

**Table. 2.11 Rate of Change in Soil Physical and Chemical Characteristics from Various Locations in Australia**

| Characteristic | Measure of change | Time for change to occur (years) |
|---|---|---|
| Surface structure | Loss | 2-10 |
| Subsoil compaction:<br>traffic pan<br>Organic matter | Formation<br>One-third loss | 1-5<br>5-8 sand<br>15-20 loam |
| pH | Decrease by one unit | 7-12 sand<br>20-30 various |
| Salinity | Not quantified | 10-100 |

**Table. 2.12 Changes in Cropping Patterns and Calculated Erosion Hazard in three Regions in Italy between 1954 and 1976**

| Location | Catchment and Area (ha) | | Change in Cropping Systems | Change in Calculated Erosion Hazard (t/ha/year) |
|---|---|---|---|---|
| Tuscany | (1)<br>(2)<br>(3) | 98<br>20<br>14 | Mixed crops replaced with monoculture, particularly vines, using mechanical, non-contour tillage; minimal pastures in new catchments | 6.4 to 7.7<br>7.8 to 8.1<br>1.7 to 16.2 |
| Emilia | (1) | 38 | Traditionally forested; catchment logged and abandoned for regrowth and not cultivated | 4.2 to 16.2 |
| Piedmont | (1)<br>(2) | 92<br>51 | Mixed cropping; some reduction in cropping while retaining contour tillage | 40.0 to 33.5<br>22.5 to 21.8 |

The African environment is being seriously degraded as a result of the over-exploitation of cropland. The degradation of cropland can best be halted by improving soil fertility, limiting soil erosion, and introducing water harvesting and dryland farming techniques.

Options for the first two include:

- Replacing shifting cultivation with perennial tree crops such as oil palm, coconut, coffee and cacao;
- Growing crops between alleys of leguminous trees and shrubs, and supplementing the nitrogen and organic matter they supply with farmyard manure;
- Using zero or minimum tillage systems to minimize soil erosion;
- Adopting integrated plant nutrition to supply nitrogen by using animal manure alone or mixed with mineral fertilizers, or by growing leguminous crops;
- Constructing physical barriers to soil erosion, such as earth bunds, bench terraces and tied ridges.

Where population pressure has led people to cultivate hillsides with marginal soils, or to settle in semi-arid areas better suited to pastoralism, three simple measures can reduce degradation: the construction of small dams to conserve water, and tree planting on upper slopes; the use of dryland farming techniques; and, finally, the use of short-season, drought-resistant cultivars.

To tackle the problem at a local level work needs to be done in cooperation with the farmers themselves: 'start with what they know, build on what they have'. Table illustrates a locally-targeted analysis of erosion risk in the hills of Italy. It combines calculations of erosion risk with on-farm assessment of changes in land use. There is a predictable increase in erosion hazard associated with deforestation and increased cropping of monocultures, especially under vines, where there is no additional ground cover and where the land is not ploughed around the contours. Erosion risk fell where cropping declined over the 20-year study period.

It seems most likely that lasting changes to cropping practice and control of erosion will be based on farmers' recognition of trends such as those in Tables, coupled with strategies which farmers find appropriate for their goals. These strategies are listed in Table 2.13, which broadly sets out the options. Soil physical sustainability depends on activities which are explicitly aimed at its maintenance, and if necessary, any activities needed to ameliorate or control damage already done. Water harvesting can be used as a complementary strategy, the options for which are summarised by Critchley and Siegert. All the strategies in Table are described above and some have been illustrated. It is appropriate to repeat, however, that few such strategies are universally applicable in detail. For example, minimum soil disturbance may, after several years, enhance sustainability in temperate semi-arid Australia and USA whereas tillage experiments in Africa and Asia support conventional, even deep, ploughing. While the philosophy of minimal disturbance may be biologically 'right', differences in soil texture may require different approaches to sustainability. For example, Sahelian soils are commonly coarse-textured with high bulk densities and form crusts. They do not readily develop macropores. Though it is desirable to mulch such soils with straw, there is none available as it is used to feed livestock.

**Table. 2.13 Aspects to Consider for Maintenance or Amelioration of Soil Physical Properties**

Maintenance: prevention of physical degradation

- Crop choice.
  - Rotations + sequential cropping
  - Mixed cropping
  - Relay cropping
  - Alley cropping, parkland + agroforestry
- Crop cultural practices
  - Tillage + residue management
  - Time of planting
  - Seed quality and soil organism symbioses
  - Inorganic fertilizers
  - Organic matter management
  - Cultivar: ground cover, complementarity with other crops
  - Biological pest + weed management
- Inter-crop ley and fallow
  - Cover crop

- Pasture ley
- Maintenance of surface litter in absence of living vegetation

• Mulches

- *In situ* live mulch
- Green manure crops
- *In situ* dead residues
- Transported residues
- Animal wastes, composts
- Industrial wastes
- Inorganic covers, *e.g.*, gravel

Amelioration to control damage

• Management of water erosion

- Contour ploughing
- Graded channels
- Bunds
- Grassed waterways
- Ponds

• Management of wind erosion

- Wind-breaks + interplanting with trees
- Shrub + tree revegetation
- Soil coverage
- Ridges

• Soil surface management

- Coverage with residues, transported waste, etc.
- Also *Inter-crop ley and fallow* and *Mulches*

• Compaction

- Deep tillage, subsoiling
- Deep-rooted 'natural plough' plants

3

# Biological and Chemical Aspects of Soil Productivity

## INTRODUCTION

Observations such as the accumulative beneficial effects of pasture, and the degradative impacts of successive cereal crops on a coarse-textured sandy loam soil in Australia shown in Figure, provide a basis for recommending rotations to maintain sustainability. There are many beneficial effects from growing legume crops and pastures in rotation. They improve soil structure, biological activity and crop yields, as well as increasing soil organic matter and nitrogen. This Chapter describes those aspects of soil biology, organic matter and soil nutrition central to the observed benefits of crop rotations.

## SOIL BIOLOGY AND THE BIOLOGICAL MICRO-ENVIRONMENT

Organic matter, microscopic and macroscopic organisms (*e.g.*, fungal hyphae and invertebrates), detritus from fungi and animals, and bacteria, and biological exudates, all assist in stabilising soil structure. The role of each part of the biomass differs according to its size. Broadly, large aggregates greater than 250 m m diameter (macro-aggregates), are stabilised by their inherent physical structure, wetting and drying cycles, and organic matter. Micro-aggregates (< 250 m m) are stabilised by live or dead roots, fungi, invertebrates and micro-organisms. The populations of soil organisms of all sizes are linked functionally through their roles in the degradation of various forms of organic material. The latter includes live and dead plant material and other live or dead organisms. A schematic food web is shown in Figure 3.1. This shows that animals such as nematodes and some fungi feed directly on live plants while other fungi and bacteria feed predominantly on litter. Earthworms and other large invertebrates create, and inhabit, burrows and pores, and are very mobile.

The most notable of these are termites, which are divided into three groups according to the structure of their nests: those that build mounds:

- Above ground.
- On the soil surface.
- Below ground.

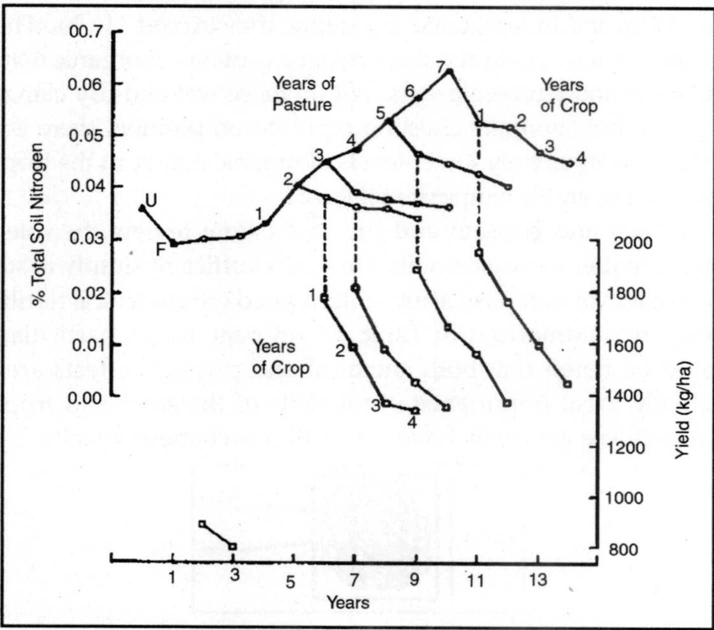


**Fig. 3.1. Trends in Total Soil Nitrogen and wheat Grain in a Long-term Rotation Experiment at Wongan Hills, Western Australia**

Small arthropods, microfauna and fungi live mostly in larger voids and in association with roots. Foster reviewed the location of the various types of soil-dwelling organisms and found that fungi, which constitute about 80 per cent of the biomass in many soils, tend to be restricted to the rhizosphere of roots, to larger pores between aggregates and to the surface of aggregates. Bacteria, by contrast, are found on roots in the rhizosphere, in small colonies in the larger micropores, within aggregates and on and within cell debris. For more information on location refer to Foster. Smiles describes the physics of the micro-environment of small soil organisms.

## ORGANIC MATTER

Both plants and animals provide inputs of organic matter to soils. Once within the soil organic residues can be distinguished on the basis of their chemical structure (*e.g.*, old lignified humic substances that degrade slowly), by their source (plant or animal) or by location. The standing crop of litter in semi-arid grasslands is usually more than 3 t/ha and in temperate dry steppe may exceed 11 t/ha. There has been much debate about the relative contents of organic matter in tropical and temperate soils. Within those wet-and-dry climates that have hot summers assisting rapid decomposition, there is no evidence of inherently lower levels of organic matter in the tropics than in comparable temperate regions.

Kowal and Kassam and Juo and Payne review the role of organic matter in tropical soils. Here, it is sufficient simply to state that organic matter has various interrelated effects on soil fertility. These are summarised in Table 3.1 on page 64. In particular it should be noted that both chemical and physical effects are of relatively great importance in the soils of the semi-arid tropics because these generally have low cation exchange capacity.

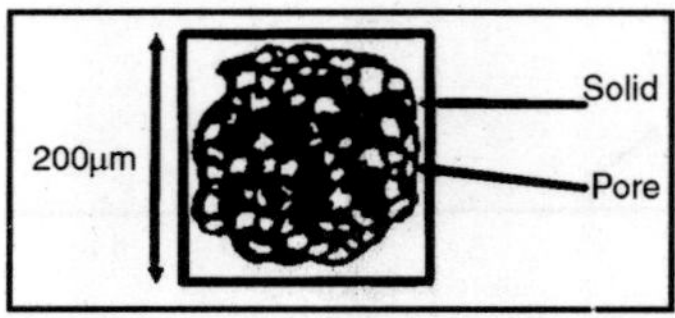


**Fig. 3.2. Model of Aggregate Organisation with Major Binding Agents Indicated**

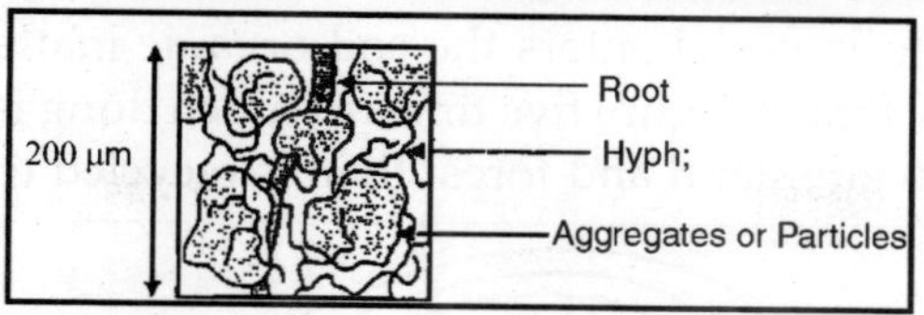


**Fig. 3.4. Model of Aggregate Organisation with Major Binding Agents Indicated**

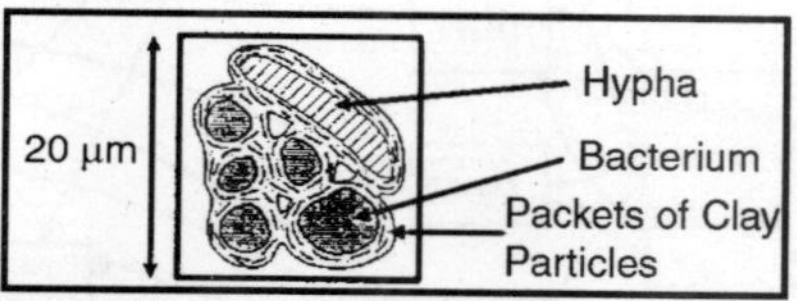


**Fig. 3.5. Model of Aggregate Organisation with Major Binding Agents Indicated**

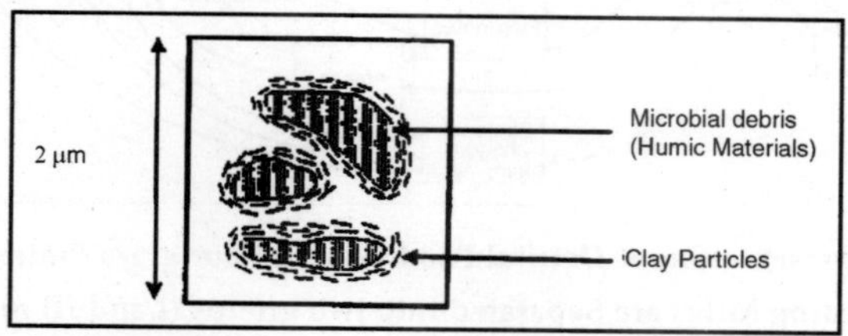


**Fig. 3.6. Model of Aggregate Organisation with Major Binding Agents Indicated**

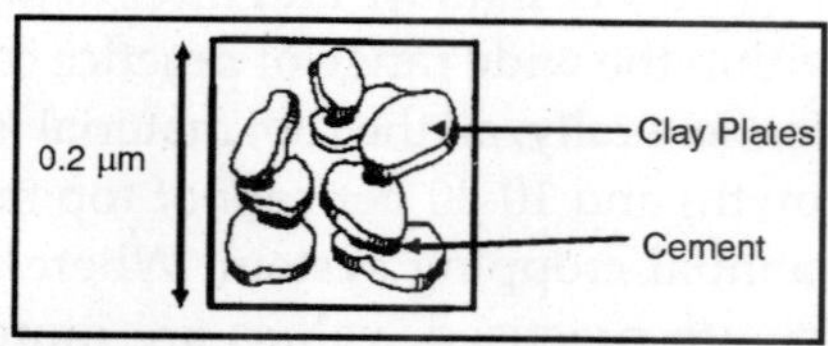


**Fig. 3.7.`Model of Aggregate Organisation with Major Binding Agents Indicated**

The relative importance of litter (crop residue) and manure as inputs of organic matter, varies between cropping systems and spatially within a system. Figure illustrates the flow of litter, manure and by-products (such as dung cake for fuel) in Indian villages practising approximately one-third single cropping and two-thirds double cropping. Here, most of the above-ground crop residue is fed to animals, but an equal amount of below-ground crop material enters the soil organic matter pool. It is noteworthy that in Figure five times as much dung is distributed naturally to grassland and forest than is recycled to the crop.

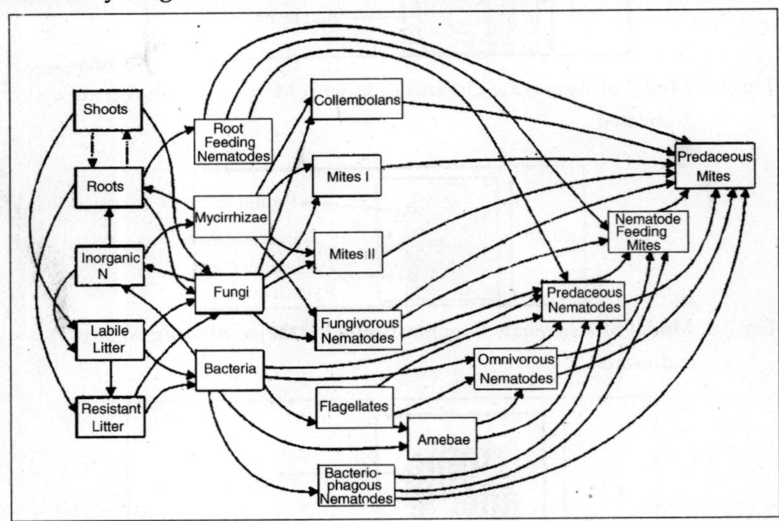


**Fig. 3.8. Representation of Detrital Food Web in Shortgrass Prairie. Fungal-Feeding Mites are Separated into two groups (I and II) to Distinguish the Slow-growing Cryptostigmatids from Faster-growing Taxa**

The pattern of flow of manure and litter to the cropping soil in Figure falls within the wide range of practice common in wet-and-dry climates. Generally, all the root material (say, 40 per cent of total crop growth) and 10-30 per cent of top material may be recycled in an annual cropping system. Where alley cropping and agroforestry are practised, values are more variable, but possible inputs could be very significant where the trees, from which the litter is taken, are grown away from the annual crops. Table 3.1 gives values for leaf production from trees.

If, say, two-thirds of the leaves from leguminous trees are harvested annually, litter values will be substantially higher and the material of better quality than the leaf and stem residue from an annual crop likely to be recycled in the field. Some qualifications, however, should be made. Tree root material is not available for decomposition in the crop field unless it is spatially overlapping (*e.g.*, as an intercrop), in which case the trees will compete with the crop for soil nutrients, water, light and space.

**Table. 3.1. Effects of Organic Matter on Soil Fertility**

| **Primary effects** | **Consequences** |
|---|---|
| **Physical effects** | |
| Binding of particles, root action leading to improved structural stability, balance between fine, medium and large pores | Improved root penetration, erosion resistance and moisture properties; water-holding capacity, permeability, aeration |
| **Chemical effects** | |
| Nutrient source, balanced supply, not subject to leaching, with slow, partly controllable, release | Including better response to fertilizers, non-acidifying source of *N*, mineralisation of *P* in available forms |
| Complexing and enhanced availability of micronutrients | |
| Increased cation exchange | Better retention of fertilizer nutrients |
| Improved availability of *P* through blocking of fixation sites | |
| **Biological effects** | |
| Provision of a favourable environment for *N* fixation | |
| Enhanced faunal activity | |

The proportion of animal and human manure used on cropland is more variable. Some farmers have developed stable systems which strongly emphasise the use of animal manure on crops. For example, Norman *et al.* describe how farmers in northern Nigeria managed to apply 4 t/ha of manure to their heavily-cropped crop land though they had only 3 cows each. Many other farmers do not ensure adequate recycling, either because they are more concerned with livestock management or they do not know the importance of maintaining a 'zero nutrient budget' to replace nutrients removed by the crop. For example, Norman *et al* also describe farmers with 10 cows each, who applied only 1.9 t manure/ha to their crops.

Within a cropping system, manuring practice varies with location. There is transference towards the centre of the system. On traditional farms, the area near the household or village is highly fertilised with human and animal manure while more distant fields receive little or no organic matter. Fussell describes such a traditional 'ring' farming system in semi-arid west Africa. Here, if houses are thatched, the village needs rebuilding or moving every 2 to 4 years. Moving takes advantage of the fertility gradient. Where the huts are not moved, the fertility gradient becomes steeper with time. Rather than trying to even out fertility by labour-intensive transport of manure, farmers vary the cropping of the fields. Continuous cropping of millet is sustainable close to the hut or village where there is plenty of human and animal manure but crop rotations are essential at the periphery.

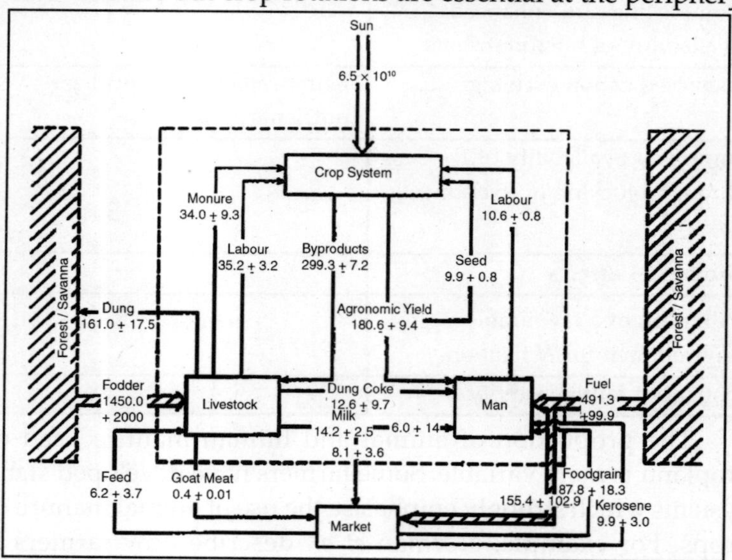


**Fig. 3.9. Energy flow through the agro-ecosystems. Values are means from five villages = 1 SE (× $10^6$ KJ/yr/ha. cultivated land solar radiation = 6.5 × $10^{10}$ kJ/yr/ha**

**Table. 3.2 Biomass Production of Leaves from Multipurpose Trees**

| Country | Land use | Tree | t/ha/year |
|---|---|---|---|
| Malaysia | Plantation | *Acacia mangium* | 3.06 |
| Philippines | Plantation | *Albizia falcataria* | 0.18 |
| Costa Rica | Hedgerow intercropping | *Calliandra calothyrsus* | 2.76 |
| Philippines | Plantation | *Gmelina arborea* | 0.14 |
| Indonesia (Java) | Plantation | *L. leucocephala, A. falcataria, Dalbergia latifolia, Acacia auriculiformis* | 3.00-5.00 |
| | | *Cordia alliodora* | 2.69 |
| | Plantation crop | *C. alliodora + cacao,* | 6.46 |
| Costa Rica | combination | *Erythrina poeppigiana,* | 4.27 |
| | | *E. poeppigiana* + cacao | 8.18 |
| Nigeria | Hedgerow intercropping | *Cajanus cajan* | 4.10 |
| Nigeria | Hedgerow intercropping | *Gliricidia sepium* | 2.30 |
| Nigeria | Hedgerow intercropping | *L. leucocephala* | 2.47 |
| Nigeria | Hedgerow intercropping | *Tephrosia Candida* | 3.07 |
| India | Plantation | *L. leucocephala* | 2.30 |

Closed systems, which rely on maintenance of fertility by recycling organic matter, are not sustainable. Nitrogen levels may be maintained or even enhanced by using legume crops or pastures in rotation but even then further inputs of nutrients are required to replace those removed by the crop. Fussell describes the inevitable need to use inorganic nutrients or organic nutrients from off-farm sources such as wastes from cities to complement farm organic matter in the African Sahel:

"Although the importance of organic manure in increasing cereal yields is well recognised, it is unlikely that there is sufficient available, on a regional basis, to sustain yields without the use of additional chemical fertilizers. For example in the Western African savannah 10 t/ha/year of manure are required for sustainable cropping of millet or sorghum.....while in northern Nigeria 2.5 t/ha/year are sufficient to maintain yields in most areas." This four-fold difference largely reflects the integration of livestock with cropping in Nigeria which results in relatively high levels of soil organic matter.

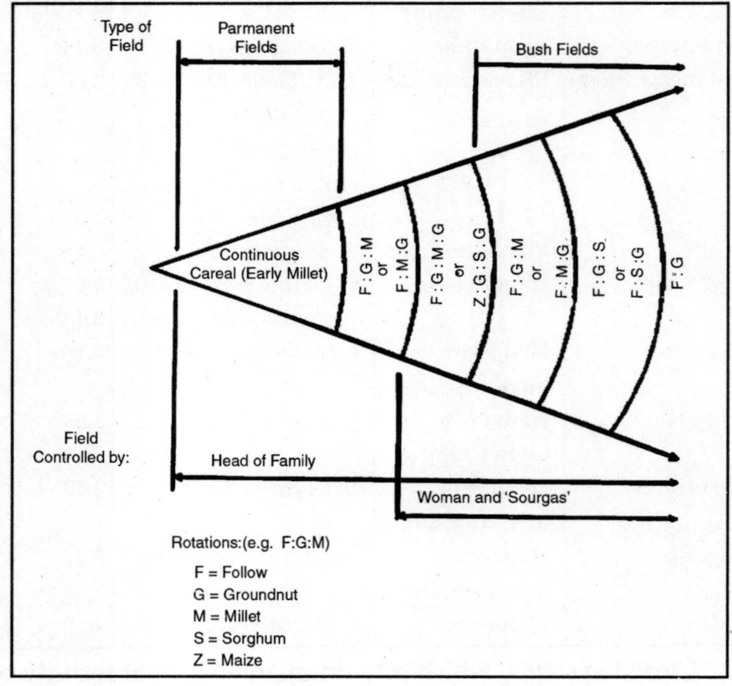


**Fig. 3.10. Fields Around the Residence, Senegal**

Farmers elsewhere, for example in Ghana, give lower priority to crop fertility, which lowers soil organic matter levels and leads to greater nitrogen loss through water erosion when there is little litter cover on the ground. Irrespective of these differences, however "It is doubtful if either of these levels of application can be achieved, as... estimates cattle and sheep manure outputs in the northern savannah zone of Nigeria are estimated to be only 1.4 and 0.25 t dry matter per head per annum respectively." Off-farm sources of manure, organic matter generally (*e.g.*, industrial by-products) and soil ameliorants will become increasingly important. Some, such as sewage from cities, are being researched. Their use in developing countries seems likely to increase, particularly as labour for transporting these materials is cheap relative to the cost of other nutrients such as manufactured inorganic fertilizers. The treatment and efficacy of various off-farm sources of organic matter are outside the scope of this *Bulletin*. It suffices to point out that substantial amounts of material are available (Table).

**Table. 3.3. Annual Production of Organic Wastes in the USA and their Current use on Land**

| Organic Wastes | Total Production | | Current Use on Land[1] (%) |
|---|---|---|---|
| | Million Metric Tons | Percentage of Total | |
| Anumal manures | 159 | 21.8 | 90 |
| Crop residues | 391 | 53.7 | 68 |
| Sewage sludge and septage | 4 | 0.5 | 23 |
| Food processing | 3 | 0.4 | (13) |
| Industrial organic | 7 | 1.0 | 3 |
| Logging and wood manufacturing | 32 | 4.5 | (5) |
| Municipal refuse | 132 | 18.1 | (1) |
| Total | 728 | 100.0 | - |

*Note*: [1] Values in parentheses are rough estimates because of insufficient data.

**Table. 3.4 Decomposition Constants, k, for Tropical Legumes. Values were Calculated with Exponential Equation for Decomposition using Data Reported in the Literature**

| Species | Location | Mean Annual Rainfall | Mean Annual Temperature °C | k/year |
|---|---|---|---|---|
| *Gliricidia sepium* | Ibadan, Nigeria | 1250 | 23-31 | 8.48 |
| *Flemingia congesta* | Ibadan, Nigeria | 1250 | 23-31 | 3.66 |
| *Cassia siamea* | Ibadan, Nigeria | 1250 | 23-31 | 2.17 |

*(Contd...)*

| | | | | |
|---|---|---|---|---|
| *Lonchocarpus cyanescems* | Ibadan, Nigeria | 1250 | 23-31 | 8.87 |
| *Inga vera* | El Verde, Puerto Rico | 4000 | 22 | 1.65 |
| *Inga* sp. And *Erythrina* (mixed) | Caracas, Venezuela | 1200 | 20 | 3.01 |
| *Erythrina* sp. (mixed with non-legumes) | Caracas, Venezuela | 1200 | 20 | 3.81 |
| *Inga edulis* | Yurimaguas, Peru | 2200 | 26 | 0.91 |
| *Cajanus cajan* | Yurimaguas, Peru | 2200 | 26 | 1.45 |
| *Erythrina sp.* | Yurimaguas, Peru | 2200 | 26 | 3.72 |

The rate of breakdown of litter and other organic materials both determines and depends on the populations and activities of organisms in the soil. It also determines the extent to which minerals taken up by a crop are released from its organic residues and made available as inorganic ions to the subsequent crop. There are numerous mathematical models of organic matter degradation. Almost all assume that the rate of degradation decreases with time, as the more soluble, digestible and accessible material is selectively and progressively degraded by soil organisms. This selectivity is often arbitrarily described by recognising several 'pools' of organic matter and, with time, 'passing' material from labile to less-labile compartments. In practice its physical and chemical composition changes gradually with time, as does its physical binding with soil particles and its relation to the predators that feed on it.

The rate of decomposition of leaf litter depends on its environment, particularly on soil temperature and soil water. Both these affect the physical breakdown of the litter and determine the population and activity of soil animals and fungi that feed on it. Decomposition also varies with plant type and age of litter, being slower for heavily lignified material. The specific properties of litter from different species, and the generally exponential form of litter decay (the rate of decomposition slowing with time) lead to values (Table) that suggest half-lives of litter ranging from 1 to about 10 years. Because of the importance of temperature in determining decomposition, rates decline from tropical to temperate locations within wet-and-dry climates.

Plant species, water and temperature are not the only factors affecting the speed of litter decomposition and mineral cycling. Management plays a role.

There are four ways for managing crop residues:

- Stubble mulch in which residues are left standing;
- Surface mulch, where above-ground residues are cut and left on the top of the soil after harvest;
- Incorporation by ploughing; and
- Cut-and-carry, in which surface residue is removed and (if not used for livestock or thatching, etc.) returned as a surface mulch about planting time for the subsequent crop; this is usually combined with ploughing of below-ground residues.

Two of the above treatments involve the fragmenting of root residues. All of them affect a range of soil properties. The degree of contact between the residue and the soil (and its organisms) and other unexplained factors affect the rate of decomposition.

Table suggests that the rates of release of minerals from organic matter, particularly litter, are a significant element in nutrient cycling and crop productivity in semi-arid environments. Such climates have a rainy season in which rainfall exceeds evaporation, so there is a risk of mineral loss through run-off and mineral loss and acidification by leaching. During the dry season there is potential loss of nitrogen as ammonia. This suggests the need to manage litter so most decomposition takes place when the subsequent crop is growing rapidly and is able to take up the nutrients released. It is wise at the same time to maintain ground cover if possible (Chapter). Manipulation of litter requires labour, which may already be in maximum demand prior to sowing.

## SOIL ORGANISMS ASSOCIATED WITH THE CROP

### BACTERIA AND NITROGEN

Cropping in dryland regions needs nitrogen to be economically successful (*e.g.*, Keating *et al.* 1991). Two sources of nitrogen are from organic matter (Chapter, section *Soil pores and water characteristics*) and from nitrogen-fixing bacteria associated with plant roots.

*Bradyrhizobium* and *Rhizobium* species infect plant roots forming galls or nodules, and fix nitrogen from the soil atmosphere directly to the plants. Locally-adapted, heat-tolerant strains survive from crop to crop in wet-and-dry climates and, whether established by natural colonisation or by inoculation of the crop seed at sowing, they subsequently fix variable quantities of nitrogen.

Where bacterial infection is effective, the bacteria commonly fix between 70-100 per cent of the nitrogen used by the crop, though the proportion is lower when the crop is given inorganic fertilizers.

**Table. 3.5 Effect of Soil Mineral N and N Fertilizers on Crop N Productivity and the Proportion (P) and Amount of crop N Derived from $N_2$ Fixation**

| Species | Location | Level | | Total crop N (kg N/ha/crop) | $N_2$ fixed | |
|---|---|---|---|---|---|---|
| | | Soil mineral N (kg N/ha) | Fertilizer N (kg N/ha) | | Proportion | Amount (kg N/ha/crop) |
| Groundnut | India | - | 0 | 196 | 0.61 | 120 |
| | | | 100 | 210 | 0.47 | 99 |
| | | | 200 | 243 | 0.42 | 102 |
| Chickpea | Australia | 10 (to 120 cm) | | 114 | 0.85 | 97 |
| | | 326 | | 184 | 0.17 | 33 |
| | | | 0 | 109 | 0.80 | 87 |
| | | | 50 | 110 | 0.55 | 60 |
| | | | 100 | 104 | 0.29 | 30 |
| Soybean | Australia | 70 (to 120 cm) | | 230 | 0.34 | 78 |
| | | 260 | | 265 | 0.06 | 16 |
| | India | - | 0* | 63 | 0.29 | 18 |
| | | | 100 | 148 | 0.26 | 28 |
| | | - | 0** | 89 | 0.48 | 43 |
| | | | 100 | 115 | 0.24 | 28 |
| Common bean | Kenya | - | 10 | 149 | 0.39 | 58 |
| | | | 100 | 158 | 0.10 | 16 |
| Cowpea | Kenya | - | 20 | 116 | 0.53 | 62 |
| | | | 100 | 137 | 0.08 | 11 |
| | India | - | 0 | 163 | 0.77 | 125 |
| | | | 100 | 138 | 0.67 | 92 |
| | | | 200 | 172 | 0.33 | 57 |

*Note:* * Uninoculated.

** Inoculated.

The extent of the effectiveness of infection of legume crops in the wet-and-dry tropics needs to be surveyed. Temperate research indicates that nitrogen fixed by bacteria ranges from 20 to 120 kg N/ha in a growing season for annual crops (Table). In the semi-arid tropics, amounts of nitrogen fixed per hectare range from none, where nodulation is ineffective, to 16 kg N in soybean naturally colonised by rhizobia, to 84 kg N when inoculated. Nitrogen fixation in soybean and groundnut of 50-70 kg N/ha/growing season is reported in Senegal. Nitrogen-fixing bacteria associated with tree legumes can fix similar quantities.

Rhizobia rarely fix all the nitrogen used by the crop and a substantial amount of nitrogen is removed from the field as grain, so the net benefit from symbiosis varies. For example, if rhizobia fix 50 per cent of the crop's requirement and 60 per cent of above-ground nitrogen is in the grain at harvest, soil nitrogen is depleted irrespective of the amount of nitrogen fixed or the grain yield. Peoples and Craswell studying 21 cases of tropical grain legumes, found positive nitrogen balances in 15 and negative ones in five. Similarly, many experiments with grain legumes in southern, semi-arid Australia show that rhizobial associations give net benefits in more than three-quarters of cases and that the benefit from lupins is substantially greater than that from field peas, largely because a smaller proportion of nitrogen is harvested and removed in lupins.

## FUNGI, ALGAE AND NUTRIENTS

Various fungi facilitate uptake of nutrients by plants, particularly phosphorus. Numerous fungi live in close association with plant roots. One group, vesicular arbuscular micorrhizal fungi (VAM), form both vesicles and arbuscules (knot-like structure) on the surface and within the root. They also colonise soil animals including earthworms and woodlice (Table).

**Table. 3.6. Nitrogen Fixation by Trees and Shrubs. Values are Per Growing Season or Per year Unless the number of Months is given in Brackets**

| Species | N Fixation (kg N/ha/year) |
|---|---|
| *Acacia albida* | 20 |
| *Acacia mearnsii* | 200 |
| *Allocasuarina littoralis* | 220(?) |
| *Casuarina equisetifolia* | 60-110 |
| Coffee + *Inga* spp. | 35 |
| *Coriaria arborea* | 190 |
| *Erythrina poeppigiana* | 60 |
| *Gliricidia septum* | 13 |
| *Inga jinicuil* | 35-40 |
| *Inga jinicuil* | 50 |
| *Inga jinicuil* | 35 |
| *Leucaena leucocephala* | 100-500 |
| *Leucaena leucocephala* (in hedgerow intercropping) | 75-120 |
| *Leucaena leucocephala* | 100-13 (6) |
| *Prosopis glandulosa* | 25-30 |
| *Prosopis glandulosa* | 40-50 |
| *Prosopis tamarugo* | 200 |
| Rain forest fallow | 400-100 |
| Mature rain forest | 16 |
| *Alachynomene afrospera* | 130 (2) |
| *Glyricidia sepium* | 100 (3) |
| *Sesbania* spp. | 125-140 |
| | 119-188 (2) |
| | 140-290 (2) |
| *Xalliandra colothyssus* | 11 (3) |

They are most prolific in the topsoil, to about 10 cm depth. They facilitate uptake of nutrients, particularly phosphorus from soils low in that element. They provide some protection to the host plant, their presence being associated with decreased colonisation by pathogens. Ellis *et al.* also found that wheat plants inoculated with VAM were more drought-tolerant than plants without VAM. Importantly, comparisons of conventional cropping systems using inorganic fertilizers and herbicides with organic systems not using herbicides have found much higher levels of infection of crop roots by these beneficial fungi in the organic system. This suggests that management for desired, associative soil organisms, should become a part of future sustainable cropping.

Other organisms associated with or infecting plants include endophytic fungi which affect plant growth rates and confer resistance to some insects. Cyanobacteria, which belong to the blue-green algae, are believed widespread in the semi-arid tropics and contribute 0.5 to 15 kg N/ha/year. *Azospirillum, Klebsiella, Enterobacter* and other species are free-living but largely inhabit the root rhizosphere; their distribution and role is still to be defined for cropping systems in wet-and-dry climates. Actinorrhizal associations are known between *Casuarina* and *Frankia* sp., but these are not exploited. It is claimed that such associations can fix as much as 60 kg N/ha/year. There are no doubt other symbioses yet to be discovered and exploited.

## WEEDS, CROP PESTS AND DISEASES

Weeds, pests and diseases all compete with or directly reduce the vigour of crops. Many pests and diseases are soil-borne. Weed life-cycles depend on replenishment of the soil seed bank and survival of the seeds against natural decay, predation by soil animals and depletion by human management, particularly cultivations. Ecological weed control thus aims to minimize recruitment of new seed into the soil as a long-term strategy as well as trying to reduce artificially the size of the weed seed bank in the soil.

**Table. 3.7. Frequency (Per cent) of VAM Fungi in Soil-dwelling Macro-Invertebrates Sampled from Natural and Agricultural Ecosystems in Ohio**

| Taxa | Ecosystem | | | |
|---|---|---|---|---|
| | Conventional tillage maize | No-tillage maize | Pasture | Old field |
| Lumbricidae (earthworms) | 25.0 | 83.3 | 50.0 | 75.0 |
| Isopoda (woodlice) | 100.0 | 35.7 | 64.7 | 36.8 |
| Carabidae (ground beetles) | 2.1 | 19.8 | 14.5 | 12.8 |

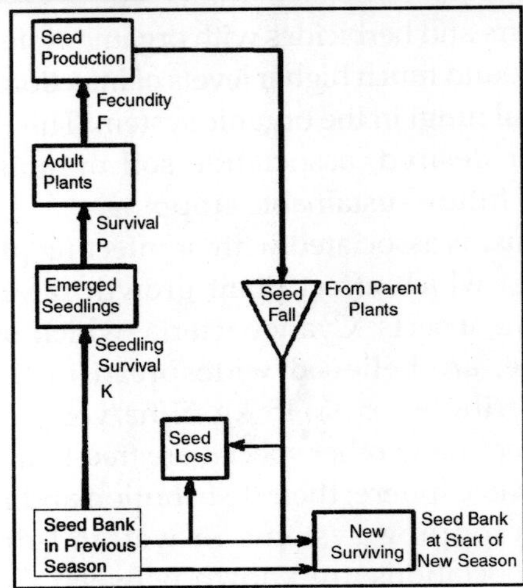


**Fig. 3.11. A General Scheme of Seasonal Cycle of Weed Population**

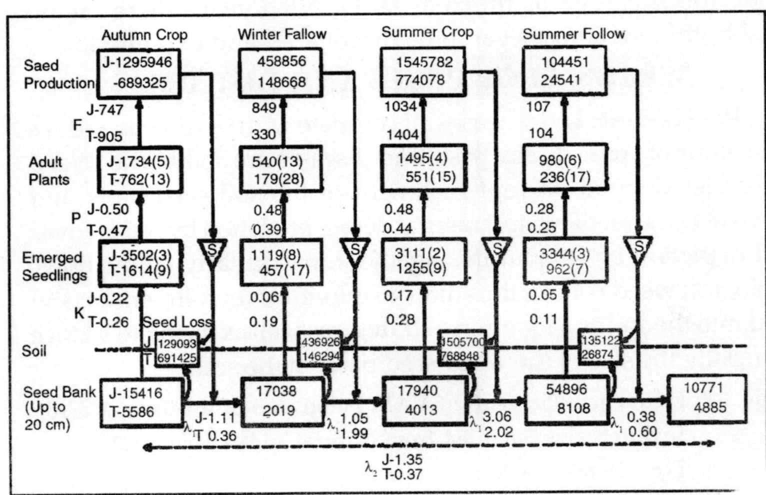


**Fig. 3.12. Total Dynamics of weed Plants and Seeds over two years. Figure gives Average weed Populations over two years in Potato Field during Autumn (September-December) and Summer (April-July) Cropping Seasons and Intervening Winter (January-March) and Summer (August-September) Fallow Periods**

Weed life cycles and strategic weed control are well understood for temperate wet-and-dry climates. Figure 3.12

illustrates the life cycle of weed populations and Figure gives informative data for weed populations in north India (2500 mm AAR of which 70-90 per cent falls in 5 months). The weed populations were measured under the contrasting conditions of slash-and-burn and terrace cultivation. Seed recruitment to the soil seed bank was higher under terrace cropping than under slash and burn but fewer survived.

It is generally accepted that there are links between weed populations, their competitiveness, and soil fertility. A good example of this is the various species of witch weed. These species infect the roots of millet, sorghum, Maize and sugar cane. *S. generioides* also infects legumes and tuberous crops. They are a serious nuisance and are widespread in semi-arid Africa. It is estimated that they currently infect 21 million ha and a further 44 million ha are at risk. Their spread and increased aggressiveness is considered to be due largely to declining fertility and soil carbon contents. The incidence of insect pests and crop diseases depends on the complexity of the cropping system and the types of crops grown. It depends too on management factors, such as the timing and type of tillage and the treatment of the crop residues. These aspects are so complex they warrant a Bulletin to themselves, so they are only touched upon here.

The incidence of pests and diseases is generally believed to be less frequent and/or intense in diverse cropping systems. Data on insects are relatively scarce but Andow is frequently quoted as showing a positive relationship between insect pest populations and the practice of monoculture.

His experience, however, is mainly with cotton, a unique crop, and wheat, though he gives a few examples from Maize and rice.

**Table. 3.8 Viruses for which Disease Incidence is Lower in more Diverse Cropping Systems**

| Pathogen | Type[1] | Vector |
|---|---|---|
| Alfalfa mosaic virus | N | Aphid |
| Bean common mosaic virus | N | Aphid |
| Bean yellow mosaic virus | N | Aphid |

*(Contd...)*

| | | |
|---|---|---|
| Beet yellows virus | P | Aphid |
| Cauliflower mosaic virus | N | Aphid |
| Chlorotic mottle virus | N | Aphid |
| Maize stunt spiroplasma | P | Leafhopper |
| Cucumber mosaic virus | N | Aphid |
| Groundnut rosette virus | P | Aphid |
| Pepper veinbanding mosaic virus | N | Aphid |
| Tomato yellow leaf curl virus | P | Whitefly |
| Turnip mosaic virus | N | Aphid |

*Note*: [1] Type of pathogen transmission system is given as P (persistent) or N (non-persistent).

Power shows that the incidence of virus diseases is less in complex cropping systems. He suggests that disease transmitted by insects is less common in multiple-cropping than in monocultures because aphids and some other insects settle on plants in response to visual cues that do not enable them to distinguish between host and non-host plants. In this way polyphagous insects can acquire a pathogen from an infected plant and transfer it when feeding on a non-host plant. If the insect is preferentially attracted to the non-host crop, it may be speculated that this crop acts as a 'trap' or 'protection' crop.

Power reviews situations where intercropping or the inclusion of a second, barrier species has led to lower disease levels. In contrast, bacteria and fungi in the root region and rhizosphere are reported to be slightly fewer in a coconut monocrop than in a multi-storied mixed cropping system. Differences in populations, and in their varied (positive or negative) effects on the food crop, are no doubt best understood through analysis of the feeding habits and predation of the organisms themselves, rather than by making superficial generalisations about their numbers. Fick and Power and Hearn and Fitt review pest management generally and pests and diseases in cotton crops specifically.

## INORGANIC NUTRITION

Inorganic nutrients occur in soil as ions and minerals, *e.g.*, as oxides, silicates and phosphates, both adsorbed onto the surface of clay particles and organic matter, and in solution.

A large proportion of some nutrients, most notably nitrogen, is found in organic matter in all but the most highly degraded soils, so organic matter and the organisms associated with it are given.

Clay particles, because of their crystalline structures, carry an inherent electrical charge. This results in attractive forces (mainly van der Waals forces) and repulsive forces (electrostatic forces) which give clay species their particular characteristics. The inherent surface charge also causes a layer of associated ions to align next to the solid particles forming a so-called diffuse double layer because it consists of a relatively inexchangeable layer (the Stem layer) closest to the surface of the particle and an outer, readily exchangeable layer, of varying thickness, called the diffuse layer. Sposito explains this more fully. In the present context, it is appropriate to describe briefly four aspects of the physico-electrical structure of soils. These are: the inherent exchange capacity; the linkage between soil particles and soil organic matter, and its effects on soil stability; ions in solution and their solubility; and the ion imbalances (from the perspective of crop growth) associated with acidity and salinity.

**Table. 3.9. Representative Cation Exchange Capacities (in $mol_C$/kg) of Surface Soils**

| Soil order | CEC |
|---|---|
| Alfisols | 0.1 2 ± 0.08 |
| Aridisols | 0.16 ± 0.05 |
| Entisols | 0.13 ± 0.06 |
| Histosols | 1.4 ± 0.3 |
| Inceptisols | 0.19 ± 0.17 |
| Mollisols | 0.22 ± 0.10 |
| Oxisols | 0.05 ± 0.03 |
| Spodosols | 0.11 ± 0.05 |
| Ultisols | 0.06 ± 0.06 |
| Vertisols | 0.37 ± 0.08 |

Adsorption is the net accumulation of matter at the interface between a solid phase and an aqueous solution. Readily exchangeable ions are those so loosely adsorbed to clay or other particles that they are replaced easily by leaching with an electrolyte solution. The ion exchange capacity of soil is the number of moles of adsorbed ion charge which can be displaced from a unit mass of soil; in most applications, this refers to readily exchangeable ions.

Sposito notes that 'Much controversy exists over the surface chemical significance of ion exchange capacities'. The maximum surface charge measurement indicates a soil's potential to adsorb ions while its actual capacity, which is more relevant agriculturally, has a lesser value. Table gives representative cation exchange capacities (CECs) for selected soil orders. It is notable that though the CEC of each order ranges widely, the predominant soils in wet-and-dry climates have low CECs.

The readily exchangeable proportion of the CEC varies with soil pH: the proportion available to readily-exchangeable bases decreases from about 1 at pH 8 to 0.5 at pH 6 to perhaps 0.2 at pH 4.5. Below pH 6 an increasing proportion is taken up by various aluminium ions and complexes, which are variably toxic to plants.

The electrical conductivity and CEC of a soil are related to its clay content. Similarly, because of the electrical charge of the clay particles, a high but variable percentage of the soil organic matter is bound to them. Table 3.10 shows that it may be as high as 90 per cent and Figure 3.13 and 3.14 illustrates the two postulated main ways that organic matter is bonded to clay. These are weak anion exchange and strongly-held ligand exchange which is a form of chemical bonding.

It follows from the electrically-charged nature of clay and organic matter and the high likelihood of their association that both contribute to the nutrient-holding capacity and stability of soils.

This intimacy led Pieri to propose that structural stability, at least of the African soils he studied, could be described by a critical value of S greater than 9, where S is the ratio of organic matter to clay plus silt, expressed as a percentage. This is shown in Figure 3.15.

**Table. 3.10. Proportion of Soil Organic Carbon in the Clay-organic Complex**

| | Per cent Organic Carbon in Soil | Per cent Soil Carbon in Clay-organic Complex[1] |
|---|---|---|
| Podzol | 1.5 | 18 |
| Solonised brown soil | 1.5 | 77 |

*(Contd...)*

| | | |
|---|---|---|
| Grey clay soil | 1.1 | 91 |
| Terra rossa | 2.8 | 82 |
| Groundwater rendzina | 5.4 | 69 |
| Black earth | 1.8 | 82 |
| Krasnozem | 4.9 | 90 |
| Red brown earth | 2.5 | 66 |

*Note*: [1] Defined as the material sinking when the soil was ultrasonically dispersed in an organic liquid of density 2 $g/cm^3$.

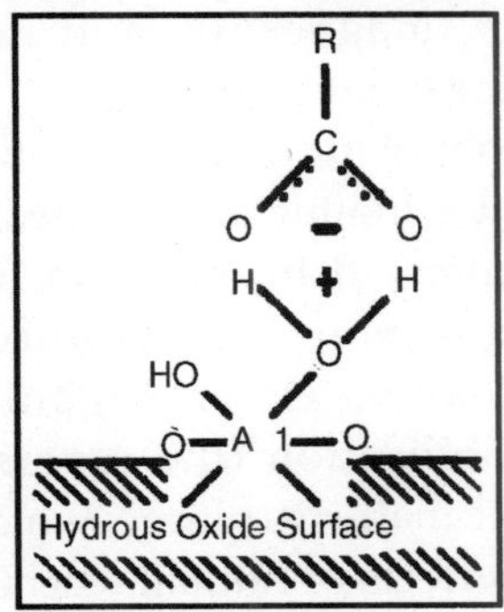


**Fig. 3.13. Diagram Illustrating Anionic Bridging: Anion Exchange. R is a Polyanionic Humic Colloid**

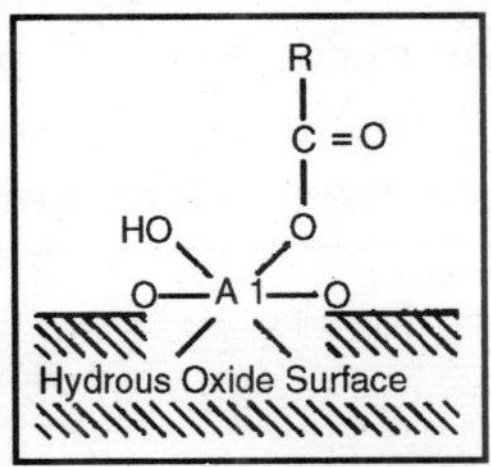


**Fig. 3.14. Diagram Illustrating Anionic Bridging: Ligand Exchange. R is a Polyanionic Humic Colloid**

Plants take up most minerals as inorganic nutrients from the soil solution (except legumes, which may fix dinitrogen gas directly from the soil air). An element is available (to the plant) if it is present as, or can be transformed into, a free ion, and it is within the plant root zone. Most elements move within physical proximity of roots through soil water movement and into the plant through evapotranspiration.

Diffusion along concentration gradients is important for less-mobile ions such as phosphorus, particularly where soil solution concentrations are weak and root densities are high (*i.e.*, the transport path is short).

Sposito and others give calculated values for the diffusivity of nutrients. Diffusion times range from 1 day for an ion to move 3 mm (which is comparable with the time it would take to move by convection in the mass flow of water) for nitrate to about 200 days for potassium, magnesium and molybdenum, and to thousands of days for other nutrients.

The concentrations of nutrients in solution fluctuate daily and seasonally. The most dynamic are nitrate and ammonium ions, which are interconverted by bacteria. Fluctuations can be explained by the effects of temperature and soil water on mineralisation (breaking down organic matter to release ammonium), immobilisation (the reverse) and nitrification (conversion of organic matter to nitrate, which is stable and highly soluble), and by the effects of rainfall leaching nitrate to depth.

In seasonally wet-and-dry cropping systems, there is a flush of nitrate following the start of the wet season and nitrate-N may accumulate in the topsoil by capillary rise of water during the dry season. Within the major seasonal patterns driven by soil water, Rochester *et al.*, found that the soil nitrate cycle lagged three months behind changes in temperature.

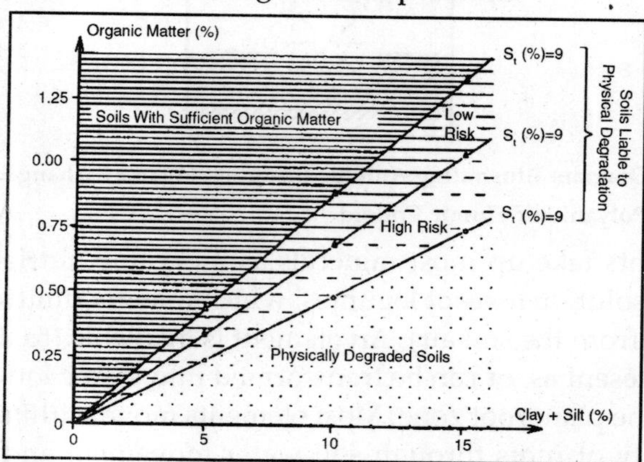


**Fig. 3.15. Critical Organic Matter Levels for Maintenance of Physical Stability**

Low soil pH affects plant roots directly because of the effects of the hydrogen ion concentration on root membrane integrity and exchange capacity. Acidity also affects roots indirectly in two ways. It alters the availability of ions in the soil solution (possibly making available toxic aluminium species, relatively toxic to plants).

It also affects mineralisation through the protons competing with cations for dissolved ligands and surface charged groups. Soil pH also affects micro-organisms, and thus the speed of transformations, for example, those between nitrate and ammonium.

Poor plant growth on acid soils may thus be caused directly by hydrogen ions, by toxicities of aluminium or manganese, or through deficiencies of calcium, magnesium, potassium, phosphorus, nitrogen or trace elements. Chase *et al* describe these relationships for sandy Sahelian soils. Variation in pH across distances of 15 m can be as much as pH 4.5 to 7.5, with associated decreases in aluminium and hydrogen ions, and increases in crop productivity. The critical pH at which crop growth is affected varies with crop, cultivar and soil type. Critical levels may be as high as pH 5 to 5.5 for less tolerant plants in soils with soluble sources of aluminium but otherwise can be as low as pH 3.9 to 4.

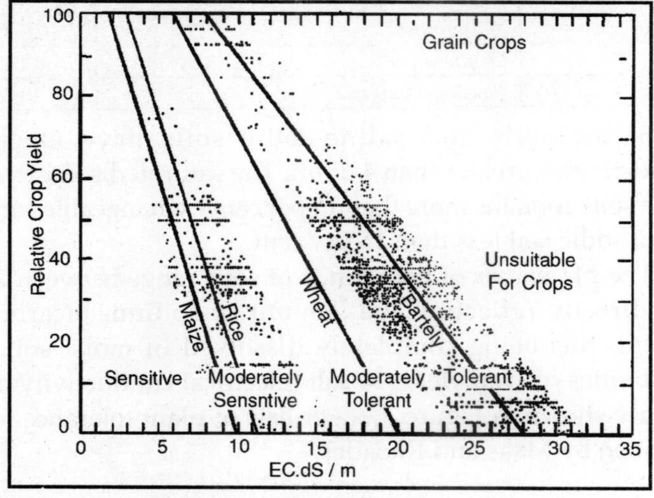


**Fig. 3.16 Salt Tolerance of Grain Crops**

**Table. 3.11. Relative Salt Tolerance of Various Crops at Emergence and During growth to Maturity**

| Crop | | Electrical Conductivity of Saturated-soil Extract | |
|---|---|---|---|
| Common Name | Botanical Name | 50% yield (dS/m) | 50% Emergence (dS/m) |
| Barley | *Hordeum vulgare* | 18 | 16-24 |
| Cotton | *Gossypium hirsutum* | 17 | 15 |
| Sugarbeet | *Beta vulgaris* | 15 | 6-12 |
| Sorghum | *Sorghum bicolor* | 15 | 13 |
| Safflower | *Carthamus tinctorius* | 14 | 12 |
| Wheat | *Triticum aestivum* | 13 | 14-16 |
| Beet, red | *Beta vulgaris* | 9.6 | 13.8 |
| Cowpea | *Vigna unguiculata* | 9.1 | 16 |
| Alfalfa | *Medicago sativa* | 8.9 | 8-13 |
| Tomato | *Lycopersicon lycopersicum* | 7.6 | 7.6 |
| Cabbage | *Brassica oleracea capitata* | 7.0 | 13 |
| Corn (maize) | *Zea mays* | 5.9 | 21-24 |
| Lettuce | *Lactuca sativa* | 5.2 | 11 |
| Onion | *Allium cepa* | 4.3 | 5.6-7.5 |
| Rice | *Oryza sativa* | 3.6 | 18 |
| Bean | *Phaseolus vulgaris* | 3.6 | 8.0 |

Saline soils and saline-sodic soils have electrical conductivities greater than 4 dS/m. The saturated soil extract of saline soils contains more than 15 per cent exchangeable sodium; that of sodic soil less than 15 per cent.

The pH values of both kinds of soils range between 7 and 10.5 directly reflecting the amount of sodium bicarbonate present, this being completely dissolved in moist soil. The sensitivities of crop yields to salt (electrical conductivity of the soil) are shown in Figure. Longer lists of plant tolerance to salt are given by Maas and Rhoades.

**Table. 3.12. Annual Rate of Organic Matter Loss Measured in the Field in the Savannah Area**

| Place and source | Dominant rotation | Clay + silt (%) (0-20 cm) | Annual rate of loss k (%) | Annual rate of loss No. of years | Notes |
|---|---|---|---|---|---|
| Burkina Faso | | | | | Ploughed |
| | Sorghum monocropping | 12 | 1.4 | 10 | No fertilizer |
| | Sorghum monocropping | 12 | 1.9 | 10 | Low rate manure |
| | Sorghum monocropping | 12 | 2.6 | 10 | High rate manure |
| | Sorghum monocropping | 12 | 2.2 | 10 | m + crop residues |
| | Cotton-cereal | 19 | 6.3 | 15 | Much erosion |
| Cameroun | Cotton-cereal | 17 | 3.2 | 5 | No fertilizer |
| | Cotton-cereal | 17 | 2.9 | 5 | Fertilizer |
| | Cotton-cereal | 17 | 2.5 | 5 | Fertilizer + kraal |
| Côte d'Ivoire | Cotton-cereal | - | 2.6 | 5 | Low rate manure |
| | Cotton-cereal | - | 2.3 | 3 | Low rate manure |
| | Cotton-cereal | - | 0.4 | 3 | Improved fallow |
| Senegal | | | | | Ploughed |
| | Millet-groundnut | 3 | 7.0 | 5 | No fertilizer |
| | Millet-groundnut | 3 | 4.3 | 5 | Fertilizer |
| | Millet-groundnut | 3 | 6.0 | 4.5 | Fertilizer + straw |
| | Millet monocropping | 4 | 4.6 | 3 | PK fertilizer |
| | Cereal-legume | 11 | 3.8 | 17 | F0T0 |
| | Cereal-legume | 11 | 5.2 | 17 | F0T2 |
| | Cereal-legume | 11 | 3.2 | 17 | F2T0 |
| | Cereal-legume | 11 | 3.9 | 17 | F2T2 |
| | Cereal-legume | 11 | 4.7 | 17 | F1T1 |
| Chad | | | | | Ploughed, v. fertile |
| | Cotton-cereal | 11 | 2.8 | 20 | Cotton monoculture |
| | | | 2.4 | 20 | Cotton-cereal |
| | | | 1.2 | 20 | + 2-year fallow |
| | | | 0.5 | 20 | + 4-year fallow |
| Togo | Cotton-cereal | 10 | 2.4 | 20 | Low rate manure |
| | Cotton-cereal | 10 | 1.1 | 20 | High rate manure |

## FIELD INDICATORS OF BIOLOGICAL AND NUTRITIONAL PROBLEMS

In this chapter, whilst reviewing relevant recent work on soil organic matter, soil biology and inorganic soil nutrients, a non-traditional perspective has been taken by placing emphasis on soil organic matter and the close chemical and functional relationship between organic matter and soil particles. It is therefore consistent to suggest that the most obvious indicator of biological and nutritional problems is the absence of, or reduction in, organic matter. Rates of loss of organic matter independent of erosion tend to be slow, but important as they are cumulative. Table suggests that under dryland cropping in west Africa, rates of loss are about 2-4 per cent per annum.

**Table. 3.13. Soil Attributes and Standard Methodologies for their Measurement to be Included as Part of a Minimum Data set (MDS) for Monitoring Soil Quality.**

| Soil Attribute | Methodology |
|---|---|
| Total organic carbon | Dry or wet combustion |
| Labile organic carbon | Digestion with KCI |
| Nutrient availability | Analytical soil test |
| pH | Glass electrode-calomel electrode pH meter |
| Electrolytic conductivity | Conductivity meter |
| Texture | Pipette or hydrometer method |
| Plant-available water capacity | Determined in field best or from water desorption curve |
| Structure | Bulk density from intact soil cores field measured permeability of Ksat |
| Strength | Bulk density or penetration resistance |
| Maximum rooting depth | Crop specific-depth of common roots or standard |

Larson and Pierce propose that minimum, analytically-gathered data sets are essential for monitoring soil sustainability.

They include two measures of organic matter among the ten attributes that they consider essential.

Their concept of requiring agreed minimum data sets is consistent with the approach to assessing sustainability outlined.

Once the minimum data set is constructed, each soil attribute is determined for a reference time (T0) and the change in soil conditions can then be measured over time (T1), which they suggest should be one to ten years.

While suggesting that agreed repeated observations or measurements are essential, it is preferable to empower farmers to take responsibility for recording their own observations of surrogate measurements rather than giving responsibility for analytically-based measurements to outsiders. Policy-makers need to address the need for analytical or surrogate assessments of soil sustainability. A first step would be to ask farmers for their observations of soil characteristics and their attitudes and concerns about soil productivity.

In the case of soil organic matter measurements, it is believed that the limited availability of expertise, the costs and the inherent sampling errors make direct measurement of organic carbon neither cost-effective nor informative. As described in Chapter, it is more likely that surrogate measures are adequate and, if sufficiently simple and cheap, have some likelihood of being used.

Pieri suggests that a bleached (possibly brittle) soil surface and plant deficiency symptoms are useful surrogates for loss of organic matter, low CEC and soil nutrient imbalances. Given that loss of organic matter is concomitant with soil structural degradation, indicators suggested in Chapter, such as turbidity of water in surface catchments, remain useful.

Indicators of plant nutrient deficiencies include: colour (*e.g.*, redness for potassium deficiency); paleness (a more general symptom, but especially obvious in nitrogen deficiency); and small leaves and plants.

Other symptoms, such as leaf curling and accelerated dropping of older leaves, may also be helpful but might equally indicate water deficits. There are several publications with photographs of nutrient deficiencies; these, however, might require further tailoring to specific combinations of crops and soils.

Soil acidity is most obviously indicated by stunted plants, by bare ground, and by better relative growth of acid-tolerant weeds in a sensitive crop.

Salinity too is indicated by vegetation changes such as trees dying for no apparent reason or an increase in the proportion of salt-tolerant herbs.

Other symptoms of salinity include: waterlogged or bare soil; livestock congregating and licking the soil surface for salt; visible salt crystals; the smell of salt; and clear catchment water because salt settles sediment.

**Table. 3.14. Mineral Nutrients and the Decline of Fertility**

| General Problems | Signs of Simple Problems | Where they Occur | Probable Causes |
|---|---|---|---|
| Limitation of nutrient supply to crops | | | |
| • Nutrient imbalance | | | |
| 1 | 2 | 3 | 4 |
| Deficiency in organic matter | Bleaching and destruction of soil surface | Senegal, Niger, Burkina Faso, Mali | Insufficient return of crop residues<br>Accelerated mineralisation of dry matter<br>Too little fertilizer |
| N (S) deficit | N (S) deficiency in cereals, legumes and cotton | Throughout area | Too little N (S) applied in fertilizers or manures. High C/N ratio<br>Very little N fixation<br>Leaching of nitrate |
| K-Ca-Mg deficit | K deficiency, Al toxicity | Frequent K deficiency in | Severe leaching of Ca, Mg, K. |

(*Contd...*)

| | | | |
|---|---|---|---|
| | | cotton<br>Al toxicity in groundnut and cotton (Senegal) | Fertilizers low in Ca, Mg, K. |
| • Low buffer capacity | | | |
| Progressive drop in CEC | Loss of fine mineral and organic soil particles | Senegal, Mali, Cote d'Ivoire, Burkina Faso, Niger, Chad | Poor erosion control<br>Rapid mineralisation |
| | Acidification | Senegal, N Cote d'Ivoire, Burkina | $NO_3$/Ca + Mg leaching |
| **1** | **2** | **3** | **4** |
| Faso, Chad | Fertilizers too | | low in Ca, Mg<br>Too little or no liming |
| Marginal soils | Nutrient deficiencies | Senegal, N Togo,S Mali, Burkina Faso | Land shortage<br>Poor cultivation |
| Inefficient utilisation of nutrients | . | | |

## MANAGEMENT FOR MAINTENANCE OF SOIL BIOLOGY AND NUTRITION

The aim of management should be to create balanced organic matter and mineral budgets. It should ensure that, over several years (a complete crop rotation), soil organic matter is not depleted and that nutrients added equal or exceed those removed by cropping or lost in various ways.

Various approaches to good management are outlined in Table. These complement the aspects listed in Table and the advice on saline water management given by Kandiah and that on water harvesting offered by Critchley and Siegert.

When managing organic matter farmers should recognise that the effects of animal and human manure, sewage sludge and plant residues last longer than those of green manure crops. Green manures, though valuable, usually last only one or two seasons because they are incorporated before they are mature and lignified. The longer-term beneficial effects of manures on soil organisms are indicated in Table.

**Table. 3.15. Aspects to Consider for Maintenance or Amelioration of Soil Biology and Nutrition**

Maintenance: prevention of degradation

- Crop choice
  - Preference for rotations and intercropping with several species, as for Table.
  - Inclusion of legume in rotation
- Cultural practices
  - Use of inorganic fertilizers to maintain a neutral nutrient budget
  - Plant litter conservation
  - Incorporation of human and animal manure
  - Incorporation of organic wastes from industry and cities
  - Tillage: minimum soil disturbance
  - Biological pest and weed management
  - Reduce rate of acidification through crop choice, litter and fertilizer management
- Water management
  - Water harvesting
  - Minimisation of salinity, if a problem is likely, through seasonal leaching and other practices Amelioration to control damage
- Nutrient imbalances and deficiencies
  - On basis of visual symptoms, use inorganic fertilizers
  - Change cropping pattern to reduce acidity
- Soil surface degradation through loss of organic matter, wind and water erosion
  - Increase organic matter through transported wastes, mulches, cover crops, etc., as in *Cultural practices*

Juo and Payne advise: 'In spite of the many proven benefits of soil organic matter, its management and recycling in an intensified, modem agro-ecosystem must necessarily revolve around two fundamental characteristics of the system, namely, the availability of organic material at the farm level, and the economic incentive for conserving and recycling organic matter'. To this may be added consideration of the benefits and costs of treating and transporting human wastes from cities (cf Table). On-site organic matter, organic material brought in from outside and industrially-produced fertilizers will be used according to their benefit cost ratios and the attitudes of governments and crop managers.

Tillage reduces the frequency of VAM, at least in invertebrates. Tillage reduces earthworm populations 10-30-fold, both killing them directly and destroying their burrows. Haines and Uren show that differences in earthworm populations between tillage treatments and stubble burning are reflected by 50 per cent differences in numbers of soil pores.

Tillage also effects the location, numbers and activity of micro-organisms within the soil, depending on the type of tillage. For example a mouldboard plough that inverts topsoil has more effect than minimal tillage. Doran found microbial biomass and potentially-mineralisable nitrogen to be 54 per cent and 37 per cent higher respectively in the top 7.5 cm of no-till than ploughed soil. These would be critical differences if translated to the semi-arid tropics. Microbial and fungal biomasses may be 20-70 per cent higher after 1 and 2 years no-till. However, conventional tillage, by burying topsoil, may cause microbial populations and their activities to be higher than under no-till at depths of say 7.5 to 15 cm. Differences in soil organisms (*e.g.*, microbial biomass) under differing tillage treatments are seasonal, generally being greatest in the period when the weather is most favourable for soil organism activity and plant growth. Rasmussen and Collins summarise many data on the impact of tillage on soil properties and conclude that stubble-mulching with zero tillage conserves up to 2 per cent more organic matter per year than ploughing.

Cropping patterns and rotations affect soil nutrition. Diversity of cropping increases the number and variety of soil organisms and reduces pests and diseases.

Soil acidification and salination are extreme cases of nutrient imbalance and, unlike other deficiencies, cannot be corrected simply by adding mineral fertilizers.

The management techniques to reduce acidification are:

- To reduce the net proton production of the system by minimising nitrate leaching (a special problem in seasonally wet-and-dry climates);
- To avoid using ammonium fertilizers and reduce the accumulation of organic matter;
- To lime the soil.

Liming is a high cost option while adoption of perennial species (to avoid seasonal accumulation of organic matter and nitrate leaching) is less costly. By contrast, salinity is usually managed by strategic leaching. This is done with the sparing use of low-salt water when both soil moisture and the water table are low.

**Table. 3.16. Micro-arthropod Populations in top 10 cm of clay soil 1 and 2 Years after Adding Organic Fertilizers in Italy. Additions were made to Achieve 4 Per cent Organic Matter and Inorganic N and P were to make all Treatments Equivalent to the Manure**

| Taxon | Control | Fowl manure | Sludge | Green manure | Straw |
|---|---|---|---|---|---|
| **One year after application** | | | | | |
| Collembola | 13209 | 31635 | 13653 | 17205 | 24642 |
| Entomobryidae | 2109 | 4329 | 2109 | 222 | 2331 |
| Onychiuridae | 1221 | 333 | 2109 | 222 | 1221 |
| Isotomidae | 9990 | 26529 | 9324 | 16650 | 20 313 |
| *C. coecus* | 8214 | 24753 | 7659 | 10101 | 18204 |
| *C. thermophilus* | 0 | 333 | 888 | 0 | 0 |
| *I. Minor* | 111 | 111 | 0 | 4995 | 0 |
| *F. Parvulus* | 0 | 111 | 0 | 0 | 0 |
| Sminthuridae | 0 | 222 | 0 | 111 | 222 |
| Neelidae | 0 | 111 | 111 | 0 | 555 |
| Acarina | 65046 | 42513 | 35853 | 43068 | 70263 |
| Pauropoda | 3108 | 1221 | 3108 | 2331 | 7104 |
| Microarthropods | 83361 | 80475 | 54834 | 65157 | 103674 |
| **Two years after application** | | | | | |
| Collembola | 4773 | 7104 | 8769 | 5328 | 5550 |
| Entomobryidae | 0 | 999 | 444 | 222 | 111 |
| Onychiuridae | 444 | 444 | 111 | 222 | 0 |
| Isotomidae | 2886 | 1998 | 6771 | 4107 | 4551 |
| *C. coecus* | 1887 | 999 | 2442 | 3108 | 3885 |
| *C. thermophilus* | 0 | 222 | 3996 | 222 | 111 |
| *I. Minor* | 222 | 222 | 0 | 333 | 0 |
| *F. Parvulus* | 333 | 222 | 0 | 0 | 333 |

(Contd...)

| | | | | | |
|---|---|---|---|---|---|
| Sminthuridae | 1221 | 3552 | 1221 | 777 | 888 |
| Neelidae | 222 | 0 | 0 | 0 | 0 |
| Acarina | 12432 | 28083 | 24753 | 27639 | 13764 |
| Pauropoda | 999 | 111 | 1554 | 999 | 777 |
| Microarthropods | 19425 | 35964 | 36963 | 35187 | 21090 |

# 4

# Sustainable Crop Rotations

## INTRODUCTION

Much has been written on the theoretical and practical benefits of mixed cropping and on its problems (*e.g.*, competition). This work is not reviewed here but the aim is to describe briefly some of the cropping patterns currently used in the semi-arid tropics and contrast them with systems used in semi-arid temperate regions.

The aims are to draw attention to practical constraints and to identify opportunities for more-sustainable dryland crop rotations in wet-and-dry environments.

The systems chosen are in Africa (the Sahel, east Africa and Ethiopian highlands), south Asia (India and east Indonesia) and in temperate Australian and Mediterranean regions. All include livestock. The climate varies within all these areas. Rainfall increases north to south in the Sahel, and changes with relief in the Rift Valley, and in the mountains and rain-shadow areas in E and NE Africa.

It increases from east to west in Indonesia and is lower inland than on the coast in India and Australia. In mountainous country in Ethiopia, tropical crops are replaced by temperate species as altitude increases. In contrast, temperate species only can be grown in the wet, cool season climates of much of Australia and the Mediterranean.

In labour-intensive Africa and Asia, villages are the units of production. They can be either traditional or, as in Ethiopia, reformed government-directed settlements. In Australia, the farm family is the decision-making and labour unit, whether they own or manage the properties.

These differences in organisation and ownership are relevant to sustainability. Where a collectively-determined cropping strategy is not sustainable, migration from the village is accompanied by necessary (often slow) changes in land use, or the village is abandoned. In extensive, mechanised, family-managed systems, economic or biological non-sustainability causes changes in ownership which are quickly followed by changes in cropping practices.

Within labour-intensive systems food security has high priority. This and family under-employment encourage the focusing of labour near the house. The importance of the household garden thus varies with the size of the property. This is more apposite in Asia and the wet tropics than in the wet-and-dry tropics, where sequential cropping of vegetables under a household tree crop (using, if necessary, hand-carried water), gives way to a seasonal vegetable crop followed by fallow in the dry season. When villages are moved and land use is changed to commercial agriculture, recreation or forestry, as has occurred to a marked extent in Thai highlands, the intensively-used household gardens are abandoned and the overall intensity of management and the fertility of the system is reduced.

**Table. 4.1. Components of Cropping Systems Illustrated in this Chapter**

| Location | Major crops | Major animals | Feed source |
|---|---|---|---|
| W. Africa Sahel | Millet/sorghum, maize, groundnuts, cowpea, sesame, cassava, yams, tree legumes | Cattle, goats, sheep, poultry | Fallow weeds, crop residue, vines, tree crop cuttings, oil cake, cull tubers |
| E. Africa | Maize/barley, sorghum, millet, tef (Ethiopia) | Donkeys, cattle, goats | Crop residues, fallow weeds, tree cuttings |
| S. Asia | Sorghum/millet (India), maize/rice (other); cassava; kenaf, wheat, groundnut, soybean, chickpea | Cattle, buffalo, goats, sheep | Bran, oil cake, crop residues |
| S. Australia | Wheat/barley; lupins, peas (subterranean clover, annual pasture medics) | Sheep, cattle | Pasture ley, crop residues |

**Table. 4.2. Land Utilisation by District, Sine-Saloum, Senegal**

| | Fatick | Foundiougné | Gossas | Kaffriné | Kaolack | Nioro | Sine-Saloum |
|---|---|---|---|---|---|---|---|
| Total area ($km^2$) (ST) | 2646 | 2 959 | 2 330 | 11 847 | 1 880 | 2 277 | 23 939 |
| Rural population | 186 973 | 98 629 | 139 775 | 283 868 | 136 602 | 154 829 | 1 000 678 |
| Density (population/$km^2$) | 71 | 33 | 60 | 24 | 73 | 68 | 42 |
| No. of farms | 20 393 | 9 781 | 15 351 | 29 635 | 15 486 | 13 969 | 104615 |
| Mean pop./farm | 8.71 | 9.58 | 8.65 | 9.10 | 8.38 | 10.53 | 9.10 |
| Livestock | | | | | | | |
| Cattle | 71 300 | 57 800 | 55000 | 157 500 | 62 000 | 114 500 | 528 000 |
| Horses | 36 700 | 8 100 | 22 400 | 48000 | 1 250 | 5 600 | 140 300 |
| Mules | 13 300 | 2 900 | 5800 | 11 900 | 7900 | 2 500 | 88 460 |
| Sheep/goats | 176 000 | 207 500 | 75 000 | 100 500 | 95000 | 122 500 | 751 500 |
| Areas | | | | | | | |
| Cultivated (ha) 83/84 | 93 649 | 96 575 | 151 379 | 285 386 | 98000 | 145 965 | 870 956 |

| Proportion cropped: | | | | | | | |
|---|---|---|---|---|---|---|---|
| Millet and sorghum | 52 | 35 | 39 | 41 | 41 | 33 | 40 |
| Maize | - | 2 | 1 | 2 | 1 | 2 | 2 |
| Groundnut | 47 | 62 | 59 | 55 | 57 | 64 | 57 |
| Area/inhabitant (ares) | 5.00 | 6.35 | 8.54 | 7.47 | 5.34 | 7.79 | 6.86 |
| Area needed for wood[a] (km²) | 37 395 | 19 725 | 27 955 | 56 774 | 27 324 | 30 966 | 200 139 |
| Area needed for livestock[b] (km²) | 256 520 | 184 460 | 172 120 | 435 860 | 185160 | 265 700 | 1 489 820 |
| Total Areas (T) | 387 564 | 290 760 | 351 454 | 778 020 | 310 484 | 442631 | 2560213 |
| Degree if exploitation (T/ST%) | 146 | 98 | 151 | 66 | 165 | 194 | 107 |

*Note*: [a]Norm at 0.2 ha forest to cover fuel needs for cooking and timber for building.

[b] Based on 1 ha pasturage per month of the dry season per LU (livestock unit). As animals are partly fed from fodder crops and harvest residues, values used are: 2 ha/LU (cattle and horses), 0.4 ha (mules). 0.2 for sheep and goats.

## EXAMPLES

In substantial areas of semi-arid west Africa and the highlands of Ethiopia the present land use is not sustainable. The areas needed for food crops, for livestock and fuel exceed the actual land available.

It is unrealistic to suggest that changing crop rotations will provide the quantitative answer needed in areas such as those in Table. The most obvious answer is to remove livestock from the system. According to Table they need one to two times the area currently under food crops. Animals are kept for prestige, for their products and for traction. Substitutes for their products (*e.g.*, soy milk and meal) might be provided more cheaply, in real terms, if soil sustainability is assigned a value. They could be traded for crop surpluses. Grain legumes can be substituted for some livestock products and increased planting of a wider variety of legumes would improve the sustainability of the cropping system. This has already be done elsewhere, for example in parts of east Indonesia.

The value of draught animals is also debatable. Sandford interprets conflicting data to suggest that farmers often use animal traction to increase the area cropped, rather than for more timely management of existing land to increase yields. If this is so, livestock reduce productivity in two ways: directly through their need for food and through their traction being used to increase the area, but not necessarily the management skill.

There are two obvious difficulties when recommending removal of livestock from a district. *First,* the livestock may be owned by people other than those who cultivate. In these circumstances, integration of livestock with cropping is unlikely. Livestock removal usually involves relocation or re-employment of the herdspeople, neither of which is easy. *Secondly,* it is not easy to identify and foster peasant-based industries to generate cash for fuel and livestock products such as milk.

Conventional wisdom is turned upside down by the suggestion that, in densely populated regions where fallows are short (<4 years) and land use is not sustainable, land used for livestock and fuelwood should be turned to food crops. For example, recent inventories and land assessments for east Africa place equal priority on livestock, fuel and food. Such equal emphasis is surely inconsistent with the belief that the priority product of a cropping system is food security

(Chapter ). Similarly, and perhaps underlying the notion that fallow-for-forage has equal status with cropping, is the widely-repeated belief that soil degradation is caused by shortened fallow periods and, therefore, that sustainable cropping depends on some minimal fallow period between crops. Many current land assessments include calculated 'fallow requirements. Fallow as such, however, does not restore soil structure, biological activity or nutrient status. A fallow, long enough to allow re-establishment of deep-rooted perennial plants crops that draw nutrients from depth and maintain soil surface cover, will improve soil productivity provided that nutrients are not removed (*e.g.*, as milk or meat) from the system. This rarely holds nowadays. Most commonly, a short fallow of weedy annual species leaves the soil bare and liable to erosion in the dry season, there is structural degradation through trampling and plant uprooting, and insufficient soil water is conserved for the next crop. There is no reason why a well-managed continuous cropping system should be less sustainable than one including unmanaged short fallows from which nutrients are removed by livestock or as fuel.

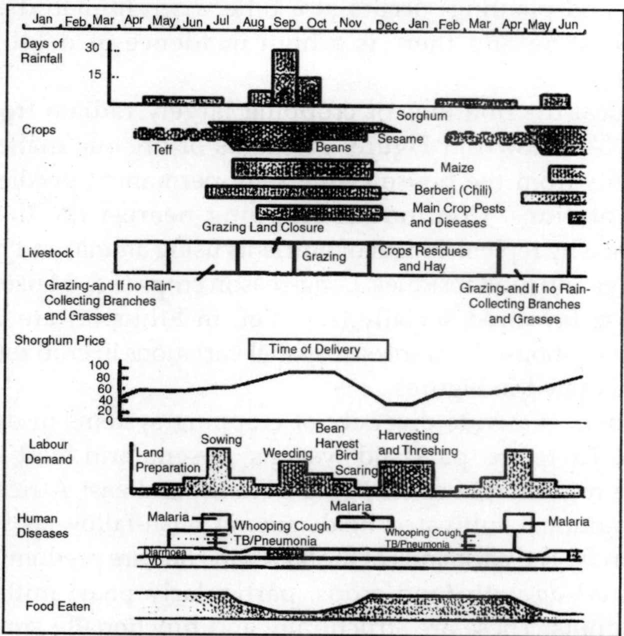


**Fig. 4.1. Seasonal Calendar of a Peasant Association in Wollo, Ethiopia**

As well as taking up land for their feed, animals are a key constraint on crop rotations. Poulain describes a typical example, in the Serere, Senegal: 'the system comprises a typically triennial rotation and the integration of cropping with cattle rearing and fodder trees'.

The herd is enclosed in one field during the crop-growing season and immediately after harvest the cattle are released to graze on crop stubble and *Acacia albida* trees. Around the village there are permanent fields of millet, cowpeas and spices fertilised with household refuse while more distant from the settlement the rotation is typically groundnut-millet-fallow.

Seasonal cropping and grasing patterns for mid-altitude Ethiopia are shown in Figure. The specific food crops favoured in Ethiopia vary with altitude, but the seasonality of crop growth, livestock needs and labour requirements, shown in Figure, are broadly typical. This figure also illustrates the pressure on human resources in the semi-arid tropics during the period around the start of the wet season, when the highest demand for labour (for tilling and planting) occurs at a time when human diets are deteriorating and there is a high incidence of debilitating diseases.

Local distributions of cropping largely radiate from the house. As shown in Figure, gradients of organic matter and nutrients from the house create semi-permanent gradients in crop rotations. Continuous cropping nearest the house is sustained by replenishment of nutrients using animal and human manures and food residues. Long-season crops (*e.g.*, Maize), and/or those favoured socially (*e.g.*, t'ef, in Ethiopia) are grown nearest the house. Examples of spatial variations in crop rotations are illustrated in Figures.

There is a wide diversity of cropping systems in dryland Africa. There are 'parkland systems' in semi-arid west Africa. On the arid margin of cropping in north and east Africa there are traditional cultivated fields among bush-fallow as well as parklands. The parklands of the Sahelian zone are predominantly *Acacia albida* with food crops, particularly pearl millet and groundnuts. These are structurally and functionally similar to the *Prosopis cineraria/pearl* millet parklands of parts of India.

One crop or, at best, two in relay, can be grown in the seasonally wet-and-dry climate of the parkland that has a perennial tree component. The cultivated ground layer carries an annual food crop, the stubble of which is grazed leaving the ground more or less bare through the dry season. The land used for food crops is traditionally cultivated, often by first cutting-back trees and bushes at the start of the wet season. The soil is ploughed and soil and organic matter piled into mounds, which are then burnt.

The ash from the mounds is then spread and the soil re-tilled as often as necessary. For t'ef in Ethiopia, there may be as many as nine tillage operations spread over three months, with consequent loss of cropping opportunity (soil water which is not used). Tillage and mounding are labour-intensive. They destroy topsoil structure and disrupt the continuity of macropores (Chapter). Nonetheless, and despite the scientifically-demonstrated benefits of maintaining soil surface cover, traditional tillage can give higher yields than minimum- or zero-tillage.

As shown in Figure, the benefits from zero tillage may take several years to accumulate so it is not surprising that one-year experiments in the Sahel failed to demonstrate the benefits of minimal soil disturbance. Ridging may also be practised. This helps to reduce wind erosion and wind-caused seedling death, improving establishment by 50 per cent in experiments. While the benefits of ridges seem intuitive, it does not follow that the ridges need to be broken and re-formed each year. Permanent ridges have the advantages of both reducing wind erosion and maintaining undisturbed topsoil.

The main food crop is usually pearl millet but sorghum and Maize are grown in more favoured areas. The cereal crop is usually planted between the trees in hills or pockets of up to ten seeds. The seedlings are thinned or compete with each other so that commonly only 2-3 survive to maturity. A low plant density, commonly 5000 hills, is equivalent to between 10 000 to 15 000 plants per hectare. In these circumstances, on-farm experiments suggest that inorganic fertilizers may give only marginal economic returns. Again, the dilemma raised biological sustainability may not equate with short-term economics. As

Figure illustrates, plant populations need to be increased substantially (with attendant risks of population-induced water deficits, in dry years) to get economic benefit/cost ratios from applied inorganic nutrients, at least in the year in which the fertilizers are applied.

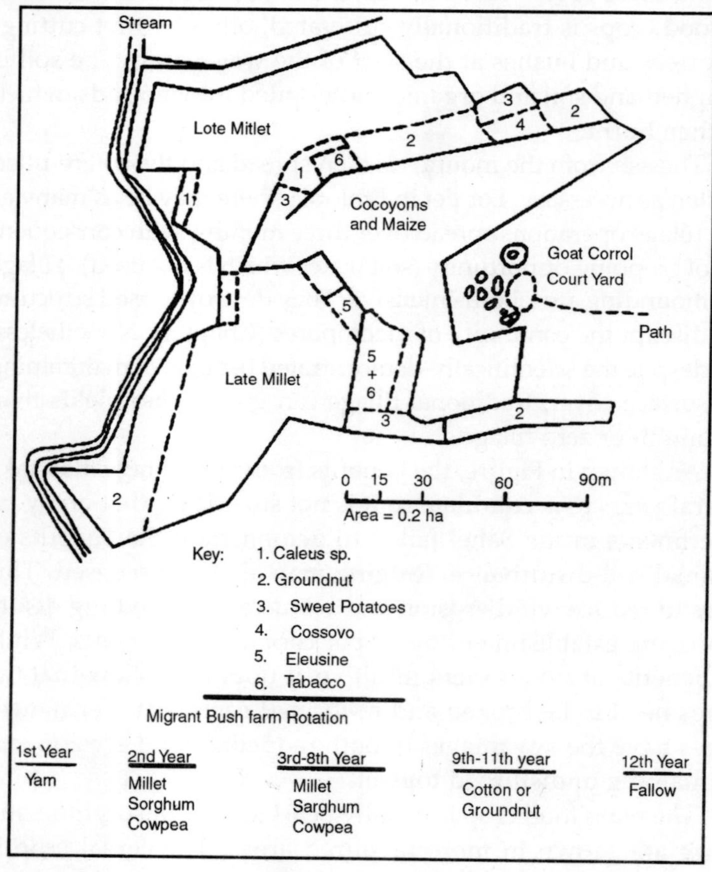


**Fig. 4.2. Homestead and Bush Field Land use and Cropping Pattern at Dalung, Benue Plateau**

However, this and similar analyses, highly relevant to short-term decisions of individual farmers, do not allow for:

- Residual benefits from fertilizers in the seasons following application of phosphorus and nitrogen, as found by Bationo *et al.*

- Indirect benefits from the fertilizers, such as, say, reduction of the incidence of parasitic weeds (*e.g.*, Striga) and the increased effectiveness of nodulation by rhizobia in subsequent legume crops.

Millet and sorghum yields are generally higher when grown the year following a grain legume. Though, on poor soils, legumes such as cowpea in rotation with millet have little effect on the millet yields if phosphorus fertilizer is not added. The beneficial effects of grain legumes are somewhat disputed.

There is substantial evidence showing relatively small residual nitrogen benefits from groundnuts and soybeans. Australian systems are similar in this respect. The benefits, associated with relatively high nitrogen fixation, only accrue when nutrients, particularly phosphorus, are adequate for both rhizobia and crop growth. The systems require small inputs of inorganic phosphorus for sustainability.

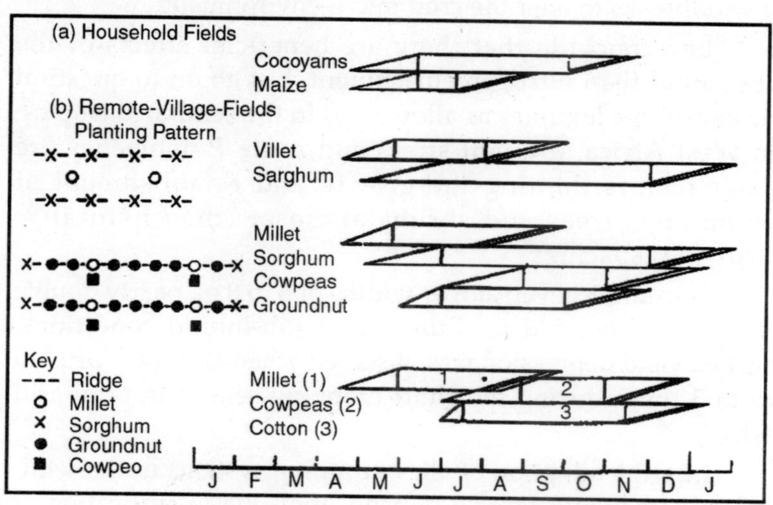


**Fig. 4.3. Cropping Schedules and Pattern of Planting for some Crop Combinations in Northern Nigeria**

Fertility is increased under tree legumes by:

- Fixation of dinitrogen gas from the soil atmosphere.

- The gathering of livestock and humans beneath their shade so concentrating their manure.
- Recycling of nutrients from the deep subsoil by leaf fall.
- Trapping and accumulation of nutrients moved laterally by wind or water from elsewhere.

Since, soil fertility is higher beneath the trees, crop yields may also be higher (though in dry years yields can be expected to be lower because of the water used by the trees).

Thus, farmers often sow sorghum under the trees to take advantage of the improved soil conditions which are not so well exploited by pearl millet, with its lower yield potential.

Figure 4.4 illustrates the nitrogen benefits from the prunings of tree legumes. Juo and Payne review the use of tree legumes as windbreaks to alter the crop micro-environment.

They conclude that there are beneficial effects of the trees other than nitrogen enrichment, but go on to question the use of tree legumes as alley crops in the semi-arid tropics: 'In West Africa, drought stress and acute P deficiency are major factors limiting the growth and establishment of leguminous trees and shrubs at closer (than naturally-occurring) spacings.

For example, even at row widths of 6 to 8 m, nearly double those recommended for humid and sub-humid conditions, marked yield depression was observed when alleys are pruned up to 3 times during the short cropping season in semi-arid India.

Thus, the adoption of alley cropping systems in the semi-arid tropics would largely depend upon the identification of specific locations where soil texture and fertility level, groundwater table and rainfall distribution are more favourable for alley establishment'. A similar view led to targeting existing fencelines as the most realistic sites for the introduction of tree legumes in Ethiopia.

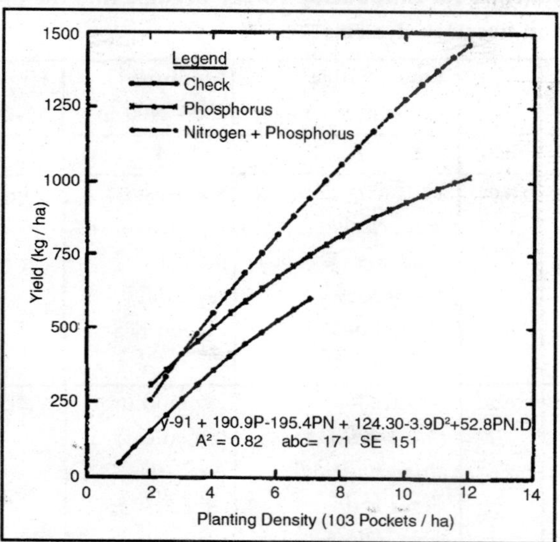


**Fig. 4.4. Effect of Plant Density and Fertilizer use Options on Millet Yield in farmers* fields where Y = grain yield kg/ha, D = Plant Density ($10^3$ Pockets/ha) and PN represent P Fertilizer only and P + N fertilizer Codes with values of 1 and 0 Represent Treatments with and without Fertilizer Respectively.**

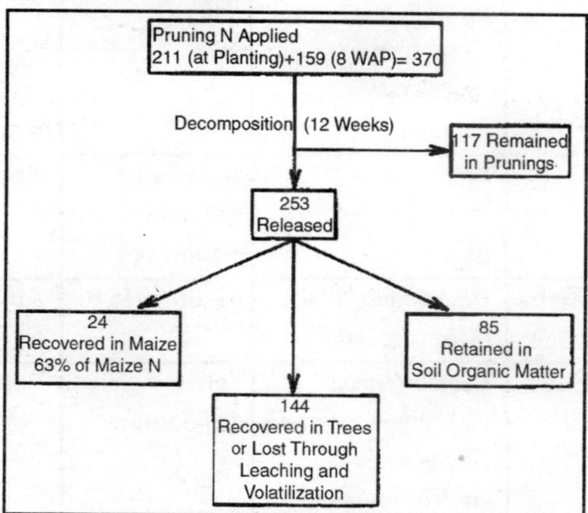


**Fig. 4.5. Partitioning of Nitrogen from Prunings of *Leucaena Leucocephala* to Crop, Tree and Soil in an Alley-cropping System on an Lixisol at Ibadan, Nigeria**

**Table. 4.3. Strategies for Introducing Forage Legume into the Ethiopian Crop-livestock Systems**

| Strategy | | Low altitude <2000 m | Medium 2000-2400 m | High >2400 m |
|---|---|---|---|---|
| 1 | 2 | 3 | 4 | 5 |
| Forage strips | Trees | Leucaena *(Leucaena leucocephala)*, Sesbania (*Sesbania brachycarpa*), pigeon pea *(Cajanus cajan)* | Tagasaste (*Chamaecytisus prolifer)*, sesbania Pigeon pea | Tagasaste |
| | Herbs | Siratro (*Macroptilium atropurpureum*), silver leaf desmodium *(Desmodium intortum)*, greenleaf desmodium *(Desmodium uncinatum)*, Verano stylo (*Stylosanthes humilis)* | Desmodium (greenleaf) Axillaris *(Axillaris* spp.) white clover, vetch | Vetch |
| Backyard forage | Trees | Leucaena, sesbania, pigeon pea | Tagasaste, sesbania pigeon pea | Tagasaste |
| | Herbs | Desmodium, alfalfa (*Madicago sativa)* | Alfalfa, vetch | Alfalfa |
| Undersown and relay legumes in crops | Herbs | Lablab (*Lablab purpureus)*, cowpea (*Vigna unguiculata*), siratro, greenleaf desmodium, Verano stylo, vetch | Vetch, desmodium | Vetch |

(*Contd...*)

| 1 | 2 | 3 | 4 | 5 |
|---|---|---|---|---|
| | | *(Vicia sativa), Cassia rotundifolia* | | |
| Oversown legumes in pasture and fallow | Herbs | Verano stylo, Siratro | ? | ? |
| Livestock exclusion areas | Trees | Leucaena, sesbania | Tasasaste, sesbania | Tagasaste |
| | Herbs | Siratro, stylos, Axillaris | Axillaris, siratro | ? |
| Conventional pastures and special-purpose forages | Herbs | Stylo (Verano), siratro, desmodium (greenleaf and silverleaf) | Desmodium (greenleaf and silverleaf), vetch | Alfalfa, vetch |

Others rightly draw attention to the need for technical packages which incorporate various options for tree legumes: intercropping and alley cropping; planting along contour lines and farm boundaries; as wood lots; as wind-breaks and the promotion of natural regeneration of trees in pastoral areas. It is best for the farmers to decide which option fits their goals.

To conclude this overview of African dryland systems, it is appropriate to consider their constraints. Obviously, the main constraint is the rainfall amount, its distribution and reliability. These severely limit the opportunities for increasing productivity per unit area.

The limitations, nonetheless, can be tackled effectively using a range of strategies. For example, in a region of Somalia, with a rainfall of 580 mm in a good year, four practices for better soil water use were tried (ridging; bunding; intercropping with a grain legume; incorporation of residue from the previous cereal crop).

Even in a season of above-average rainfall, all increased the yield of sorghum, the main crop, by 30-50 per cent. Clean fallow (a crop- and weed-free season), with the aim of conserving water for the next crop, did not improve the sorghum yield. In areas with higher and more reliable rainfall, opportunities for water conservation and relay cropping increase.

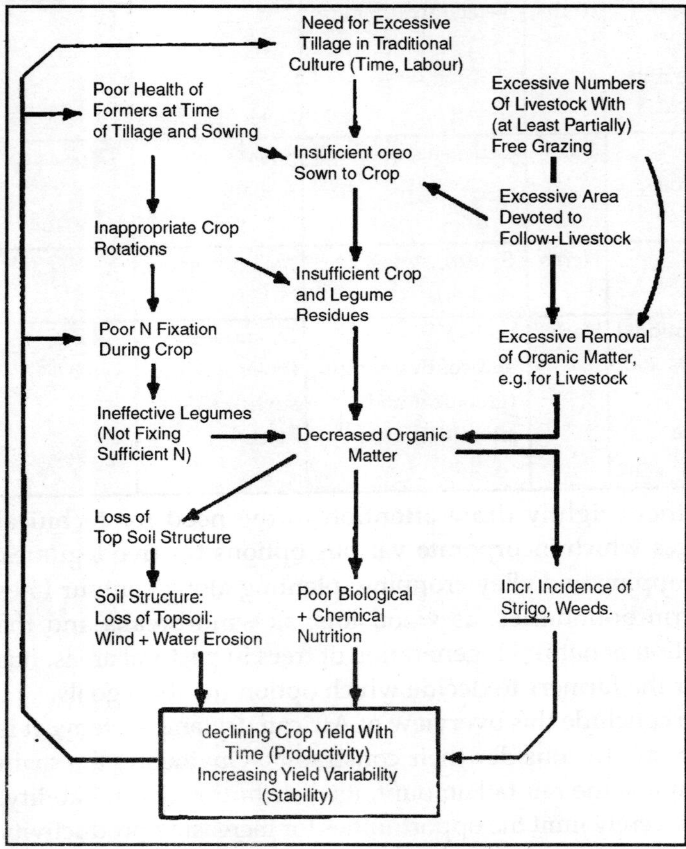


**Fig. 4.6. Scheme to Illustrate how Observed Deterioration in Agriculture may be linked back to Root Causes, which are Themselves Interrelated**

## KEY RESOURCE

In regions where single crops are the most realistic expectation, the seven aspects outlined below may be considered 'key local resource issues which are involved in production and sustainability. They are not listed here for prescriptive purposes. Any prescriptive list should be compiled by people working and living in the relevant regions. They can, however, be used as realistic examples of the resource issues/problems/opportunities related to sustainable rotations for the semi-arid tropics. It is useful to link these issues schematically, and attempt to make their root causes explicit, perhaps through a flow diagram as in Figure. Similar diagrams could provide a basis of discussion and, perhaps, action which may lead to changes in cropping practice and agreement with farmers as to how to monitor the sustainability of their system.

- Too large a proportion and area of land is used for livestock or fallow which is marginally beneficial for livestock and fuel production. Reducing livestock numbers and/or keeping them penned in a cut-and-carry forage system, rather than allowing them to graze freely for most of each year, frees land for food cropping. Fallow as such confers no positive benefits to the sustainability of cropping. Indeed, contrary to the implication in Kassam*et al.* poorly-managed short fallows grazed by livestock can be associated with degradation of soil structure and chemical depletion.
- There are too few local markets to generate cash so that farmers aiming for food security could purchase livestock-products and fuel. There is a need for more markets to overcome the constraint described in 1 above. There are opportunities to add value, for example small-scale processing of soybean meal. Such steps are immediate and create local employment, and are presumably more realistic than suggesting that semi-arid Africa tries to compete internationally with, say, the USA for markets in soybeans. Subsistence farmers competing with mechanised agribusiness may be likened to a runner competing against a fast car.
- The health and strength of human (and animal) labour varies seasonally. Labour is needed for tillage when debilitating disease is most likely and when seasonal deterioration in diet starts. Sowing and weeding

coincide with the seasonal minimum in diet. Thus, human labour constraints enhance traditional conservatism with respect to maintaining uncropped areas and, combined with traditional high intensity tillage, reduce the area of crops sown and make sowing untimely.

- For cropping systems to be sustainable, nutrients other than nitrogen need to be imported. This constraint cannot be overcome even if recycling of manures is made more effective and degrading practices such as mounding, burning and ploughing are stopped. It follows that cash generation (2, above) is essential to increase purchases of fertilizers.
- To sustain nitrogen levels, crop legumes are essential. Their absence near homesteads needs to be balanced by giving legumes a dominant role in rotations in outer fields.
- Parts of the cropping system with herbaceous legumes do not currently dominate cropping systems in dryland Africa nor are they likely to with present species and cultivars. Groundnuts are highly competitive and have poor water-use efficiency. They, however, have an appreciable, largely un-exploited, variation in nitrogen-fixing capacity. Cowpeas have a longer growing season and are more susceptible to pests and diseases than is desirable. For legumes to dominate part of a cropping system there is a need to move, for example, to 1:1 intercropping with cereals and 3:1 years legume/cereal rotations to maximise the net benefits of legumes to soil structure and fertility. The adoption of such rotations requires:
  - Legumes that can be used as an alternative to groundnuts;
  - Legumes which are promiscuous, that is able to be infected by many naturally-occurring rhizobia; and
  - Legumes which are more effective at nodulating and can benefit more from their rhizobia. These opportunities are developed in Chapter 5: they can

be seen as part of a system that focuses on the improvement of a few selected grain legumes, and their processing. In this way the present causes of non-sustainability listed in 1 to 4 above can be addressed

Naturally-occurring tree legumes that have been sustainably managed by trimming and browsing can be augmented with the same species or introduced species, particularly as part of stable land systems, along fencelines or on permanent soil ridges.

**Table. 4.4 Traditional and Improved Crops and Cropping Systems for Selected Locations in the Semi-arid Tropics of India**

| Location | Crops | | Stable cropping systems | |
|---|---|---|---|---|
| | Traditional | Improved | Intercrop | Sequential |
| Cambisols | | | | |
| Jodhpur (380 mm, 11 weeks) | Pearl millet<br>Moth bean<br>Cluster bean<br>Mung bean<br>Sesame<br>Rapeseed-mustard | Hybrid, pearl millet<br>Improved mung bean<br>Castor bean<br>Cluster bean<br>Sunflower<br>Safflower | Green gram or cluster bean/pearl millet (BJ 104)<br>*Cenchrus ciliaris* mung bean (T 44) (normal rain)<br>*Cenchrus ciliaris* cluster bean (FS277) (for >500 mm rain) | Pearl millet-fallow<br>Pearl millet (BL 104)-mustard (T 59) (for >500 mm rain) |
| Hisar (400 mm, 13 weeks) | Pearl millet<br>Cluster bean<br>Mung bean<br>Chickpea | Hybrid pearl millet<br>Cluster bean<br>Improved mung bean<br>Rapeseed-mustard | Pearl millet/mung bean<br>Pearl millet/cowpea (fodder) | Pearl millet-chickpea<br>Mung bean-mustard |
| Shallow Luvisols | | | | |
| Anantapur (570 mm, 14 weeks) | Groundnut<br>Pigeonpea<br>Foxtail millet<br>Sorghum | Groundnut<br>Castor<br>Pearl millet or sorghum<br>Pigeonpea<br>Mesta (rozella) | Groundnut (Kadiri-1)/pigeonpea (PDM 1)<br>Groundnut/castor bean<br>Pearl millet/pigeonpea | - |
| Medium Vertisols | | | | |
| Rajkot (625 mm, 17 weeks) | Pearl millet<br>Cotton<br>Sorghum<br>Groundnut | Sorghum<br>Cotton<br>Castor<br>Groundnut | Groundnut (J-11)/<br>Groundnut (J-11)/ pigeonpea<br>Cotton/green gram | - |

(*Contd...*)

| | | | | |
|---|---|---|---|---|
| Shallow Luvisols | | | | |
| Hyderabad (770 mm, 17 weeks) | Sorghum<br>Castor bean<br>Pearl millet | Castor bean<br>Sorghum<br>Foxtail millet<br>Pearl millet | Sorghum/pigeonpea<br>Pearl millet/pigeonpea<br>Castor bean/cluster bean<br>Pigeonpea/mung bean | - |
| Deep Luvisols | | | | |
| Bangalore (890 mm, 32 weeks) | Finger millet<br>Maize<br>Groundnut<br>Horse gram | Finger millet<br>Maize<br>Groundnut | Finger millet (PR 202)/ soybean<br>Groundnut/pigeonpea<br>Finger millet/maize or pearl millet (fodder) | Cowpea-fingar millet |
| Shallow to medium Vertisols | | | | |
| Solapur (722 mm, 23 weeks) | Pearl millet<br>Sorghum<br>Safflower<br>Chickpea | Hybrid pearl millet<br>Sorghum<br>Groundnut<br>Chickpea | Pearl millet/pigeonpea | Pearl millet-chickpea<br>Mung bean-rabi sorghum |
| Bijapur (680 mm, 17 weeks) | Pearl millet<br>Groundnut<br>Cotton | Hybrid pearl millet<br>Foxtail millet<br>Sunflower<br>Green gram<br>Safflower | Groundnut/pigeonpea<br>Pearl millet/pigeonpea<br>Chickpea, safflower | Green gram-rabi sorghum<br>Green gram-safflower |
| Deep Vertisols | | | | |
| Hyderabad (770 mm, 25 weeks) | Sorghum<br>Maize<br>Safflower<br>Chickpea | Sorghum<br>Safflower<br>Chickpea | Sorghum/pigeonpea | Sorghum-saff lower<br>Sorghum-chickpea<br>Maize-chickpea |
| Bellary (500 mm, 8 weeks) | Cotton<br>Rabi sorghum<br>Safflower<br>Coriander | Rabi sorghum<br>Safflower<br>Field beans<br>Chickpea<br>Cotton/setaria | Sorghum/coriander<br>Cotton/chickpea | |

## AREAS

The largest areas of seasonally wet-and-dry climate in south Asia are the 12 zones in India and the II and 12 zones in Laos and Cambodia. There are also much smaller, densely populated, areas, in east Java and the eastern islands of Indonesia.

Venkateswarlu and others review rotations in the Indian semi-arid tropics. As in west and north-east Africa, tree and shrub legumes are sometimes present and planting of elite crops such as pigeonpea, (*Cajanus cajan*) are encouraged. Annual crops, however, are dominated by pearl millet and sorghum, as in the Sahel.

Table lists traditional crops and their association with the length-of-growing season. As explained earlier this varies substantially with soil water-holding capacity in areas having the same annual rainfall. Maize is grown on favoured microsites, on soils with relatively high water-holding capacity and on the wetter margins of the region.

Animals are important in Asian farming economies, cut-and-carry systems of feeding being more common, for example, in Indonesia than in India or Africa. It is common practice at the end of the wet season, before the crops are harvested and residues available to livestock, for farmers to strip leaves from the Maize or sorghum during grain filling. As Pearson and Hall have shown, lower leaves can be removed to provide nutritious feed without harming the food crop, but removal of upper leaves, which is not uncommon, reduces grain yield.

**Table. 4.5. Management of two Cropping Patterns Commonly used in Upland Areas of Indonesia**

| Cropping pattern | | | | | | | | | | | | Crop | Spacing (m) | Population per ha (1000 plants) |
|---|---|---|---|---|---|---|---|---|---|---|---|---|---|---|
| O | N | D | J | F | M | A | M | J | J | A | S | | | |
| - - - maize - - - | | | | | | | | | | | | maize | 2.0 × 0.4 | 25 |
| - - upland rice - - | | | | | | | | | | | | upland rice | 0.4 × 0.2 | 125 |
| | - - - - - - - cassava - - - - - - - | | | | | | | | | | | cassava | 4.0 × 0.4 | 6 |
| - - - maize - - - - | | | | | | | | | | | | maize | 2.0 × 0.4 | 25 |
| - - - upland rice - - - | | | | | | | | | | | | upland rice | 0.4 × 0.2 | 167 |
| | - - - - - - - - cassava - - - - - - | | | | | | | | | | | cassava | 4.0 × 0.4 | 6 |
| | | | | groundnuts | | | - - - rice beans - - - | | | | | groundnuts | 0.2 × 0.2 | 250 |
| | | | | | | | | | | | | ricebeans | 0.4 × 0.2 | 250 |

**Table. 4.6. Relative Yield of Transplanted and Dry-seeded Rice Obtained from on-farm trials in Iloilo and Pangasinan**

| Location | Seedling Establishment | No. of Fields | Grain yield (t/ha) |
|---|---|---|---|
| Iloilo | Dry-seeding | 12 | 5.0 |
| | Transplanting | 9 | 5.0 |
| Pangasinan | Dry-seeding | 50 | 4.5 |
| | Transplanting | 26 | 4.0 |

As in Africa, trees for firewood are important in India. Shortage of fuelwood has caused other communities (*e.g.*, in east Java) to trade crop surpluses for petroleum products. Budgets of fuel and forage needs for farms and regions are published by Srivastava and Rao and others.

Where community populations are sufficiently sparse, it is realistic to recommend one-fifth of available land for silviculture and a substantial proportion for tree alley crops (16 per cent). Planting of trees for fuel and forage on 'alternative land' which has been degraded and is unstable, should be seen as a conservation measure and not as a cost against food cropping.

Tandon and Rego review crop responses in India to inorganic nutrients other than nitrogen. They conclude that responses are often large and that phosphorus and zinc are of major importance, though yield responses to potassium and sulphur are also common on some soils and iron chlorosis is an emerging problem.

Published figures giving areas of grain legumes (mostly chickpea, cowpea and gram), suggest that cereal-legume rotations and intercropping mixtures are, in practice, about 4:1 cereal and oilseeds: legumes. Thus, cropping systems in India have similarities with the Sahel though differing soils, social factors and markets should caution against extrapolating, or trying to transfer, solutions from one to the other.

Semi-arid cropping systems in India, and to a greater extent in Indo-China and east Indonesia, use dryland or upland rice when possible during the wet season. Table 40 shows typical dryland cropping patterns in east Java, with rice the preferred wet season crop if the length of the growing season (duration of rainfall), or the availability of runon water, permit. Otherwise, monoculture Maize is grown, with little interplanting of grain legumes. The grain legumes are used as a second, relay crop, often hand-broadcast into the rice stubble or as a marginal wet-season crop, planted late and on less-favoured fields.

The advantage of semi-arid south-east Asia over, say, the Sahel, is its varied topography, so that many areas are able to capture run-on water which allows extension of the growing season. Thus, dryland rice grown with a significant period in standing water is possible. In India, ICRISAT has successfully popularised water harvesting to create local areas suitable for rice or relay cropping in less hilly regions. This increases both crop diversity and economic and ecological stability.

Traditionally, rice has been grown largely by transplanting seedlings from nurseries. Societal change, driven by women preferring to do piece-work for cash instead of maintaining transplant gardens, is encouraging direct seeding. This has several advantages. It shortens the crop life cycle allowing two crops in some situations (Gomez and Gomez 1983). It is less labour intensive and avoids transplant shock. Transplanted rice has no inherent yield advantage over directly-seeded rice.

A list of constraints on and opportunities for dryland cropping in south Asia might identify similar key issues to those listed in the previous section. Livestock is segregated from cropping in parts of the region, though notably not in India. The absence of livestock and dearth of trees for fuel elsewhere in Asia, however, illustrate that communities may move from devoting land to livestock and fuel crops to essentially food-crop only systems. Recognition of the benefits of tree legumes and their adoption seems broadly feasible. Within the food crop component of the cropping system, there remains the problem of having insufficient legume cropping to maintain a neutral nitrogen budget. The productivity of the herbaceous legumes currently grown is of the order of 0.3-0.9 t/ha only.

Thus, to achieve sustainable cropping in south Asia attention is needed to the following constraints:

- The proportion of herbaceous legumes in crop mixes, and the effectiveness of nitrogen fixation (residual value) of the legumes need to be increased.
- Visual symptoms should be used to diagnose the need for inorganic fertilizers, particularly those containing phosphorus and zinc.

Soybean and mungbean are currently grown, and may be more nitrogen-effective and less degrading than groundnuts. They are, however, less extensive than cereals, which suggests that more legumes should be grown as intercrops. Table summarises potential intercropping systems, including crop legumes, shown by ICRISAT to be agronomically viable.

**Table. 4.7. Promising Intercropping Systems that Include Legumes in India**

| System | Row Ratio | Potential Areas |
|---|---|---|
| 1 | 2 | 3 |
| Sorghum + pigeonpea | 2:1 | Semi-arid red soil regions of southern Telengana, semi-arid black soils of Vidarbha region and semi-arid black soils of Malwa plateau |
| Pearl millet + pigeonpea | 2:1 | Semi-arid black soils of Deccan region of Maharashtra as well as Karnataka and semi-arid black soils of Saurashtra |
| 1 | 2 | 3 |
| Pigeonpea + soybean | 1:1 | Semi-arid/sub-humid black soils of Madhya Pradesh and sub-humid red soils of Chotanagpur region |
| Sorghum + mung bean | 1:1 | Semi-arid black soils of Bidarbha and Marathwada region |
| Pigeonpea + sunflower | 1:1 | Semi-arid black soils of Deccan region of Maharashtra |
| Finger millet + pigeonpea | 4:2 | Sub-humid red soils of Orissa and semi-arid red soils of southern Karnataka |
| Groundnut + pigeonpea | 5:1<br>3:1 | Semi-arid red soils of Rayalaseema |
| Maize + mung bean | 1:1 | Sub-humid submontane regions of northwest Uttar Pradesh and Jammu and semi-arid black soils of Malwa plateau |

In parts of Asia, for example northeast Thailand and east Indonesia, root crops, particularly cassava, are grown extensively for local consumption, local processing (*e.g.*, into packaged chips) and for export (*e.g.*, as stock-feed to Europe). The profitability of root crops for export varies widely. Their local use, however, and their good storage properties and transportability once processed, suggest that root crops will remain a component of semi-arid cropping. Inter-planting of a non-competitive legume crop shortly after planting cassava stakes could substantially increase the area sown to grain or forage legumes. The low yields of legumes suggest a need to improve both inorganic nutrition and rhizobial effectiveness.

## CROPPING

Cropping in temperate dryland climates is based on cereals, mainly wheat and barley, as is cropping in the wet-and-dry regions of north east Africa above 2400 m and in the Near East. Although the climates in Australia and the Mediterranean areas under discussion are similar they have different traditions, the Mediterranean systems being aimed towards village food security until recently while the Australian systems, developed since, the 1880s, are aimed at producing bulk grain for export. Farm size differs, Australian mechanised farms averaging 2800 ha. Mediterranean systems recognise traditional practices and farmers' values, and there is more local consumption of food crops, so there is a variety of cropping systems around the theme of cereal/fallow or cereal/hay crop/fallow. Australian systems have developed more limited options around crop/legume pastures or crop/volunteer weedy species rotations. On the Australian dry margin and on fine-textured soils the systems usually include a long fallow (9-12 months), primarily to conserve water but also to assist the mineralisation of nitrogen, and control weeds and diseases. The efficiency of the system, as assessed by water use (WUE), generally ranges from 10 to 16 kg grain/ha/mm, which is very similar to that of cereal crops in the United Kingdom and Syria.

Table. 4.8. Main Rotation Patterns in Mediterranean Cropping Systems

| Country | Main rotation |
|---|---|
| 1 | 2 |
| Italy | Cereal-hay crops-cereal<br>Fallow-cereal-cereal-fallow (has grasing value)<br>Cereal-tobacco, sugar beet, grain legumes |
| Greece | 70 per cent cereal-cereal<br>10 per cent cereal-hay crops<br>2 per cent cereal-grain legumes<br>18 per cent with other alternatives (cotton, sugar beet, tobacco) |
| Portugal | Cereal-fallow (falow has grasing value)<br>Fallow-fallow-cereal<br>Fallow-cereal-subterranean clover<br>Annual cropping:<br>Cereal-cereal-hay crop<br>Cereal-sunflower (grain legumes are being abandoned due to broomrape) |
| Spain (rainfed)<br><br><br><br><br><br>Algeria | 40 per cent fallow-cereal<br>25 per cent annual cereal<br>10 per cent cereal-sunflower<br>10 per cent cereal-hay<br>5 per cent cereal-grain legumes<br>10 per cent others (mainly grazed forage)<br>80 per cent fallow-cereal (fallow has grasing value)<br>15 per cent cereal-hay crops<br>5 per cent cereal-grain legumes |
| Egypt | Usually 3-year rotation including cotton, Maize, rice Morocco: |
| Low rainfall | 25 per cent fallow (has grasing value)<br>75 per cent continuous cereal |
| High rainfall | 15 per cent continuous cereal<br>79 per cent grain legumes<br>15 per cent fallow (grazed) |
| Tunisia | 16 per cent fallow-fallow-cereal<br>42 per cent fallow-cereal<br>17 per cent cereal-cereal<br>14 per cent cereal-hay crops<br>11 per cent cereal-grain legumes |

(*Contd...*)

| 1 | 2 |
|---|---|
| Cyprus | 20 per cent fallow<br>6 per cent continuous cereal<br>20 per cent cereal-hay crops. Nigligible grain legumes |
| Jordan | Fallow (no grasing value) exists only in low rainfall.<br>The majority of the area is cereal-grain legumes or cereal-vegetables |
| Lebanon | Little remaining fallow. Where it exists it has grasing value except in low rainfall zone Rotations are wheat-barley-wheat-alfalfa and wheat-lentils |
| Turkey: | |
| Low rainfall | 95 per cent fallow-cereal<br>5 per cent grain legumes |
| High rainfall | 50 per cent continuous cereal<br>10 per cent hay crops |
| | 10 per cent grain legumes<br>30 per cent others |

**Table. 4.9. Major Small-grain Production Systems of Australia Subdivided on Rainfall and Soil Texture**

| Winter Rainfall | | | | Summer Rainfall |
|---|---|---|---|---|
| Low (<300 mm) | | Medium | High | |
| Coarse-textured Soils | Fine-textured Soils | | | |
| C-(VP...) | F-C | C-(P...) | C-(P...) | SF-C |
| C-GL | C-C | C-C | C-P-P | F-SC |
| | F-C-(P...) | C-GL | | SF-C-SF |
| | C-GL | C-GL-C-(P...) | | -F-SC |
| | | F-C | | |

*Note*: Key: C, cereal crop; GL, grain legume; SF, summer fallow; VP, volunteer pasture; F, fallow; P, legume pasture.

The soil treatments were cultivation and lime 2.5 t/ha (•): cultivation and nil lime (O); direct drill and lime 2.5 t/ha (■); and direct drill and nil lime (□). The dashed line at 1.0 log rhizobia/g soil denotes the limit of detection using the most probable number method. Different letters notate significant difference. Rutherglen, Australia sandy clay loam ph 4.2

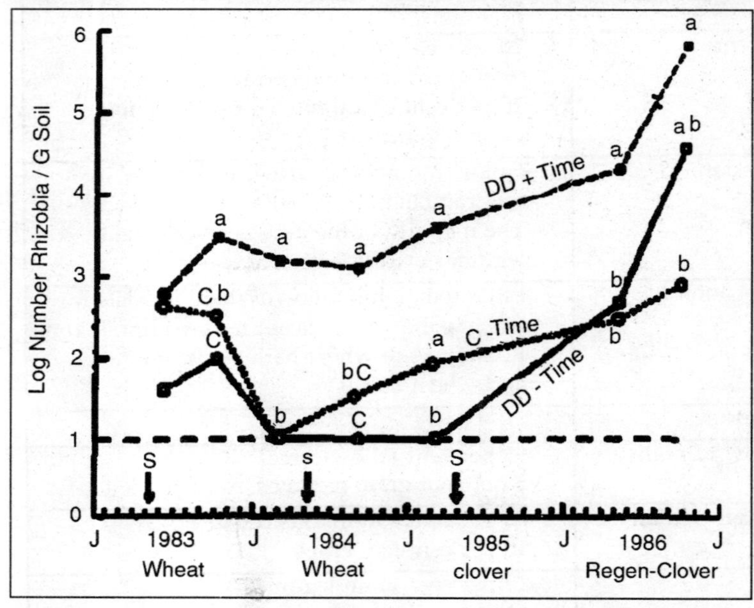


**Fig. 4.7.** ***Rhizobium Trifolii Soil*** **Populations over Four Seasons with Wheat and Direct-sown**

Land use in Mediterranean climates presents problems for soil sustainability, particularly on hill land. These are not so much directly related to cropping practices (although contour ploughing, for example, is not uniformly practised) but to deforestation and depopulation of hill country (S. Orsi, personal communication). In Australia, land preparation methods vary greatly with location and season and may confer non-sustainability. Land to be cropped is usually heavily grazed shortly before the wet season; residual vegetation (pasture or weeds) is then killed with desiccant herbicide. The crop is then sown four hours to four days later either with minimum soil disturbance, or conventionally using 3-5 passes of a tined implement. There is some attendant loss of topsoil organic matter and structure. It is noteworthy that, in a system depending on the survival and growth of rhizobia, direct drilling creates lower bulk densities and maintains higher rhizobia populations than tillage.

**Table. 4.10. Estimates of Equilibrium Values of the Amount of Soil Organic Matter Nitrogen which Builds up under Various Cereal Crop-legume Pasture Rotations, and its Mineralisation in the Crop year, in Australia**

| | Equilibrium Soil N (kg/ha) | Mineralisation (kg/ha/yr)[1] |
|---|---|---|
| Continuous pasture | 3350 | 134 |
| 2 crop: 4 pasture | 1925 | 77 |
| 1 crop: 1 pasture | 1450 | 58 |
| Continuous crop | 500 | 20 |

*Note*: [1] A decomposition constant of 0.04 is assumed, but this would vary with season, crop and cultural condition.

Australian cereal-based cropping systems need to maintain a neutral nitrogen budget through the non-cereal phase. They require addition of phosphorus and other elements as inorganic fertilizers. Organic matter levels need to be kept up.

Dunne and Shier criticised the rotations used then as not maintaining fertility for cropping. As a result pasture legume periods were lengthened. From about 1950 to 1980, pastures were widely included in rotations, the period in pasture commonly being one and a half to three times that of the crop. The accumulation of nitrogen under pasture is illustrated in Figure 4.8.

The average annual increment of soil nitrogen from 22 estimates was 67 kg N/ha/year, the highest value being 182 kg/ha/year. Perry argues that the key to the functioning of the system is the rate of mineralisation which makes the nitrogen available to the crop. Table 4.11 shows a 4-fold range in rate of mineralisation among four common crop-pasture rotations.

Nutrient elements other than nitrogen, particularly phosphorus, sulphur, zinc and molybdenum, are routinely added at sowing in quantities sufficient to compensate for their removal in the grain. As well as giving economic crop yield responses in the year of application, these nutrients have indirect benefits. Heavy applications of inorganic nutrients reduce the incidence of root diseases.

The cereal-legume pasture system, so widely used from 1950 to 1980 and publicised internationally, depended on relatively favourable international prices for grains and sheep products, especially wool, and a balance between them. Successive years of drought with high grain and relatively low wool prices in the early 1980s led to intensification of the cereal crop phase. Continuous cropping became widespread and fewer legume pastures were sown.

Then, in the early 1990s, following a short period of artificially high wool prices and increased sheep numbers, wool became marginally economic so sowing and management of legume pastures were again largely abandoned. Recently, concern about erosion associated with overgrasing and the extent of bare soil that occurs under annual pasture species such as *Trifolium subterraneum* and medicago, has shifted attention towards the inclusion of grass, particularly perennial grass, in the non-cereal phase of rotations.

This is supported by research which shows that the rate of soil acidification beneath perennial grass is slower than under annual ryegrass (*Lolium rigidum*) pasture in a seasonally wet-and-dry environment.

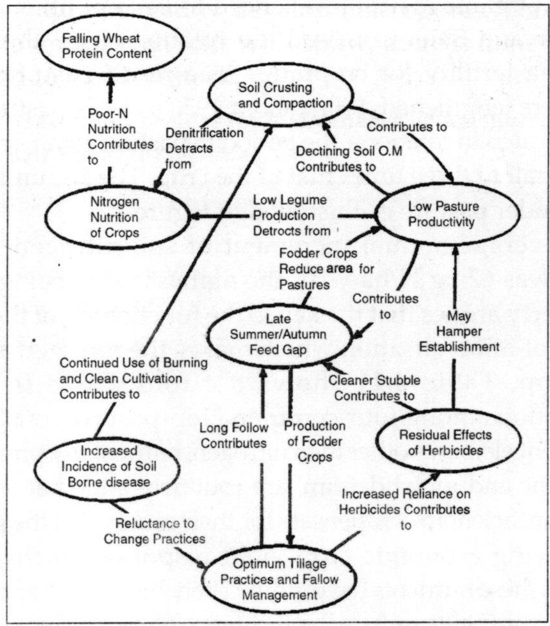


**Fig. 4.8. Linkages between Major Agronomic Problems or Issues Identified from the Conduct of a Topical rapid Rural Appraisal in the Forbes Shire in Australia**

**Table. 4.11. Impact of Lupins on Soil Nitrogen under Cerealxand Cereal-Legume Rotations: Mean Soil MineralxNitrogen ($NH_4$+$NO_3$+$NO_2$ kg/ha, 0-20 cm) after Growing Wheat (W) and Lupins (L) in Rotation**

| Soil Mineral Nitrogen after | | | | | | | | | |
|---|---|---|---|---|---|---|---|---|---|
| Year 1 | | Year 2 | | | | Year 3 | | | |
| W | 71.2b[1] | WW | 79.6d | WWW | 65.8c | WWL | 99.6b | | |
| L | 105.7a | LW | 102.5c | LWW | 66.4c | LWL | 109.2ab | | |
| | | WL | 127.8b | WLW | 78.0c | WLL | 120.5a | | |
| | | LL | 172.3a | LLW | 77.7c | LLL | 126.1a | | |

*Note*: [1] Within columns, values not followed by a common letter differ significantly ($P<0.05$).

The present system is arguably not sustainable, because of the changes in markets and attitudes, depending as it does on nitrogen fixed by a pasture phase that is increasingly botanically-impoverished. This is illustrated by farmers' perceptions that the nitrogen concentration of the cereal grain is declining, and that pasture and soil factors are causing this.

The Australian system described above is a good example of how biological and soil sustainability depends on markets, in the absence of policies of land management agreed by land managers. It shows how sustainability and agronomic practices can change rapidly. Another issue raised by recent changes in Australia is the need for adapted grain legumes. The system is likely to return to sustainability only by introduction of legume crops, particularly field peas and lupins (*Lupinus angustifolius* and *L. albus*).

These fix more nitrogen than legume-based pastures and, depending on the proportion of nitrogen removed from the field as grain, usually give a residual benefit of about 20-50 kg N/ha (field peas) and 50-90 kg N/ha (lupins). The latter value exceeds that for many tropical grain legumes (Table). As Table shows, the soil nitrogen responds positively, quickly and substantially to the inclusion of a temperate grain legume (in this case, *Lupinus angustifolius* in NE Victoria).

Grain legumes currently occupy only 12 per cent in west and 4 per cent in the east of the cereal areas. These areas need to be increased to help maintain general levels of soil nitrogen, organic matter and good soil structure.

One aspect, perhaps better documented for semi-arid Australia than elsewhere is that of timeliness. As Loss *et al.* (1990), Perry (1992) and others have described, there is a window of opportunity for sowing at the beginning of each wet season. Any delay in sowing causes substantial reductions in grain yield.

This is a universal phenomenon that emphasises the need for:

- Knowledge of the probabilities of an effective beginning to the growing season, so that sowing will be neither premature and unreasonably risky or, as is common in developing countries, delayed so much by late, excessive cultivation that yield potential is routinely lost;
- Sufficient knowledge by the farmer of the best timing and type of soil treatment at sowing for plant establishment. This requires ready availability of machinery and the use where possible of minimum tillage. Where cultivation is necessary because of local conditions, it should be coupled with sowing, so that at least some fields are sown in a timely manner and are not delayed until cultivation of the last field is complete.

Sowing is only one of several recurring operations in both crop and fallow phases (Figure 4.9). For each, timeliness may be critical. In some cases it is doubtful whether the operation should be undertaken at all. For example, ploughing and grasing at unsuitable soil-moisture contents can be detrimental to soil structure. Grasing is most beneficial if timed so that the livestock eat immature weed seeds, but it is detrimental if delayed until after seed fall and causes uprooting of plants when the topsoil is friable and dry. Within both Australia and Mediterranean regions there are examples of family farmers and large corporations with an ethic of land care who manage their soils for sustainability, and others who do not.

Table 4.12 summarises some of the characteristics of these extremes in Australia. Unsustainable management is almost always oriented to short-term market prices without knowledge or interest in the biological mechanisms which underlie soil and crop behaviour, and the patterns which characterise sustainable crop rotations. Table, although necessarily general, illustrates the fifth premise of this *Bulletin*, namely that tailoring an understanding of generic mechanisms to local situations is a powerful way of creating sustainable cropping systems.

Figure 4.9 illustrates a non-sustainable situation in east Australia. The key indication that the system is not sustainable (declining protein concentration in grain) is linked to its root causes within the system. Similar schemas, together with local knowledge of seasonal work demands and social constraints, can form the basis for debate about any action to be taken.

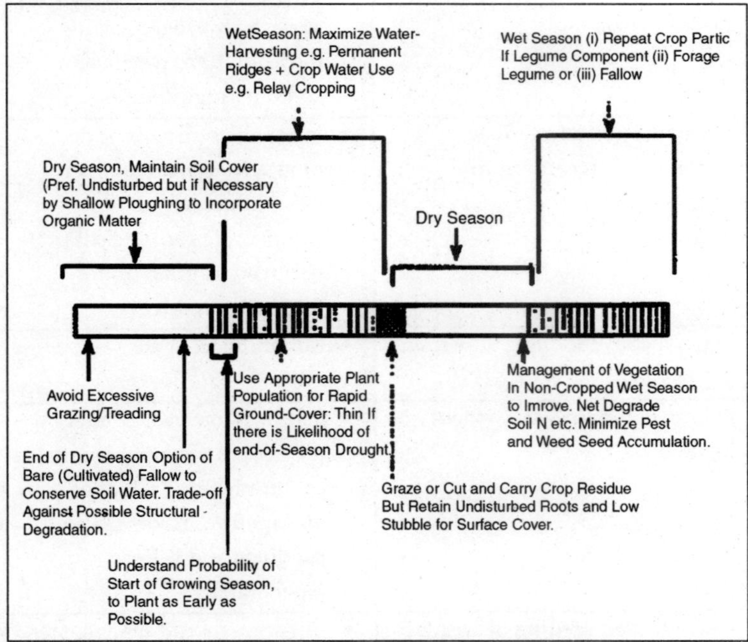


**Fig. 4.9. Scheme to draw Attention to the Need for clear time-lines, and Critical Timeliness of Operations, in Cropping in the Semi-arid Tropics**

**Table. 4.12. Management Aspects of Dryland Cropping Systems from an Australian Perspective**

| Not Biologically Sustainable | Sustainable |
|---|---|
| 1 | 2 |
| • Cropping decisions made annually only on grain and livestock prices | • Cropping broadly based on rotations and ethic of land care |
| • Focus on few products: 2 crops, 1 -2 crops, 1-2 livestock (*e.g.*, wool, sheep meat) | • Diversity of products |
| • No rotations; grasses dominate system | • Rotations with balance between grasses (cereals and legumes) |
| • Full utilisation of crop residues for livestock, hay, etc.; bare soil in dry season | • Organic matter and soil biology management: soil surface coverage, residue incorporation, permanent contour ridges/bunds |
| • Inorganic nutrients added (sometimes) according to product prices | • Inorganic nutrients added regularly to maintain zero-loss budget, *i.e.*, to compensate for nutrients removed in grain and livestock products |
| • Annual conventional cultivation (>2 passes) | • Minimum tillage |
| • Fallow not managed; without legume | • Fallow perceived as integral part of crop rotation: contains pasture legume which is managed to maximize seed products and self-regeneration |
| • Uncontrolled seeding of weeds including annual grasses during fallow | • Conscious weed management to minimize weed seed rain |

(*Contd...*)

| 1 | 2 |
|---|---|
| • No perennial grasses or trees | • Some perennial vegetation: grasses in waterways, exposed hillsides; tree legumes |
| • Livestock populations high; grasing pressure uncontrolled, causing, *e.g.*, soil structure degradation in wet areas | • Livestock populations conservative, flexible for surviving drought |

## ROTATIONS AND SOIL PRODUCTIVITY

On the balance of experimental evidence, those cropping elements that help to maintain soil productivity in parts of Africa, Asia and Australia have been emphasised.

These include:

- The need to retain organic matter and soil structure.
- The need for appropriate tillage which, in many situations, involves minimal soil disturbance.
- The need to replenish the nutrients removed in grain, straw and livestock products.
- The essential need to maximize ground cover.
- The desirability of mixing crop species, particularly to include legumes with effective nodulation (grain crops, forage crops, trees and shrubs).
- The need for any fallow period to be managed rather than to be left bare to be exploited by livestock, or for weed seeds and pests to accumulate in the soil.

The question arises: how are these conceptual elements best exploited in crop rotations? Table provides a framework, and Figure illustrates the dynamic, and recurring, nature of decisions involving the choice of rotations and techniques for the maintenance of soil productivity.

Figure illustrates the value of effectively-nodulated legumes (in this case, a pasture ley) in increasing soil nitrogen, as long as the nitrogen is not removed as a product. Figures show associated increases in soil rhizobia and vesicular arbuscular miccorhizae under undisturbed pasture legumes. Tables show the impact of plant architecture and ground cover on soil loss and mineral leaching.

All the above give estimates of the benefits, to soil biology and chemistry, of the crop elements in a rotation. The aspects they illustrate are reflected by some Australian farmers' practices, under which the rotations chosen appear to maintain soil productivity though soil nitrogen levels at equilibrium may be only half those under continuous legume pasture. However, there are very few long-term studies which quantify the effects of different crops on soil conditions. Indeed, such studies seem to be a priority to encourage changes in cropping systems. For example, there are few data on nitrogen fixation by legumes on farms in Africa and Asia, and no known studies, that compare the effects of groundnuts on soil structure and fertility (which are possibly degrading) with other legumes such as soybeans.

There is little information on the effects of fallow management on soil biology, particularly on weed seeds, pests and diseases. On many farms, weeds spread uncontrolled during the fallow period, while experiments often unrealistically contrast weed-free extremes. Caporali and Onnis, in re-affirming the importance of crop/legume rotations, interestingly also show that weed density increased more during ten years of sunflower-based cropping under sunflower monoculture than under a sunflower-lucerne rotation. They show too that there are more weeds after mechanical- than chemical-control.

There is much information available on the effects of tillage and litter/stubble treatments on soil properties. The data, however, are not always consistent. This is not surprising as the timeliness of an operation is relevant to its effects on the soil and there are rapid changes in soil properties in the days following sowing. Moreover, several years of treatment are often needed before there are lasting effects upon soil characteristics that influence crop growth, for example, root length density.

Notwithstanding the variation, and at times the ephemeral effects of management on soil properties, it is clear that there are benefits from those crop rotations that enable crop residue retention. Three examples follow. Gill and Aulakh show that zero tillage for three years gave the lowest soil bulk density and highest crop yields. Radford *et al.* found that zero tillage plus stubble removal gave the least soil water storage but that zero tillage plus stubble retention gave the greatest soil water capacity.

Chan *et al.*record that ten years, conventional (three-pass) cultivation and stubble burning gave least soil organic matter whilst direct drilling plus stubble retention gave most organic matter. In this study, tillage had a cumulative effect, causing 31 per cent differences in organic matter (2.42 per cent as against 1.68 per cent organic carbon); a loss of 1 per cent organic carbon was calculated to result in a loss of almost 3 cmole of negative charge per kilogram of soil. As a working hypothesis, it seems that stubble and litter retention (and incorporation if necessary to avoid removal by grasing or wind) is the key to sustainable rotations. Bearing in mind soil organisms, however, it may be necessary occasionally to till and mix the soil layers.

Mineral nutrition is, together with crop choice, stubble/litter treatment, and soil management, a key to sustainable rotations. For example, the removal of a 600 kg grain crop requires 1.8 kg phosphorus to be replaced using manure or mineral fertilizer. Nine kilograms of nitrogen are also needed (most realistically, from the breakdown of a previous legume crop or pasture, or by application of manure). A long fallow, in which deep-rooted perennials draw nutrients from depth, may help to balance the loss of nutrients. However, nitrate may move down the profile during the fallow, commonly giving a net annual decline in soil nitrogen in the absence of legumes, however, found that there was an increase (of 30 kg N/ha) during a short (7-8 months) fallow which balanced the loss during the crop phase. If weeds or pasture grow during the fallow and are grazed, then nutrient losses of about 20 per cent are common. These losses are by removal of animal products and volatilisation of urine. Grasing can also redistribute nutrients as dung from one field to another.

5

# Farming Techniques

## INTRODUCTION

Over 70 per cent of the people of Africa live in rural areas, and almost all of them depend directly on their smallholdings for a living. Although many people are moving to the cities, apparently mainly because they hope for a better standard of living there, it is common knowledge that even in the cities many people still try to cultivate small plots to obtain some of their food. Thus, it is clear that farming is by far the largest economic enterprise in Africa, and it is vital for the well-being of most people.

Although no two farms are exactly alike, it is obvious to anyone who has traveled in the countryside anywhere in the world that most farms in a particular area usually have many common features. Depending on the environment in that area, most of them grow the same crops, keep the same animals, and go about their farming in roughly similar ways. Therefore, they can be said to practice similar farming systems.

Farmers have to adapt their farming to their natural environment—to succeed, they must work with nature and not against it. They must also adapt their systems to infrastructural factors, such as land-tenure arrangements, and the availability of inputs such as water, power, fertilizers, pesticides, labour, advice, and information. External economic factors such as location, availability of roads, communications, markets for selling produce, prices, credit, produce subsidies, and other features affect the attractiveness and profitability of different farming systems.

Internal factors such as farm size, the available labour force, resources that can be invested, and fixed improvements are other obvious determinants. Finally, personal choice and preferences may influence the system.

Although one must be cautious in grouping farms in an area, however large or small, as practicing a common farming system, this approach has several advantages, provided that both the similarities and the differences between the farms are borne in mind. One advantage is that research can be designed to produce technologies directed to reduce similar constraints on large numbers of similar farms. Similarly, economic and infrastructural interventions can be designed for particular farming systems. In recent years, a large body of literature has grown up around the whole discipline of farming systems research.

Although I do not propose to describe details of this methodology here, farming systems researchers described most of the systems summarised in Part II.

Three critical aspects of savanna farming receive particular attention in both this and the following chapters.

These are:

- *First,* soil fertility problems—Soil conservation and the maintenance or improvement of soil fertility are crucial to sustainable and productive tropical farming systems.
- *Second,* risk and uncertainty—Some of the risks facing farmers because of rainfall uncertainty have been described in Chapter. Farmers must cope with many other risks, including crop and animal diseases and pests, and economic uncertainties.
- *Third,* labour productivity—The marked seasonality of savanna farming means that there are peak labour demands for fairly short periods, followed by longer periods with lower demands. Under these conditions, with a relatively inelastic labour supply, farmers find it difficult to increase their labour productivity.

## FARMER-MANAGED ECOSYSTEMS

Farms can be considered as ecosystems managed by farmers; thus agriculture is concerned with farmer-managed ecosystems. In his classic work on tropical farming systems, Ruthenberg points out that a farm is both an ecosystem and an independent unit of economic activity, and it is but one system, albeit an important one, among many rural systems. He further suggests that

Farmers use land which originally was part of a natural system, and most ecological systems untouched by man show a 'zonal' type of vegetation which is typical for the given natural conditions and which is close to a 'steady state'.... Natural systems, however, are unproductive in terms of human objectives. The basic principle of farming is to change the natural system into one which produces more of the goods desired by man. The man-made system is an artificial construction which requires continuous economic inputs obtained from the environment to maintain its output level. Farming thus implies the abolition of an unproductive 'steady state' in favour of a man-created, more productive but unstable 'state,' and much of the farm input (tillage, fertilizers, weeding, etc.) is nothing but an effort to prevent the new state from declining towards an unproductive low-level steady state.

## FARMING SYSTEMS—INTENSIFICATION

Ruthenberg traced the process of intensification of tropical farming systems, resulting from increasing population pressure on the land, as passing from shifting systems through fallow systems to permanent upland systems, sometimes with perennial crops and irrigation.

Boserup pointed out that each stage in this process required more labour to produce the same amount of output with a given level of technology, thus there was a direct incentive to practice extensive rather than intensive farming provided that sufficient land was available. Only when land became limiting because of population pressure would farmers intensify their production, and even then they would continue to use techniques adapted to more extensive systems as long as possible, until forced by starvation to adopt more labour-intensive techniques such as manuring and soil conservation, and then, and only then, would they adopt or invent labour-saving technologies such as the plow. She showed that, throughout the world and all through history, some societies had failed to make these adaptations in time, with the result that soil exhaustion and erosion had ruined their land, so that they died out or were conquered by more powerful people, who used them as forced labour to intensify production.

**LAND USE**

In their major contribution to the understanding of African smallholder landuse and farming systems, Allan, with Trapnell and their colleagues, working in the country that is now Zambia, stated their basic concept

In an underdeveloped country the study of vegetation in relation to soils, climate, and other environmental factors, and the classification of plant associations in accordance with these factors, should provide the most practical single guide to agricultural and forestry potentials.

Allan pointed out that the shifting cultivator worldwide has always needed a detailed knowledge and understanding of the environment to survive.

[The cultivator] can rate the fertility of a piece of land and its suitability for one or other of his crops by the vegetation which covers it, and by the physical characteristics of the soil, and he can assess the 'staying power' of a soil, the number of seasons for which it can be cropped with satisfactory results, and the number of seasons for which it must be rested before such results can be obtained again.

His indicator of initial fertility is the climax vegetation, and his index of returning fertility is the succession of vegetational phases that follows cultivation. In many cases his knowledge is precise and remarkably complete. He has a vocabulary of hundreds of names of trees, grasses and other plants, and he identifies particular vegetation associations by specific terms. This fund of ecological knowledge is the basis of 'shifting cultivation.'

Perhaps the major contribution of Allan and his colleagues was in conceptualising and reducing to quantitative terms some of the complexities of shifting cultivation. These terms included Cultivable Land, the Land-use Factor, the Cultivation Factor, and Critical Population Density. All these terms could be quantified, and together they could give an accurate understanding of the land use under a particular farming system.

Allan found that the Cultivation Factor, which he defined as the area cultivated per head of population, varied very little between four distinct and widely separated farming systems in Zambia. Farmers were growing Maize or sorghum in three of these systems and cassava in the fourth as staple foods. The average cultivated area per person was almost the same in these different systems, varying from 0.41 to 0.45 ha. On soils of lower fertility, a larger area of 0.68–0.73 ha had to be cultivated to obtain sufficient food.

Comparing these data with those from other countries, Allan found that in the parts of Kenya and Uganda with two rainy seasons per year, where bananas or other perennial crops were grown with annual crops, average areas under cultivation for subsistence were somewhat lower, at 0.17–0.27 ha/person (some of this land was cropped twice a year with annual crops). In Teso District, Uganda, however, where ox-plows were widely used, and where the second rains were often uncertain, the area was about 0.37 ha/person. In West Africa, the average food-crop area per person in the rain forests of the Congo, Ghana, and Liberia appeared to be about 0.18 ha, whereas in overpopulated areas of northern Ghana where ox-plows were used, the area varied from 0.27 to 0.72 ha.

The data quoted on other African farming systems later show that although the 45 countries of the African savanna contain an enormous variety of environments and peoples, there are remarkable common features in the farming systems throughout the continent. With the exception of an almost negligible number of larger-scale 'commercial' farms, the vast majority of African farmers cultivate 0.2–0.4 ha of subsistence food crops per person. If the full-time work of an adult man or woman is taken as a 'man-equivalent' (ME), and the number of

MEs often seems to be about half the number of people in a family, the area per ME is about double the above. Thus, the lower figure of 0.2 ha/person, or 0.4 ha/ME, appears to be about the minimum for survival in most grain-producing areas, giving about 200 kg of grain per person in an average year, at a yield of about 1 t/ha, or the equivalent in other crops. Any additional production from the average of 0.4 ha cultivated per person was described as the 'normal surplus' by Allan.

Because crop yields were frequently well below 1 t/ha, this 'normal surplus' was essential to allow some storage of grain against one or more poor harvests. Where crops are also grown for sale, an additional 0.2–0.4 ha/person may also be cultivated, particularly when simple mechanisation such as the ox-plow is used. Then the upper limit seems to be an average of about 0.8 ha/person or 1.6 ha/ME. With an average family size of about 5–6 people, this gives a cultivated area per family of about 1–5 ha (some extended families living together are considerably larger).

Obviously, these overall average figures conceal considerable local variation. In Malawi, for example, with a relatively dense population, the average holding size was 1.16 ha, with a mean population per holding of 4.5 people, giving an average area per person of 0.26 ha. However, 48.6 per cent of the resident population lived on holdings smaller than 1.0 ha, 43.8 per cent on holdings of 1.0–3.0 ha, and only 7.6 per cent on holdings over 3.0 ha.

Mean farm size per family appears to vary from about 1 to 10 ha or more, but in areas where population pressure is low and shifting cultivation or its variants are still practiced, farm size may not mean much. Farmers use the land that they need, and other land is usually held communally. Although accurate statistics over wide areas are difficult to obtain, Harrison (1987) suggests that 66 per cent of all holdings are smaller than 2 ha and nearly 96 per cent cover less than 10 ha.

## RING CULTIVATION

Pelissier gives a generalised view of a Senegalese village, which can also be taken to represent villages or farms throughout the savanna.

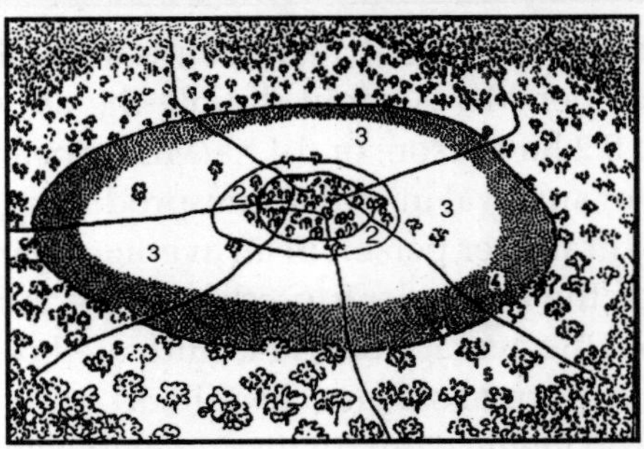


**Fig. 5.1. A Generalised Diagram of a Senegalese Village Showing Ring Cultivation**

The intensity of cropping decreases in concentric circles or rings from the land immediately around the houses to the outermost fields. The houses in the centre of the village are surrounded by a limited area of permanently cultivated 'garden' land in which a high state of soil fertility is maintained with animal droppings, household refuse, and ashes. Fruit trees provide shade and food and also protect the soil. The next area of land surrounding the village often has reduced fertility because of over-cropping without sufficient addition of materials such as manure to maintain fertility. The area around this (4) may be more fertile because of less intensive use and longer fallows, and the surrounding forest or bush may only be used on an intermittent shifting-cultivation basis.

As already outlined, the process of intensification of tropical farming systems under increasing population pressure passes from shifting systems through fallow systems to permanent cultivation systems, sometimes with perennial crops or irrigation. It is of considerable interest that, in Pelissier's diagram, this is the same as the progression from the shifting cultivation area far from the village to the permanently cultivated 'garden' land with perennial crops around the houses. (Small irrigated areas may also be cultivated where water is available.) In other words, all the stages of intensification are already present in most villages when land pressure is low, and intensification could be expected to increase as pressure on the land rises, and fallow land becomes limited.

## LIVESTOCK

Livestock ownership is variable, but a high proportion of farmers keep a few goats or sheep, perhaps averaging about 2–6 animals/farm, and some poultry. A similar average number of cattle are owned by a smaller proportion of farmers, depending on the incidence of trypanosomiasis and other factors. A few farmers keep donkeys, horses, and, in the arid areas, camels. Livestock are not usually closely integrated into the farming system, being mainly grazed on communal grasing lands, often by herdsmen from a different tribe. They may graze stubbles and other crop residues after harvest. Cultivators sometimes provide incentives to herdsmen to herd their cattle on the stubble to manure the land. Farmers under considerable land pressure, such as the Kofyar hill farmers of Nigeria (Netting 1968) or those of the Ukara Island in Lake Victoria, have adopted methods of making larger quantities of manure in small enclosures that are then used to manure larger areas.

In this way, the 'garden' land can be enlarged, depending on the number of livestock and the amount of manure that can be made. In both these examples, however, it was striking that when additional fertile land became available to some of the farmers by migration, they immediately expanded their cultivated areas and abandoned most of their intensive practices, as predicted by Boserup.

## ECOLOGICAL ANALYSIS

Although this description paints a relatively simple picture, it is important to stress the complexity and variety of tropical farming systems. The humid zone systems are probably the world's most complex in terms of numbers of crop species involved and their interactions. Also, the 45 countries represented in the African savanna have an enormous diversity of environmental, ecological, and socio-economic conditions, which lead to a great variety of farming systems.

The relatively simple view of farming systems as farmer-managed ecosystems appears useful for the present purposes, but farms are, of course, parts of many other systems, and they interact in many ways with these systems. These hierarchies of systems have been discussed by Ruthenberg, Norman *et al*, and Okigbo among others. Fresco applied ecological systems theory to the study of agricultural production in the Kwango–Kwilu region of Zaire. This approach has the advantage that it provides a theoretical framework for the study of the hierarchy of systems that make up the whole agricultural sector of a region or country.

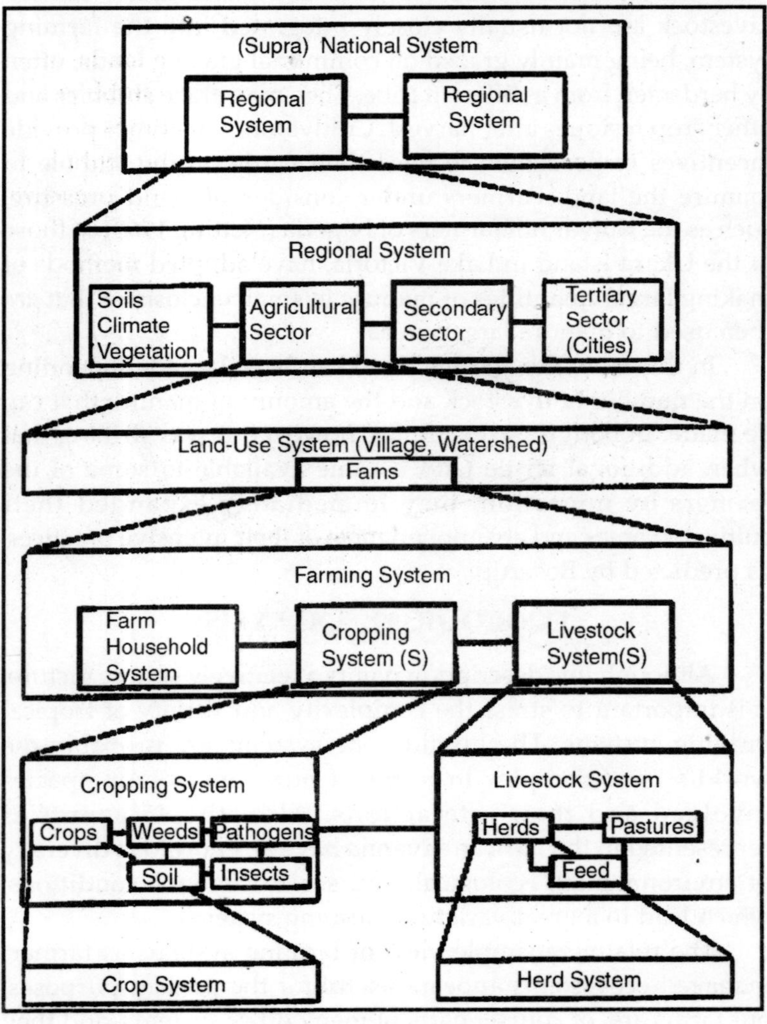


**Fig. 5.2. Agriculture as a Hierarchy of Systems**

This hierarchy is summarised as showing how each level depends on, and interacts with, the levels below and above it. In this example, the crop system and the herd system are at the lowest level (these could be divided into subsystems of individual plants or animals, and subdivided again, even down to cells). Taking the crop system as an example, it can be described in relation to the cropping system of which it is a subsystem.

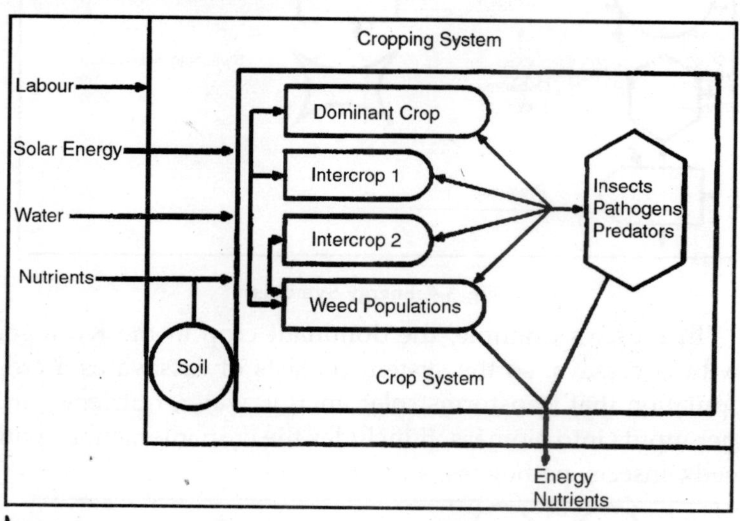


**Fig. 5.3. The Crop System**

All systems involve an arrangement of parts (components or subsystems) that interact according to some process (transform inputs into outputs). The structure of a system is defined by the quantitative and qualitative characteristics of the components and the interactions between them. The way in which inputs are processed into outputs determines the function of a system. Within the boundaries, all relevant interactions and feedbacks are included, so that all those components that are capable of reacting as a whole to external stimuli form a system; however, boundaries can be difficult to define in complex systems.

The hierarchy involves successive energy quality transformations. At each step, much of the energy is used in the transformation and only a small amount is transformed into higher quality. A higher level in the hierarchy implies a higher level of energy and a larger scale of time and space. The symbols in Fig. are some of those used by ecologists to indicate what happens to this energy.

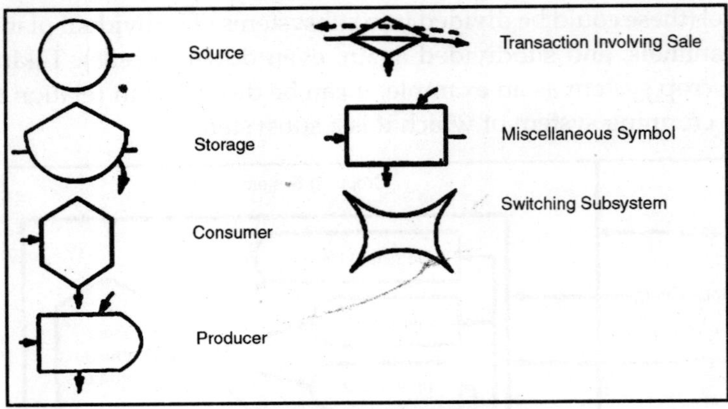


**Fig. 5.4. Energy Symbols**

In Fresco's example, the dominant crop in the Kwango–Kwilu is cassava, so the system consists of cassava as a crop population that transforms solar energy, water, nutrients, and other inputs into biomass. It includes the crop interactions with weeds, insects, pathogens, and predators.

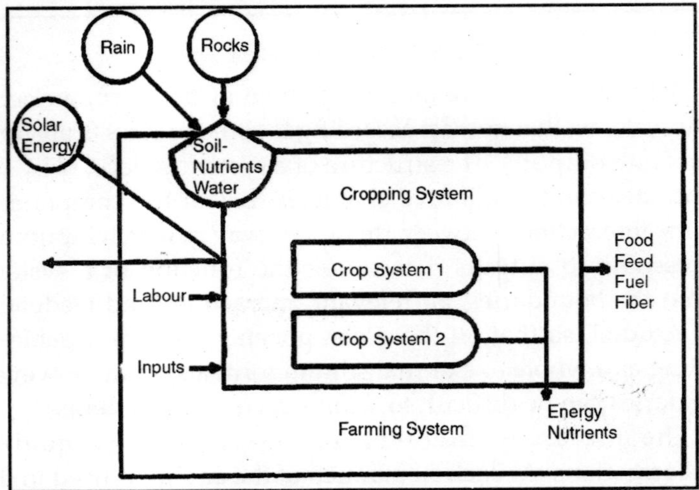


**Fig. 5.5. The Cropping System with two Crop System**

The next level above the crop system is the cropping system, which is a land-use system comprising soil, crop, weed, pathogen, and insect subsystems that transforms solar energy, water, nutrients, labour, management, and other inputs into food, feed, fuel, and fibre.

The unit of observation relating to the cropping system is the field, and fields with similar crops, soils, and so forth are considered as belonging to the same cropping system.

The various cropping systems, together with the livestock systems on a farm make up the farming system. This is defined as a decision-making and land-use unit, consisting of the farm household, cropping, and livestock systems that produces crop and animal products for consumption and sale. Unlike the cropping and livestock systems, the farming system is defined by socio-economic as well as physical boundaries.

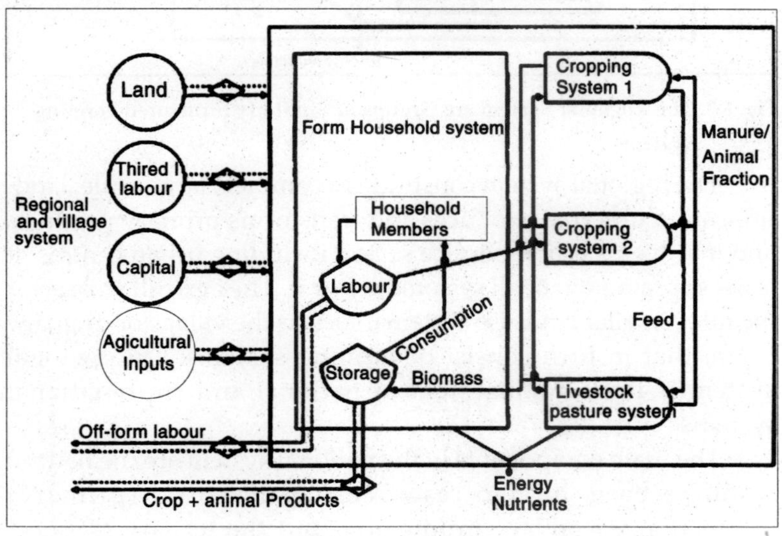


**Fig. 5.6. The Farming System**

The socioeconomic boundaries determine the people who are involved in farming (the farm household) as well as all the resources and inputs, capital, and information managed by the farm household. Its physical boundaries are those of the farm. These boundaries can be difficult to define in shifting cultivation systems.

In some societies, the farm household may consist of several units of the extended family, and other neighbouring households may also be units of the same family, and may share resources, labour, and so on. These more complex units might need different boundaries for the system. Other land-use units such as the village or watershed may form intermediate system levels between the farming system and the regional system.

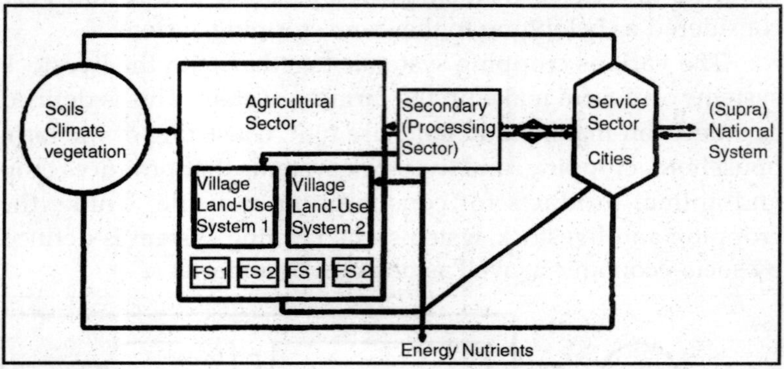


**Fig. 5.7. The Regional System are Groups of Similarly Structured Farming Systems**

The regional system constitutes a complex, large-scale, land-utilisation unit that produces and transforms primary products and involves a sisable service sector, including urban centres. It is the suprasystem of all systems below it. The agricultural sector includes smaller land-use systems, such as the village or drainage basin, that in turn consist of farming systems. The regional system is itself a subsystem of national and supranational systems.

The main components in the regional system are the natural resource base, human resources, agricultural (primary) production, secondary production, and the tertiary (service) sector and their interactions.

The natural resource base, that is, climate, soils, vegetation, and fauna, can be considered as external inputs, as well as components of the regional system. They are components of the system to the extent that they are changed in interaction with other components, but at the same time they provide the environment in which the entire hierarchy of systems is situated. In this the natural resource base is, therefore, partly drawn within the regional system boundary and depicted by the symbol (a circle) for source. Human resources are part of the primary, secondary, and tertiary sectors and do not exist outside these components.

The unit for the regional system may be an administrative unit such as a district or province, but for the purpose of defining boundaries it may be better to select a unit with some natural geographical boundaries, when possible.

Although some areas of mainly traditional agriculture such as the Kwango–Kwilu may be fairly slow to change, it must be emphasised that all ecological systems are always in a process of dynamic change. It seems likely that although many of the interactions may be difficult to quantify, the ecological framework described here could well be used for economic studies both at the farming systems and the higher levels.

# 6

# Typologies of Farming Systems

## ANALYSIS

It is essential to clarify the conceptualisation of the farming system as it relates to the objectives of the present Study.

Farming systems may be analysed at four levels:

- The field or flock/herd;
- The management unit ('unit de production ou exploitation');
- The community ('collectivit rurale'); and
- The territory ('petite rgion naturelle' or 'grande rgion')

At the level of the *management unit*, livestock and crop production may be regarded as subsystems of the same farming system. Traditional farm management studies operate at this level, and extension services are aimed at decision makers at this level, who are responsible for factor allocations. According to Jahnke, the individual farm Unit is the 'building block' of a production system: 'A livestock production system in the simplest sense is then nothing but a group of similar management units'. There are however, four reasons why neither of the first two levels is adequate for the analysis of farming systems having a livestock component in the SAZ.

## EXTERNAL RESOURCES

Livestock operations depend heavily on resources (common or open access grasings, browse, and water) outside the arable farm. At the level of the household or management unit such resources have to be treated as externals whose boundaries and capacity, because shared, cannot be defined. Yet they are not infinite*, and the manner of their use has an important bearing on the sustainability of the system. Cook *et al.*, argue that household-oriented approaches, if they fail to investigate the impact of these externalities on households and their feedback relationships, may run the risk of promoting interventions that contribute to the degradation of the environment.

## DEFINITION OF UNITS

At the level of the household, Boulier and Jouve distinguish four units: residential, consumption, accumulation and production units. They show how among six ethnic groups in West Africa, three different conformations of these units are found, and in only two of the groups are all four units coextensive. These differences have extension implications.

## BOUNDS OF UNITS

In livestock management, loaning, sharing, entrustment and other transactions are common; an owner sometimes does not manage all or any of his livestock and a manager may not own all or any of his flock or herd. Furthermore, patterns vary between seasons and from year to year.

## ECONOMIC DIFFERENTIATION

It is well known that livestock ownership tends towards inequality, notwithstanding various mechanisms for redistribution within the community.

This arises from the fact that livestock are:

- A form of investment producing a current income (in which they resemble farm land).
- A self-reproducing asset (in which they differ from farmland).

Inequality may be expressed both in the numbers of livestock (*e.g.*, cattle) owned per household or per individual, and in the type owned (cf. cattle versus sheep or goats). In mixed farming, livestock may be owned by all or by only some farm units, whereas it is uncommon within an ethnic group for land ownership to be similarly restricted. Thus the presence of a non-owning sub-group, and the greater and cumulative inequality that often characterises livestock ownership, differentiates the livestock component from the crop component of a mixed farming system.

It makes poor sense to exclude non-owning units from the production system, since, they live among the livestock owners, interact with them, and may re-enter or drop out from the livestock-owning segment from year to year.

For these reasons it may be questioned whether 'management units which are similar in their structure and in their production functions' accurately describes mixed farming households, and whether they can simply be grouped into an hierarchical farm system. The concept of the system has to incorporate diversity even competing interests, at the level of the community.

The *community* level, on the other hand, allows common access resources to be explicitly quantified and their management institutions to be identified. At this level, conflict or competition in the demand for common access resources must be resolved. The community (a village, hamlet, clan or kinship group) has rights to arable land, grasings, woodland, water and wildlife in areas that may not necessarily be contiguous. But in principle, the community system is capable of analysis in terms of soils, hydrology and agro-climatic potential.

At the level of *territory*. In addition to the diversity contained at the level of the community, functionally or ethnically distinct communities cohabiting a given area for a part or all of the year (*e.g.,* Fulani nomadic cattle breeders and Hausa sedentary farmers) may be analysed explicitly in terms of interaction, contracts, competition and complementarily in resource exploitation. Open access resources must be addressed explicitly at this level of analysis. Environmental and agro-climatic potential can be related to human and livestock populations, and ecological sustainability. Such a territory may be defined as an agro-climatic unit, a river basin or ecosystem; or as an administrative unit.

From the practical standpoint of livestock production and environmental management, a level of analysis higher than that of the single management unit is desirable, for the following reasons:

- Livestock, being mobile, are not confined within the boundaries of the farm unit, and may graze or be fed on feed obtained from resources exogenous to the farm unit, but within the community area of territory.
- Common or open access resources are subject to management decisions and regulations which are derived from custom, negotiation, or administrative dictate at the community or territorial level, and these are relevant to the question of sustainable resource management.
- Interactions amongst dissimilar livestock and non-livestock breeding communities, exploiting ethnically or functionally defined niches in the same ecological territory, are also relevant to defining the impact of livestock on the environment.
- Discrete territories may be used, not only by individual livestock keeping units, but in combination with others; the concept of the system has to take in such spatially dispersed patterns of resource use.

From the standpoint of environmental management, the territorial level of analysis is appropriate, and later in this study a framework of agro-ecological units is proposed for this purpose. Except where a single community operates a homogeneous farming system, such a territory will encompass a mix of farming systems. From a systems typological standpoint, the extent of dissimilarity amongst systems that may exist in a single territory is unmanageable, and therefore the community level is preferred. The level of the single management unit is only appropriate when crop-livestock integration is complete and the use of common or open access resources insignificant.

Water resources for livestock may be controlled at the level of the management unit or the community, or be uncontrolled under open access; this has many implications. The levels described above are defined in terms of area as follows:

**Table 6.1**

| | |
|---|---|
| Management unit | Area over which a management unit exercises controlling rights (residence, arable, fallows) |
| Community | Areas controlled by constituent management units plus common access resources where community members exercise customary rights (grasings, woodland, river valleys.) |
| Territory | Area however defined, used by one or more communities, including community areas, plus open access resources subject to no community or management unit control (though customary usage by migrants of grasing or other resources may acquire some recognition). |

## TYPOLOGY

In their current phase, four of ILCA's six research thrusts are planned to have substantial involvement in the SAZ:

- Small ruminant meat and milk.
- Animal traction.
- Animal feed resources.
- Livestock policy and resource use.

Recurrent themes in the research topics proposed for these thrusts are:

- Production systems, crop-livestock integration and productivity.
- Feed resources and management.
- Technologies, including draft.
- Breeding, reproduction.
- Stability and sustainability.
- Markets, prices, credit.

Given such a diversity of research objectives, it is legitimate to ask whether a multipurpose typology is a practicable objective. It cannot serve every need. The justification for a typology arises from the need to order diversity, as a step towards improved understanding.

It is known that livestock producers in the SAZ vary on at least seven scales:

- Household dependency on livestock
- Market integration of the livestock enterprise
- Herding movements
- Interactions with farmers
- Integration of crop and livestock production
- Size (and value) of livestock holdings
- Types and breeds of animals kept.

However Jahnke's advice is that to derive groupings from 'a theory of their differentiation (*e.g.*, the distance from the market or factor proportions available) results in a typology that reflects too narrow a spectrum of reality... judgement and pragmatism must still take precedence over principle and rigour'. Jahnke therefore adapts Ruthenberg's functional classification to the specifications of livestock production. Before following down this road of theoretical agnosticism, a brief review of some available topologies is given.

This review concludes that a number of existing or proposed typologies the functional farming systems of Ruthenberg, classifications based on economic specialisation or livestock dependency, typologies of herd movements, systems based on livestock ratios or characteristics of animal traction-have either theoretical or practical limitations from the standpoint of the present Study. A proposal is made to develop McIntire et al's (1989) sequence of crop-livestock interaction and integration into a tool for inventorying mixed farming systems. But the large number of component elements make an aggregated 'integration score' rather meaningless. Finally, a typology based on farming intensity is proposed, which includes four major types: intensive farming, enclave grasing, enclave farming and grasing. Such a typology has a strong theoretical basis and provides a framework for assigning environmental sustainability ratings to mixed farming systems.

## FUNCTIONAL FARMING SYSTEMS

Ruthenberg used a 7-fold typology of tropical farming systems in which crop-livestock interactions may be summarised as follows:

**Table 6.2**

| System | Interactions |
|---|---|
| 1 Shifting cultivation | Few livestock in the forests large scale animal rearing in the dry savannas (no reference to interactions) |
| 2 Fallow systems | livestock ownership restricted communal use of feed resources (grasing, fallows, residues) manuring exceptional degeneration of livestock performance/condition when feed becomes scarce |
| 3 Ley and dairy systems | Livestock ownership widespread privatised grasing on enclosed holdings improved cattle breeding intensive fodder production |
| 4. Permanent upland | Livestock ownership widespread cultivation traction land manure used residues used grasing, fallows scarce entrustment for seasonal transhumance fodder crops uneconomic substitution of small livestock for cattle |
| 5. Arable irrigation | Cattle not intensively organised large numbers, poor performance |
| 6. Perennial crops | (no reference to livestock) |
| 7. Grasing systems | *a.* Total nomadism<br>*b.* Semi-nomadism with little or no supplementary arable<br>*c.* Ranching |

Ruthenberg gives livestock no integral role in his classification of farming systems, nor in the evolution from less to more intensive systems which is implicit in his typology. No explicit recognition is given to 'mixed farming systems', though they receive special mention as a separate class in an otherwise similar classification proposed by McDowell and Hildebrand. Livestock are rarely differentiated: cattle most often seem to be implied by the context. Types 1, 2, 4 and 7(b) occur in the SAZ and may qualify for the designation 'mixed farming'. But this general functional typology is not ideal for present purposes because it does not derive from differences in the livestock component of the systems, nor from the nature of crop-livestock interactions, but from differences in cropping practice. Its implications for environmental management are not clear either.

Jahnke, however, follows Ruthenberg in proposing the following five classes of livestock production systems in tropical Africa:

- Pastoral range systems;
- Crop-livestock systems in the lowlands;
- Crop-livestock systems in the highlands;
- Ranching systems; and
- Landless livestock production systems.

The interest of the present study mainly concerns the second class, and then only in the SAZ. Jahnke does not propose a subdivision of this class but suggests four gradients, that could conceivably be used as the basis for such a subdivision:

- Agroclimate (cropping system).
- Population pressure (cultivation intensity).
- Tsetse challenge.
- Livestock dependency (density, species).

The first three will be incorporated in the environmental disaggregation of the SAZ; the last is considered below.

## ECONOMIC SPECIALISATION, OR LIVESTOCK DEPENDENCY

Wilson *et al*, working in Mali, recognise three classes of dependency on livestock on the basis of household revenue or food energy derived from livestock-related activities;

**Table. 6.3**

| | |
|---|---|
| 1. Pastoral | > 50 per cent gross household revenue or > 20 per cent food energy |
| 2. Agro-pastoral | 10-50 per cent gross revenue (*i.e.*, > 50 per cent derived from crops or non-agricultural activities) |
| 3. Agricultural | < 10 per cent gross revenue (*i.e.*, > 90 per cent derived from crops or non-agriculturalactivities) |

Gross revenue is defined as the value of subsistence plus marketed production, plus the value of transport animals, traction and manure. The study was carried out in Mali, but Swift (nd: 1990?) has proposed to generalise such a classification.

For present purposes, this classification has two limitations: first, household level (management unit) output and income data are not sufficiently widely available in the SAZ; and second, as explained above, the management unit level of analysis does not satisfy the requirements of the present investigation. Also, a finer mesh is needed to capture the diversity contained in the second and third classes. In a study of the livestock economy of northern Nigeria, Fricke proposed an elaborate 'social-agrarian-geographical' typology of cattle keeping systems. First published in 1969 (in German), this study broke new ground in elevating economic specialisation to prime place over the social criteria traditionally dominant in anthropological studies. Such included: political status (independent/dependent; rulers/ruled; upper/middle/lower classes); value systems (positive/negative attitudes to field cultivation; 'cult' reasons for keeping cattle); and patterns of herd movement (nomadism/transhumance).

Fricke's four classes of economic specialisation are:

- Full time cattle-keeping enterprises;
- Mixed enterprises;
- Part-time enterprises; and
- Special types.

The resulting typology is, however, complex, and the 4 classes and 23 subclasses are not all empirically related in his study to identifiable groups in northern Nigeria, still less are they capable of easy quantification or mapping. The social overburden of this scheme renders it impracticable for extension beyond the Nigerian context, and marginal to the management focus of the present study.

Baxter and other writers on East African pastoralism use the following typology of pastoral peoples:

- 'Pure' pastoralists who do not cultivate (subdivided into *(a)* those producing for the wider economy and *(b)* those only marginally involved in the wider economy).
- Primarily pastoral people, frequently transhumant,

who cannot subsist by their stock alone (often called agro-pastoralists).

- Primarily agricultural people who maintain strong pastoral values.

  In the wider context of livestock production, the emphasis on 'values' calls for a fourth type to be added to this scheme:

- Agriculturalists who also keep livestock.

Such a scheme cannot adequately cope with the variety of mixed farming systems. While it appears to apply at the community level, recent events in parts of East Africa (impoverishment by war or drought losses) suggest that within a given community, households may end up in different classes, according to their livestock wealth. Households may also (presumably) reclassify themselves as they lose or reconstitute their herds through time.

A typology based on the degree of dependency on livestock may be expected to yield important insights on the choice of economic options at the household level. But it does not directly confront the relations between the livestock and crop production subsystems and the impact of management practices on the environment.

## PATTERNS OF MOVEMENT

Wilson *et al* reject using livestock movements as the basis for classifying livestock production systems in Mali because although the nature of such movements is an important aspect of the system, it is contingent upon it, and diverts attention from the degree of dependency on livestock. It may be noted that the movements of cattle may be quite different from those of small ruminants, whose importance in mixed farming systems is sometimes greater.

On the other hand, Van Raay argued a consistent relationship-in northern Nigeria—between the movement patterns and socio-economic characteristics of the Fulani stockowners. While this typology is sufficiently closely related to management to have potential as a framework for policy, its usefulness may be restricted outside the Fulani-occupied areas of West Africa.

Table. 6.4

| Movement Category | Socio-economic Characteristics |
|---|---|
| 1 Nomadic | large herds, migratory grasing<br>No farming<br>No settlements<br>Fulfulde language<br>Strong cultural separatism |
| 2 Semi-nomadic | Smaller herds, transhumance<br>Some farming<br>Settlements for the elders<br>Fulfulde language<br>Strong cultural separatism |
| 3 Semi-settled | Small herds, transhumance<br>Committed farming<br>Permanent settlements<br>Hausa language<br>Cultural absorption |
| 4 Settled | Few animals, no transhumance<br>Committed farming<br>Permanent settlements<br>Hausa language<br>Cultural identity |
| also: | Elite cattle ownership<br>Commercial herds |

## LIVESTOCK RATIOS

The ratios between cattle and small ruminants would have obvious practical value in extension work, and within a homogeneous cultural area (such as Fulani areas of West Africa). They would be useful proxy indicators of such variables as household livestock wealth, movement patterns, and extent of commitment to farming. They are also relatively sensitive to short-term dynamics in animal ownership, responding (for example) to cycles of impoverishment and reconstitution, following periods of drought-induced mortality or destocking. However from the standpoint of research targeting, such a dynamic indicator may be insufficiently stable in the medium term (10-15 years). Ratios between breeds would be of interest from a breeding or nutritional perspective, but they provide only very indirect indicators of system properties, unless combined with other variables. For a typology applicable throughout the SAZ, livestock ratios suffer the fatal flaw of rarely being known on a comparable basis. Since, census data are either unreliable, or insufficiently detailed, in most countries, the only source of data is low level aerial surveys. Where these have been carried out, livestock ratios may be available on a country or subregional basis, but unless they can be linked to herd or management units, they remain a poor guide to system operations.

## ANIMAL TRACTION

Animal traction appears to lend itself to a taxonomy of mixed farming systems, because more is known about systems using animal draft power than about others. The presence or absence of draft, the frequency of draft using or owning management units, the relative importance of different draft animals (oxen, donkeys, horses) and the size of plough team or span all suggest themselves as possible taxonomic criteria. Such a classification would have obvious value for animal traction research and extension Ownership (as distinct from hiring) of draft cattle has implications for the size of the herd and milk output, especially in Southern Africa where spans of 6 or 8 oxen are used.

McIntire *et al.* investigating the hypothesis that animal traction is the central element of crop-livestock integration, failed to find a general association between animal traction and other techniques, and concluded that the role of draft power is badly understood. Certainly the determinants of the pattern of adoption of animal traction cannot be generalised for tropical Africa as a whole. Its impact on the farming system is difficult to separate from that of other variables. In West Africa, its implications for the livestock component of the farm system are quite different depending on whether draft power is owned or hired. In Ethiopia, the use of draft power is ancient, and apparently unrelated to commercialisation. In Botswana, cattle owning mixed farmers have adopted the plough for subsistence production, using teams of a size that, had they been necessary, would certainly have curtailed adoption of the technology in a non-cattle owning society in West Africa. Animal traction characteristics, therefore, are not suitable as criteria for a general taxonomy of mixed farming systems.

## CROP-LIVESTOCK INTEGRATION

This issue is central to improving land productivity in the SAZ. It is integral to labour intensification, for which the necessary condition is population growth. A large literature supports the thesis that rural population density explains a high proportion of the observed variation in smallholder farming intensity (defined in terms of frequency of cultivation cycles and labour inputs per ha) in tropical Africa. In the SAZ, livestock are usually a central component in such intensification under smallholder conditions.

McIntire et al argue strongly that 'farming intensity and crop-livestock interactions increase with population growth and with market infrastructure. The intensification of animal production allows more interactions: farmers invest in cattle, herders manage them, stock eat more crop residues and byproducts, and produce more manure'. Crop-livestock interaction follows an inverted U-pattern through time. 'First, specialised farming and herding societies that trade products give way to mixed farming societies, in which cropping and animal activities are in the same management unit. This movement to mixed farming, which we call the first transition, occurs when opportunities for using less labour intensive techniques of soil fertility maintenance are exhausted as population densities increase, and as the opportunity cost of labour rises. The latter encourages farm mechanisation, usually via animal traction; as draft power becomes more valuable, crop farmers start to manage livestock and herders begin to cultivate. As exogenous markets and technologies develop further, there is a reverse movement away from integration and towards specialisation, which we call the second transition. These technical changes-fertilizers replacing manure, tractors replacing animals, and supplements replacing fodder crops and pastures-eliminate the cost advantages for a mixed enterprise to provide some of its own inputs. As population density rises, causing land pressure, resource competition occurs within the farm which induces further specialisation'.

On the basis of such an hypothesis the following sequence of types can be suggested:

**Table. 6.5**

| | Increasing population density | Increasing market Integration |
|---|---|---|
| 1 No interaction between specialist herders & farmers | [] | |
| 2 Interaction between specialists | [] | [] |
| 3 Interaction and some integration (farmers acquire livestock; herders take up farming) | [] | [] |
| 4 Full integration (no livestock specialists) | [] | [] |
| 5 Specialisation (commercial crop and livestock production) | | [] |

Such a scheme must apply at the level of the territory, because in the early stages of the sequence, interactions occur between specialist (community level) systems. In practice, types 1, 4 and 5 are rare in the SAZ, leaving only types 2 and 3 to represent rather a wide range of diversity. At the community level, specific elements of the system may be inventoried and a score assigned on the basis of a scale of integration numbered 0-3, as follows:

**Table. 6.6**

| | Elements | | Integration Score |
|---|---|---|---|
| 1 | 2 | 3 | 4 |
| 1 | Residues | 0<br>1<br><br>2<br>3 | Not used for fodder<br>Open access (0A) grasing of Stover and stubble<br>Privatised stover + 0A to stubble<br>Privatised stover + stubble |
| 2 | Fodder trees | 0<br>1 | None on farmland<br>Volunteers protected, 0A browsing |

(*Contd...*)

| | | | |
|---|---|---|---|
| | | 2 | Plantings + protection, 0A browsing |
| | | 3 | Privatised, browsed, cut and carried |
| 3 | Fodder production | 0 | None |
| | | 1 | Cut and carried (C & C) from natural vegetation |
| | | 2 | C & C + bought/sold |
| | | 3 | Grown on farm and C & C + bought/sold |
| 4 | Manure | 0 | Not used for fertilisation |
| | | 1 | 'Farm' system (field grasing, night paddocking) |
| | | 2 | Dry pen system, + carrying, + farm system |
| | | 3 | Composting, + carrying, + farm system |
| 5 | Traction | 0 | No animal draft power used |
| | | 1 | Draft animals owned or rented by minority |
| | | 2 | Draft animals owned or rented by majority |
| | | 3 | Draft animals owned by majority |
| 6 | Transport | 0 | No transport animals |
| | | 1 | Owned or rented by minority |
| | | 2 | Owned or rented by majority |
| | | 3 | Owned by majority |
| 7 | Cattle movements | 0 | Off farm whole year |
| | | 1 | Outside community area* for part of year |
| | | 2 | In community area whole year, but off farm part of year |
| | | 3 | On farm all year |
| 8 | SR movements | 0 | Off farm whole year |
| | | 1 | Outside community area for part of year |
| | | 2 | In community area whole year, but off farm part of year |
| | | 3 | On farm all year |

This scheme will be applied to the systems inventoried later in the Study. An aggregate score can be assigned to a system.

An absence of any significant indicators of crop-livestock integration will produce a total of 0; the highest possible score is 24.

However it is doubtful if such a score will have more than an academic value. It is the ratings for individual elements that have practical significance.

## FARMING INTENSITY

There are strong grounds for attempting to base a typology on farming intensity (frequency of cultivation cycles, or labour inputs per ha):

- Under smallholder conditions, farming intensity tends to correlate positively with rural population density.
- Observations support the thesis that in the SAZ, farming intensity tends to correlate positively with crop-livestock integration.
- The more frequent the cultivation cycle, the shorter the fallow cycle tends to become, eventually threatening the sustainability of the fallow system and calling for alternative methods of soil fertility maintenance.
- A growing population with shortening fallows is expressed in a negative change in the grasing: arable land ratio. This, it is often argued, threatens the viability of the system of arable fertilisation via nutrient transfer by grasing animals.
- Given the value of livestock, the ease of acquisition of small ruminants, and low costs of maintenance under conditions of common access grasing, an increase in the small livestock population is often a corollary of growth in the human population. On the other hand, cattle densities fall when grasing and fodder are scarce.

The cultivated percentage provides an indicator of farming intensity (the higher the percentage, the more frequent the cycle of cultivation and the higher the labour inputs per ha) writing with primary reference to the sub-humid zone, argue that the 'land use factor' provides a guide to the progression from arable cropping to integrated crop and livestock production. Data on cultivation frequency and labour inputs are not often available, however. Using the cultivated percentage, four qualitatively distinct types may be proposed

**Table. 6.7**

| | Zone | Characteristics |
|---|---|---|
| 0 | Grasing | No farming except by livestock specialists (<5 per cent cultivated) migrant herds |
| 1 | Enclave farming | Low cultivated percentage (<20) low degree of integration common access grasing extensive many livestock specialists migrant herds visiting little nutrient cycling some nutrient transfer long fallows-main fertility strategy no trees on arable |
| 2 | Enclave grasing | High cultivated percentage (20-70) high degree of integration common access grasing restricted some livestock specialists transhumance for cattle nutrient cycling (residues-manure) nutrient transfer (paddocking, field grasing) short fallows-insufficient to maintain fertility of arable some trees on arable |
| 3 | Intensive farming | Very high cultivated percentage (>70) highest degree of integration common access grasing limited to residual, marginal or flooded land livestock owned by farmers transhumance or stall feeding for cattle intensive nutrient cycling (residues-manure) very short fallows, or none trees important on arable |

## MODEL OF FARMING

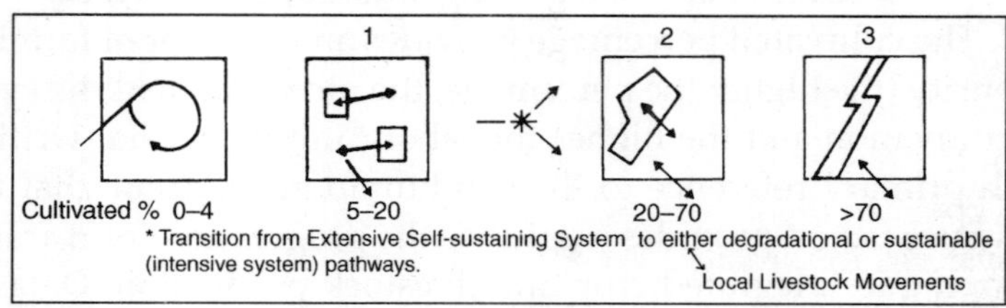


Fig. 6.1

Assigning threshold values to the model must be inexact at present. With regard to Types 2 and 3, Hendy, in a study of animal production in the Kano Close-Settled Zone, Nigeria, plotted the human population/km$^2$ against livestock/km$^2$ and livestock/head of human population. The density of about 80 persons/km had a threshold significance. At lower densities of the human population, the numbers of cattle, donkeys, sheep and goats/km$^2$ all rose with the human population density, and also rose on a per capita basis. Above the density of 80 persons/km$^2$, cattle numbers fell on a per capita basis and the other animals showed no clear trend. This meant that they increased in density/km$^2$, whereas cattle densities declined. A human population density of about 80/km$^2$, in Northern Nigeria at the time when Hendy's data were obtained (late 1960s), corresponded to a cultivated percentage of about 70. Areas above this figure are assigned to Type 3.

More recent work by ILCA shows that cattle densities increase with those of the human population until the cultivated percentage reaches about 50 (in the Nigerian Sub-Humid Zone) and about 25 (in the SAZ); thereafter they decline. Above a cultivated percentage of 85, fallows and common access grasing virtually disappear, residual land being mainly used for settlements, rivers, roads, etc; this may be recognised as a sub-type of Type 3, but it is rare to find such high intensities (densities of population over 150/km$^2$) in the SAZ, and there is no evidence of a significant change in livestock management at this level.

With regard to Types 1 and 2, work in the Maradi area of Niger indicates that at a regional population density of 30/km$^2$, and a cultivated percentage in the range 35-65, fallows are insufficient to maintain the fertility of arable land. The livestock supported by the grasings and farm residues provide manure for only 25 per cent of the cultivated area.

There is a shortage of land and of fodder, and by implication, of fallows and manure. This area may be assigned therefore to Type 2. In their analysis of the impact of drought on six farming systems in semiarid West Africa, Boulier and Jouve discern no land shortage in systems operating at human population densities of 10/km$^2$ or less. This corresponds to a cultivated percentage of about 10-20, at 1-2 ha/person. Such an area can be assigned to Type 1.

The level of analysis for such a categorisation is that of the community or the territory. The model takes no account of uncultivable land and river valley land, (bas-fond, dambo, fadama, flood plain etc.). The first is included in uncultivated land and is assumed to be available for grasing. However, where the percentage of uncultivable land is high, ceiling is set on the cultivable percentage, lowering the threshold percentages for Types l and 2 accordingly. As for river valley land, its effect depends on whether its predominant use is for cultivation, or for dry season grasing. If the first, the grasing sector is weakened; if the second, strengthened. Adjustments could be made for local situations. The model is based on West African experience and requires verification. The national livestock census, presently in progress in Nigeria, may provide an opportunity to test the model in a range of ecologies and human densities.

None of these types has necessary consequences for degradation or conservation, and therefore one cannot be said to be more sustainable than another.

Sustainability depends on:

- The nature of the cropping system, with regard to the protection of the physical and chemical properties of the soil.
- Rhe level of stocking.
- Rhe management of localised pressure points such as overgrazed village peripheries, denuded environs of water sources, exposed topographical sites (steep slopes, wind-blown crests).
- Annual variability in rainfall and vegetation cover.

However, if these variables are known, the typology provides a framework for assigning environmental sustainability ratings to mixed farming systems. There is plenty of evidence that the choice between a sustainable or degradational pathway involves decisions about labour allocation, and that under conditions of scarce capital, labour-intensive sustainable systems can only evolve where population density is high or increasing. Since, the typological sequence suggested above is fundamentally related to population density, as is the integration sequence of McIntire *et al*, it may be expected that both sequences, if found valid, will correlate in practice. Farming intensity therefore emerges as the most powerful typological principle for the purpose of understanding both crop-livestock interaction/ integration and environmental management.

## GEOGRAPHICAL ASPECTS

This subdivision embodies the contrast between the relative uniformity and continuity of the W & N region on the one hand, and the diversity and discontinuity of the E & S region on the other. At a gross level of generalisation, the W & N region (from Senegal to the Sudan) can be characterised in terms of the following properties:

- A lowland plains topography;
- A uniform, unimodal rainfall regime;
- A transitional location between the Sahara Desert and the Subhumid Zone, reflected in a strong latitudinal bias in most ecological distributions;
- Spatial and ecological continuity across its entire breadth;
- Horizontal (south-north) aridity gradients and associated dispositions of tsetse;
- A history of cultural interaction, including the co-residence, in the same territories, of specialist pastoralists and farmers, with resource-sharing agreements;
- An absence of colonial land alienation, and the spatial continuity of its farming systems.

The SAZ of eastern Africa is very different, having:

- Both highland and lowland areas;
- Both bimodal and unimodal rainfall regimes;
- A weak relationship between ecology and latitude, and abrupt ecological gradients, owing to highlands;
- A discontinuous spatial distribution;
- Both vertical (altitudinal) and horizontal (multi-directional) aridity gradients, and complex associated patterns of tsetse challenge;

- A lack of notable historical uniting influences, with pastoralists and farmers often separated and competing for resources;
- Extensive land alienation under colonial rule (in some countries), and discontinuous, diverse, sometimes isolated, or administratively confined farming systems.

The SAZ in southern Africa does not conform in all respects with the eastern African pattern. There is less highland, stronger latitudinal control, and more consistent ecological gradients. But it contains a comparatively small proportion of the African livestock (and human) populations. Since, the E & S region is defined essentially in terms of its diversity, it makes practical sense for present purposes to include southern with eastern Africa, at this level of generalisation, It is implicit in the foregoing that there are limits to the transferability of research and experience between the W & N and the E & S regions.

## LGP SUB-ZONES

FAO land inventory data, and variables used for estimating population supporting capacities in the study carried out jointly by the FAO and IIASA, are available for LGP sub-zones broken down by thermal zone and by country. The sub-zones are:

**Table. 6.8**

| | |
|---|---|
| M 1 | 150179 growing days |
| M 2 | 120149 growing days |
| D 1 | 90119 growing days |
| D 2 | 7589 growing days. |
| *The thermal zones that occur in sub-Saharan Africa are:* | |
| MC 1 | Warm tropics |
| MC 2 | Moderately cool tropics |
| MC 3 | Cool tropics |
| MC 7 | Warm sub-tropics (summer rainfall) |
| MC 8 | Moderately cool sub-tropics (summer rainfall) |
| MC 9 | Cool sub-tropics (summer rainfall). |

When overlaid on national territories, the variables listed above generate a three-dimensional matrix of more than a hundred cells. The data relevant to the present study are summarised in Appendix 3. These have been selected from a list of 16 soil constraints and 29 population and productivity related variables.

Leaving aside the thermal zones, which have less relevance for livestock production systems, some of the data on the LGP sub-zones are aggregated at the regional level in Table.

The FAO offers the only source of standardised physical land inventory, land use, and productivity data for all of sub-Saharan Africa, though the time-base for these data is 1975, and their reliability can be no better than that of the primary sources used. According to FAO the growing periods are classified as follows with regard to agroclimatic suitability for the major crops, pearl millet, sorghum and Maize, at existing (low) input levels:

**Table. 6.9**

| LGP (days) | 7589 | 90119 | 120149 | 150179 |
|---|---|---|---|---|
| **Pearl millet** | | | | |
| Yield (t/ha)<br>Suitability | 0.30.4<br>MS | 0.50.8<br>S | 0.50.8<br>S/VS | 0.71.0<br>VS |
| **Sorghum:** | | | | |
| Yield (t/ha)<br>Suitability | <br>NS | 0.30.5<br>MS | 0.50.7<br>S | 0.91.3<br>VS |
| **Maize:** | | | | |
| Yield (t/ha)<br>Suitability* | <br>NS | 0.40.5<br>MS | 0.71.0<br>S | 1.21.8<br>VS |

*Note*: * Suitability classes: NS-Not Suitable; MS-Marginally Suitable; S-Suitable; VS-Very Suitable.

In the two drier sub-zones (75119 days LGP), millet is the most suitable staple crop. However, the correspondence between these suitability ratings and actual practice may not be very close. For example, if the LGP isolines are superimposed on a map of major crop regions in the Francophone West African countries (Figure 6.2), it appears that other factors besides agroclimatic suitability (so defined) have influenced the pattern.

Table. 6.10. The SAZ of sub-Saharan Africa by Length of Growing Period (LGP) Zone

| | W & N Region | | | | E & S Region | | | | All Regions | | | | Total |
|---|---|---|---|---|---|---|---|---|---|---|---|---|---|
| | M1 | M2 | D1 | D2 | M1 | M2 | D1 | D2 | M1 | M2 | D1 | D2 | |
| Total area (000km$^2$) | | | | | | | | | 1,822 | 1,207 | 1,311 | 856 | 5196 |
| Population (1975, millions) | | | | | | | | | 31.2 | 26.7 | 17.1 | 11.2 | 86.2 |
| Density (persons/km$^2$) | | | | | | | | | 17.1 | 22.1 | 13 | 13.1 | 16.6 |
| Agricultural land available (000 km$^2$)[1] | 934.8 | 660.4 | 484.1 | 402.7 | 587.7 | 379.1 | 733 | 384.4 | 1,522.5 | 1,039.5 | 1,217.1 | 787.1 | 4566.2 |
| Cropland (rainfed and irrigated: 000 km$^2$)[2] | 787 | 457.5 | 129.1 | 90.2 | 469.9 | 298.9 | 170.6 | 130.4 | 1,256.9 | 756.4 | 299.7 | 220.6 | 2533.6 |
| Rangeland (000 km$^2$) | 30.6 | 115.5 | 287.9 | 262.1 | 45.3 | 119.8 | 424.8 | 234.1 | 75.9 | 235.3 | 712.7 | 496.2 | 1520.1 |
| Percent cropland | 84 | 69.3 | 26.7 | 22.4 | 80 | 78.8 | 23.3 | 33.9 | 82.6 | 72.8 | 24.6 | 28 | 55.5 |
| Percent rangeland | 3.3 | 17.5 | 59.5 | 65.1 | 7.7 | 31.6 | 58 | 61 | 5 | 22.6 | 58.6 | 63 | 33.3 |

*Note*: 1. The amount of agricultural land available allows for deducting estimated nonagricultural land from total land.

2. Cropland and rangeland do not add up to agricultural land available. We assume that the balance is unused.

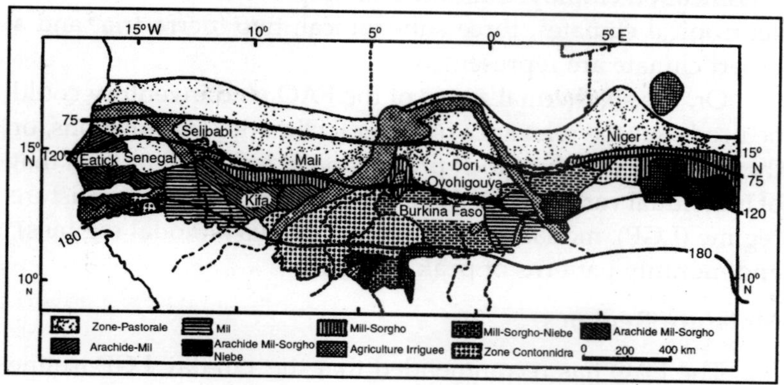


**Fig. 6.2. The SAZ in the W. & N. Region, with the 120 Day LGP Isoline Added, and Major Crop Regions**

Functions linking LGP sub-zones with livestock-related variables have not been developed. Two variables of obvious importance are pasture production and availability of suitable crop residues.

On the first, Le Hourou has proposed a link between annual rainfall and the production of dry matter above the ground, or rain use efficiency factor (RUE: kg DM $mm^{-1}ha^{-1}yr^{-1}$). Studies in the Sahel yield averages ranging from 2.2 to 3.6, and in East Africa, from 3.2 to 6.0.

He cautions, however, that differences in the length of the growing season between the unimodal rainfall regimes of the Sudano-Sahelian region and the bimodal regimes of East Africa cause fundamental differences in range type, composition and forage quality during the annual cycle. More work is therefore necessary before linkages between LGP and forage availability can be stated with any confidence.

## AGROCLIMATIC SUB-REGIONS

Sub-zones based on the use of LGP as a sole criterion do not take account of other agroclimatic variables. Thermal zones, or a general climatic classification, could be used to break the SAZ down into smaller units having more internal homogeneity. Figure, for example, shows the SAZ superimposed on a climatic classification employed for the Soil Map of Africa. No less than six tropical climates, three sub-tropical, two 'tierra fria' and a desert climate are represented.

Or, the six thermal zones of the FAO land inventory could be used. But the relevance of general climatic classifications, or thermal zones, to livestock production is less evident than that of individual variables. Of these, the most important are moisture regime (LGP), modal type (unimodal versus bimodal regimes), and monthly patterns of peak rainfall.

## Moisture Regimes

The FAO has recommended that the 120-day LGP isoline should demarcate the moist from the dry semi-arid zones:

| | |
|---|---|
| Dry semi-arid | 75119 days growing period |
| Moist semi-arid | 120170 days growing period |

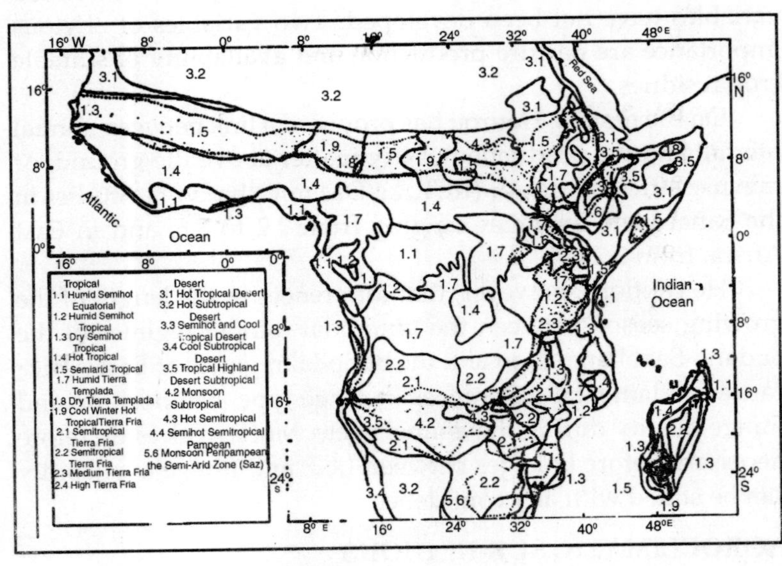


**Fig. 6.3 The SAZ in Relation to Major Climates**

This two-fold division of the SAZ has greater practical utility than the four-fold division used in the preceding section since, it reflects noticeable differences in livestock management in many areas.

These differences are most apparent in the W & N region which is characterised by relative homogeneity from east to west and an ecological gradient from south to north. Therefore it is proposed to divide the W & N region into two sub-regions, Moist W & N and Dry W & N.

In the E & S, the same distinction produces a complex spatial pattern having less usefulness for regional subdivision, though the importance of such distinctions for farming systems is clear at the micro-regional level.

**Unimodal and Bimodal Regimes**

This property has a significance for farming systems second only to that of the growing period. Following Leroux, the SAZ can be subdivided on this basis. Unimodal regimes occur throughout the W & N region (with the exception of a small area of Mauritania, which it has been decided to ignore), and in NW Ethiopia, in the E & S region.

Bimodal regimes occur throughout the E & S region from NE Ethiopia to Tanzania. From Tanzania (which is transitional) until the Tropic is reached, unimodal regimes occur. In the sub-tropical part of the E & S region, unimodal regimes occur in S. Mozambique, E. Swaziland, and Madagascar, but complicating factors extend the length of the rainy season in S E Botswana and W. Lesotho.

**Monthly Patterns of Peak Rainfall**

In the W & N region, under unimodal regimes and strong latitudinal influence, August is the peak month in normal years. In the E & S region, the latitudinal range of the SAZ (from 15N to 30S), and the influence of highland masses, create considerable variability in the monthly patterns of peak rainfall. These variations need to be taken into account in proposing sub-regions of homogeneous agroclimatic properties.

**Functional Definition of the SAZ**

Before combining the above three variables into a scheme of agroclimatic sub-regions, it is appropriate to examine some anomalies in the definition of the SAZ which arise near the upper and lower (75 days LGP) limits. In several locations the reliability of these limits, as indicators of semi-arid ecological conditions for farming systems, may be questioned.

The following functional modifications to the SAZ are therefore proposed, for the reasons given; and the boundaries shown in Figure (AH):

- W & N region, arid boundary; rainfed farming occurs extensively on the north side of the 75-day isoline in the Sudan, and sporadically elsewhere. On the Qoz Sands of Kordofan, rainfed cultivation extended beyond 14 until 1980. This line is proposed instead as a functional limit (Figure).
- E & S region, Kenya-Uganda borderlands: NE Uganda (Karamoja) received 650-850 mm of rainfall during the first half of the present century, characterised by extreme variability, supporting a vegetation of dry thorn scrub and a mixed pastoral-farming economy with cattle keeping both economically and culturally dominant. From Dyson-Hudson's account, it appears that the whole area (except possibly the mountains), up to the 210 day isoline, is best described as semi-arid. The boundary has been adjusted to *include* this area. On the Kenyan side of the border, almost all the territory with 75 or more growing days is rated as arid, with a very low stock carrying capacity, in Kenyan ecological classifications.
- *E & S region, S Somalia*: Rainfed agro-pastoralism extends well beyond the Bay region of southern Somalia to the central rangelands between 3 and 5N. Rainfall, although low, is distributed through a long season. It is proposed to extend the functional boundary to *include* this area.
- *E & S region, W Kenya and SW Uganda*: Notwit-hstanding anomalously short growing periods (less than 120 days according to FAO), ecology and farming systems in the environs of Lake Victoria are subhumid in character; in the Kenya portion only a small strip of territory receives less than 800 mm of rainfall annually. Both

these areas, with the Lake Victoria coast of Tanzania are *excluded* from our functional definition of the SAZ.

- E & S region, Zambia: there are major differences between the LGP zones according to FAO and those estimated by an independent country study . These latter indicate shorter growing periods. Nevertheless, the ecology of most parts of Zambia is not semi-arid, and the farming systems have more in common with subhumid systems elsewhere. Altitude and latitude, through the temperature regime, must influence the effectiveness of Zambian rainfall, which appears to have a different relationship between annual total precipitation and length of growing period (more rainfall, shorter GPs) than is observed generally in the SAZ. For present purposes, Zambia is *excluded* from the SAZ, together with adjacent territory in Malawi.
- *E & S region, Tanzania*: Certain areas in central Tanzania falling below the 75 day isoline are *included* in the SAZ on the grounds of their relatively small size and fragmented pattern.
- *E & S region, N & W Mozambique*: The first of these zones (N Mozambique) carries a broad-leafed woodland, is heavily infested with tsetse, only moderately populated and appears to have few livestock. The second is a small, sparsely inhabited area almost devoid of livestock. Although no farming system characterisations have been found, it is believed that they are neither truly semi-arid nor significant to the livestock economy of Mozambique, and they are therefore excluded.
- *E & S region, E Botswana*: The 75 day isoline understates the extent of rainfed farming in E Botswana significantly.

**The Sub-regions**

These revisions made, the sub-regional classification is tabulated below and shown in Figure (AH).

**Table. 6.11**

| Rainfall regime[1] | Subregion number[2] | Subregion W & N | Rainfall peak months: Single | Double |
|---|---|---|---|---|
| A | – | Dry semi-arid | Aug | |
| A | – | Moist semi-arid | Aug | |
| | | E & S | | |
| A | 1 | NW Ethiopia | Aug | |
| B | 2 | NE Ethiopia | | Mar–Apr: July–Aug |
| | 3 | S Ethiopia | | April: Oct |
| | 4 | N Kenya | | Apr–May: Jul |
| | 5 | E Kenya | | April: Nov |
| | 6 | Coastal Kenya | | Apr–May: Nov |
| | 7 | S. C Somalia | | Apr-May: Oct–Nov |
| | 8 | Tanzania [3] | Jan | Mar–Apr: Dec–Jan |
| A | 9 | Southern tropics (S Zimbabwe-N Botswana-NE Namibia-S Angola) | Jan–Feb | |
| | 10 | Coastal Angola | Mar | |
| C | 11 | Southern sub-tropics (S Mozambique, E Swaziland) | Jan–Feb | |
| | 12 | SW Madagascar | Jan | |
| | 13 | SE Botswana | | Oct–Apr[4] |
| | 14 | W Lesotho | | Dec–Mar[4] |

*Note*: 1. A: unimodal; B: bimodal; C: subtropical.

2. Subregion numbers are shown in Figure 6 (AH), where they are further sub-divided into environmental units (see below).

3. In Tanzania there is a complex transitional pattern of bimodal and unimodal regimes.

4. No clear peak in a long sometimes irregular. rainy season.

## ENVIRONMENTAL UNITS

The foregoing regional subdivisions leave much environmental diversity unaccounted for, being confined to agroclimatic variables. Soil-related variables need now to be conjoined with other relevant variables in order to delimit smaller units having a greater degree of homogeneity with regard to the primary resources of farming systems.

In principle, a GIS-overlay computerised technique offers a method of unifying the variable distributions of different data sets. The nearest approaches to an operational GIS including environmental variables in sub-Saharan Africa are the FAO Land Inventory and UNEP's GEMS development. In the time available for the present study it has not been possible to explore the capability of the GEMS. The FAO Land Inventory has been used in Section 2 (above) to catalogue certain variables against LGP sub-zones. As mentioned above, the LGP sub-zones, when overlaid on thermal zones and countries, generate over 100 cells. If the soils map is superimposed on the map of LGP sub-zones, the number of cells is excessively large 1,213 for Kenya alone. Something much simpler is needed for present purposes.

## The Sources

The objective is to search the patterns of the mapped variables for convergent spatial distributions that provide a basis for environmental units. Land inventories have been developed, and published, for a number of national and sub-national areas including or impinging on the SAZ of sub-Saharan Africa. The resources available for such studies (*e.g.*, those conducted by the LRD/LRDC/ODNRI/NRI of the UK Overseas Development Administration, the IEMVT in France, and the FAO/UNDP) permitted the processing of large quantities of primary data air photography, soil samples, etc. and their incorporation into hierarchical procedures for taxonomy and aggregation of environmental units. These cannot be used for present purposes, because there is no way of bridging the gaps, or ensuring zonal compatibility.

The present attempt at a preliminary approximation of environmental units for the SAZ relies, therefore, on a manual assessment of output from the sources listed above. There are many anomalies in the data which could not be solved given the time available. Also, the benchmark dates of the sources vary from the 1960s to (perhaps) the 1980s. A hazard that is intrinsic to any attempt to evaluate environmental trends is that such benchmarks may not be made clear in the sources, and in any case such data compilations have to make use of primary studies differing in date and reliability. The least reliable data probably affects the population, livestock and land use estimates. Desertification risk classes also cannot carry much weight, since, only the briefest description is given of the method used to derive them (UNEP, 1977). There are anomalies apparent on several of the maps.

**Method**

The method used is as follows:

1. The 75 and 180 day LGP isolines are superimposed on country sections of the Soils Map of Africa at 1: 5M.
2. Generalised soil units are derived in three classes:
   - One soil dominant >50 per cent area (with or without associated soil >25 per cent area)
   - Two soils dominant, total >66 per cent area
   - No soils dominant (complex pattern).

   It should be noted that the map units shown on the Soils Map of Africa are associations of dominant, associated, and included soils, and that each of the 20 soil classes used is further subdivided into several soil units. In order to simplify, we used only the soil class (designated by a capital letter) and reduced the number of classes from 26 to 17 by omitting 9 classes considered to have minor importance in the SAZ. For example, Environmental Unit 35 in Sudan has associated soils described as follows:

   **I/R + J**

   *i.e.*, a dominant soil class, lithosols (I) with regosols (R)->50 per cent area occurs with an associated soil class, fluvisols (J)->25 per cent area.
3. If the 120-day isoline bisects the unit thus recognised, it is subdivided into two, identified as d (dry) or m (moist). If the isoline divides the unit very unequally, the lesser part is included under the dominant moisture regime.

4. Where data are available, a degradation risk value is assigned to the unit.
5. The dominant grassland community and descriptive category (*e.g.*, savanna) are recorded, followed by the vegetation class number and a summary description of the woody vegetation.
6. The dominant desertification risk category is recorded.
7. An estimate of cattle density in each unit is obtained by choosing a representative 1 cm2 (10,000 km2 at 1: 10M) and counting the dot symbols.
8. The units are overlain on the population density map and the dominant range estimated, omitting urban and peri-urban agglomerations.
9. The presence of tsetse and species is recorded.
10. The environmental unit boundaries are revised when necessary at stages (4), (5), and (8) to better harmonise the variables.

### Stratification

Environmental units having the same specification but separated in space or by national boundaries are combined under one identification number but retain alphabetical suffixes (the first letters of the country name) in order to facilitate matching with third order subdivisions and to make it possible to arrive at national evaluations.

## EFFECT OF ENVIRONMENTAL DEGRADATION

The present Study is undertaken at a time when reservations about the conventional view of degradation in the SAZ are becoming commonplace, and both its linkages with management, and the evidence for its progression are being questioned. It is difficult to reconcile this perspective with the orthodox view of desertification as a man-made and irreversible process consuming large areas of productive land every year. In mixed farming areas, both the degradation of arable land under cycles of cultivation, and the degradation of rangeland under various levels of stocking, are issues. Relevant to both cropping and animal husbandry, as well as to the status of the environment in general, is the management of the woody vegetation.

## FUNCTIONAL *VS* ECOLOGICAL DEGRADATION

Environmental status has traditionally been left to ecologists to define, even though it has long been recognised that low nutrient status in cultivated soils is primarily an aspect of their economic management, and may be remediable given the right incentives. Work on common access grasings in the Communal Areas of Zimbabwe has challenged conventional notions of carrying capacity and overstocking. Optimum stocking levels for commercial beef cattle may be lower than those of dairy herds whose functions include household subsistence, investment, breeding, manure and traction, and which are fed partly on residues and browse.

What may appear as overstocking to the ecologist may be economically efficient to the stockowner. Alteration of the vegetation is not irreversible. The opportunity costs of alternative forms of management are more relevant to an understanding than a comparison between observed and potential vegetation; also, annual primary productivity may be higher under intensive grasing.

It appears necessary to distinguish between ecological degradation (in the sense of the loss of primary potential productivity) and a functional, remediable degradation that reflects the economic rationale of a particular management system under certain constraints of capital, land or labour.

## DIAGNOSTIC *VS* LONGITUDINAL EVIDENCE

Reliance on diagnostic evidence (*e.g.*, a substitution of annual grasses for perennials, of unpalatables for palatables, the appearance of bare ground, gully erosion, etc.) supported by intuitively convincing hypotheses linking management (or mismanagement) with degradation, has tended to obscure the scarcity of longitudinal data that would allow the rate and nature of degradation to be established.

Proper examination of such data, increasingly available from the interpretation of air photos and earth satellite imagery, exposes many ambiguities and tends to emphasise the impact of rainfall fluctuations.

Meanwhile the efficiency of some pastoral nomadic systems, in terms of energy conversion under conditions of fluctuating climatic stress, is becoming better understood. Such studies would be appropriate in the SAZ also.

## STOCKING RATES AND DEGRADATION

If the condition of the vegetation is not always a reliable guide to the quality of management, neither can stocking rates be used as a short cut to assessing degradational status. Overstocking (however defined) may occur at any point on the scale of farming intensity. If it truly occurs, then unless the livestock are fed from imported feed, there must be either cumulative ecological degradation, losses from sale or starvation, or both. It is a transitional, not a permanent condition. The persistence of livestock populations that are supposed to be much higher than local carrying capacities for decades, if not generations, is therefore of obvious significance.

Carrying capacity estimates tend to be related to the area of available land rather than to the total capacity of the managed ecosystem to feed livestock (natural grasing, browse, crop residues, weeds, fodder crops, field boundary plants, irrigation canal-sides, etc). Arable encroachment on grasing land has major implications for cattle management, even though the crop residues may support more LUs/ha on an annual basis than the natural grasings. A switch into small ruminants, however, may sidestep such problems, and there are mixed farming systems where comparatively high small ruminant stocking levels are maintained, although natural grasings have all but disappeared.

## DENSITY, INTEGRATION AND SUSTAINABILITY

The following model is advanced linking human and animal population densities, farming intensity, crop-livestock integration and environmental management.

The first stage of the model is a low population density associated with farming enclaves and a predominance of grasing land. With increasing human population density, which is expressed in increasing availability of family labour, and given the economic conditions (uncertain market supply/prices of foodstuffs) that encourage a subsistence priority in the household economy, arable land expands at the expense of natural grasings. As the human population rises, and given the multipurpose value of livestock, so does the livestock population, subject to constraints imposed by household poverty, disease or starvation in drought. Diminishing natural grasings may favour small ruminants at the expense of cattle, or necessitate transhumance. The loss of natural woodland encourages the protection and eventually planting of browse (especially valuable for small ruminants) and other trees on farmland. Increasing frequency of cultivation (increasing labour inputs/ha) necessitates the use of animal manure and enhances this function of livestock, as well as favouring grain/legume crop mixtures.

Crop residues increase in importance relative to natural grasings as sources of fodder. Leguminous trees, providing dry season browse as well as benefiting crop growth, increase in importance in the system. Trees and planted field boundaries (also sources of fodder) stabilise soil wash and reduce aeolian activity.

The rising scarcity of land intensifies individual claims to access rights, and eventually raises the market price of land and the frequency of sale relative to other forms of transfer. Labour and capital investments are made in order to raise the productivity of land. Labour diversification out of agriculture, in response to alternative income-earning opportunities, need not cause the system to decline owing to the investment value of both the land and the livestock. Primary productivity of the system is low (constrained by the manure supply) but stable, and degradation is held in check.

This model provides a rationale for linking sustainable environmental management with high human and livestock densities, in contrast with much conventional wisdom that sees-rising tendencies as a certain road to environmental degradation. According to such a model, degradation is more likely to occur earlier in the sequence, if an increasing human population density is not associated with the introduction of intensive practices and crop-livestock integration.

The implication is that the link between the characteristics of mixed farming systems and environmental degradation, or sustainability, should be sought in the management of intensification, achieved through the integration of crops, livestock and (probably) trees.

## LINKING THE SYSTEMS TYPOLOGY TO ENVIRONMENTAL MANAGEMENT

It has not proved possible to identify direct and unambiguous linkages between system characteristics and trends in environmental degradation, or in other words, to link ecological sustainability to properties of system management on the basis of measured observations.

- The distribution of case studies on the map of Environmental Units leaves many EUs unrepresented by a system characterisation. A larger sample is needed. However the literature is unevenly distributed and many EUs will remain unrepresented even if a more thorough search is undertaken.
- There is little reason to suppose that a system case study is always reliably representative of the EU in which it is situated. There is also little reason to expect that there is any general correspondence between system properties and EUs, since, some of the criteria used for delimiting the EUs may have marginal significance for system management.
- No clear pattern of degradation risk or status emerges from the mapping of the EUs. This is partly because the sources are inadequate-the assessments of degradation risk are only available for areas north of Lat. 2N, and elsewhere the broad categories of desertification risk provide an insufficiently detailed guide. More fundamentally, it is because actual degradation is linked to management as well as to environmental characteristics.
- Characterisations of mixed farming systems often ignore questions of sustainability, or deal with them in a superficial way. This arises from the differences

in the professional skills required for the investigation of socio-economic, technical, and environmental variables, and from the relatively late arrival of sustainability on the research agenda of management-related studies.

- Unlike the EUs, the mixed farming systems identified in the present study do not comprise a spatially complete set, which, if it were available, would invite correlation with the map of EUs. Not only are many systems unrepresented in the literature, but of those that have been described, the territorial limits are rarely known.

Because it has not proved possible to link in a systematic way the organisational (management) aspects of systems directly to reliable indicators of environmental status, as set out in Term of Reference, it has been necessary to proceed independently with the generation of Environmental Units and with the taxonomy of mixed farming systems.

However, in setting out a rationale for both of these operations, the present study provides a basis for further work.

## ENVIRONMENTAL CLASSIFICATION

- A refinement of the EUs as defined and classified. Further subdivision is not considered useful since, it would increase the number of units in the SAZ as a whole, and in some individual countries, to a level that would be complex. On the other hand, amalgamating the EUs into a smaller number would increase the internal variability of the units, and it is preferable, if a smaller number is required, to use divisions based on a smaller number of criteria, *i.e.*, the third order (LOP) subdivisions or the second order (agroclimatic) subdivisions.
- Further analysis of the FAO Land Inventory data with a view to.
  - Revising the system of 83 EUs derived from conventional published maps, and extending the scope of the accompanying inventory.

– Linking the LGP sub-zones with livestock-related variables such as biomass production in natural pastures, and the availability of crop residues as fodder.

- Exploration of the GEMS system's capability for supplementing the FAO's LGP zonation and the system of EUs employed here. It may prove possible in future to substitute a computerised GIS-based regionalisation.

**Systems Typology**

- An extension of the systems review to a larger number of cases, an intensification of selected cases from additional literature, and the filling of some gaps in the map of mixed farming systems. Given a larger and more complete set of case studies, systematic analysis of the patterns of similarity may be attempted.
- Cross tabulation of selected system characteristics in order to explore in a preliminary way the existence of linkages between, say:
  – Stocking rates (LUs/$km^2$) and integration scores.
  – Cultivated percentages and human/livestock densities.
  – Access rights and market impact.
  – Livestock types and economic integration.
  – System integration and environmental sustainability or degradation.
  – Investment value and effects of drought.

This has not been attempted in the present study. It would be desirable to strengthen the review of the systems before doing so.

- Incorporation of livestock census data at the national level into the systems typology (and EUs), where available. The National Livestock Census of Nigeria, presently in progress, offers an opportunity.

The difficulty we have experienced in identifying clear patterns linking the systems typology with the environmental variables, notwithstanding the priority of the degradation-sustainability issue in the SAZ, underlines the need for both

- More system characterisations
- A format to expose such linkages on a compatible basis.

7

# Farming Systems and Environment

## NUTRIENT DEFICITS

The mixed farming systems of the developing world contain about 67 per cent of the cattle and 64 per cent of the small ruminants of the world. Throughout the world, animal numbers are growing in the mixed farming system, most rapidly in the humid/sub-humid regions. Sheep and goat numbers show the fastest growth rates in the humid/sub-humid region, underlining how human population pressure is reducing farm size and access to and use of resources.

Irrigated mixed farming systems have shown the greatest increase in productivity, particularly in the humid regions of Asia. This is clearly a result of the strong growth in demand for animal products and better access to feed resources and other types of infrastructure in Asia. Milk production is important, particularly in south Asian countries, due to the growing demand in the region and the favorable policies that many governments have created for the dairy sector. Although the growth of dairy production can place more pressure on land resources, it can also increase the use of crop by-products which in turn improves nutrient recycling and, if of high quality, can diminish methane production.

### STATE

There is a considerable range of positive and negative interactions between livestock and the environment within the different sub-systems. These interactions can affect land quality in its physical (soil erosion) and chemical properties (soil fertility), the use of non-renewable resources, such as fossil fuels and fertilizer, and the conservation of agricultural (plant and animal) biodiversity. They are detailed below.

*Soil erosion* is probably the most pervasive form of land degradation in the developing world. Erosion rates are particular high in Asia, Africa and South America where they average 30 to 40 tons/ha/year, compared with an average soil formation of 1 ton per ha/per year. In Africa, 60 per cent of soil erosion damage occurs in the semi-arid and dry sub-humid regions where cropping and livestock co-exist, with strong interlocking factors of cropping, fuelwood collection and grasing.

**Table. 7.1. Effect of Soil Erosion and Nutrient Export on Mixed Farm Productivity in Ethiopia**

| | | |
|---|---|---|
| Soil losses | Grasing systems | 5t/ha/year |
| | Crop land | 42t/ha/year |
| Crop production losses | | 500,000 ton |
| Livestock production losses | | 1,000,000 TLU |
| Gross Annual Immediate Losses | | US $ 100 million |
| Gross Discounted Cumulative Losses | | US $ 1.9 billion |

The nutrient export results from the use of dung and crop residues as fuel. The Gross Discounted Cumulative Loss captures the cumulative nature of the land degradation, in which each year's erosion and nutrient loss is followed by another, adding layers of losses and hence, cost on top of each other.

Soil erosion is even more damaging on sloping lands. Poorly managed sloping terraces under crops and degraded rangelands can lose up to 100 MT/ha/year. Conversely, well managed pasture land loses 7 MT/ha/year or less and well managed forest land losses range from 0-10 MT/ha/year. Bojo and Cassells quantified these losses in the degraded Ethiopian Highlands. Their results showed the effect of including pastures in those environments as a means of reducing erosion.

### *Soil Fertility*

Livestock play a significant role in maintaining soil fertility. In partially closed mixed farming systems, livestock can replenish a substantial share of soil nutrients, and therefore reduce the need for inorganic fertilizer, with corresponding savings for farmers in terms of cash outlay, for the country in foreign exchange, and for the world in non-renewable resources.

The total value of this contribution is not known, although approximate figures are given by Jansen and de Wit for the irrigated mixed farming systems of Asia. Assuming manure production of about 1 ton dry material per year per Tropical Livestock Unit[1], and an effective availability[2] of 15 per cent of the nutrients in the case of stall fed and half that amount for grasing animals, the amount of nutrients under stall fed conditions is about 8 kg N and 6 kg P per year per TLU. Under those assumptions, livestock in the mixed irrigated farming system can supply between 2 and 10 per cent of the nitrogen requirements for rice, and about 40 to 120 per cent of the requirements for phosphorus in cassava.

As can be clearly seen, nitrogen is the most depleted nutrient, with the amount lost varying, depending upon the technology used in collection, storing and application practices. How farmers approach these three factors largely determines the effectiveness of the recycling process and therefore provides an avenue for intervention. As shown, stall feeding significantly increases the amount of nutrients available from manure.

To demonstrate the importance of these contributions, an estimate was made of the amount of fertilizer that would be required to replace the manure that is used in the irrigated system of the humid tropics. The value of this is estimated to be between US$ 700 to US$ 850 million per year, depending on various assumptions.

The economic benefits of improved soil structure as a result of adding soil organic matter from manure are more difficult to estimate. Adding manure to the soil increases cation exchange capacity, and improves soil physical conditions by increasing the water-holding capacity and improving soil structure stability. When adding the manure output from pigs and ruminants together, livestock may contribute up to 35 per cent of the soil organic matter requirements. This is a crucial contribution because this is the only avenue available to many farmers for improving soil organic matter.

**Table. 7.2. Estimated Contribution of Livestock to Crop nutrient Requirements in Irrigated Systems in Asia (Per cent N and P removed by Crops)**

| System | Rice | | Cassava | |
|---|---|---|---|---|
| | N | P | N | P |
| Pigs | 2 | 21 | 4 | 42 |
| Ruminants-grasing | 4 | 19 | 10 | 38 |
| Ruminants-stall-fed | 8 | 38 | 20 | 75 |
| Pigs+Ruminants-grasing | 6 | 40 | 14 | 79 |
| Pigs+Ruminants-stall-fed | 10 | 59 | 24 | 117 |

Assuming rice yields of 4 tons per ha, and cassava yields of 10 tons per ha.

***Non-renewable Resources***

Draught animal power, in addition to other economic benefits, provides an important source of energy in the mixed farming systems of the world and helps to reduce dependence on non-renewable fuel resources. In developing countries, animal power is used to cultivate about 52 per cent of the 480 million hectares of cropland. Draught animals provide between 25 to 64 per cent of the energy needed for cultivation in the irrigated systems of the world.

Worldwide 300 million draught animals are used in smallscale agriculture, while 30 million tractors would be needed to make the same contribution. This is equivalent to an US$ 200-300 billion investment in tractors plus a $5 billion annual fuel cost. Assuming that approximately 50 per cent of the arable land is cultivated in the world's irrigated areas with draught animal power, complete replacement by tractors would require annually 888 million litres of diesel at a cost of US$ 222 million, and US$ 429 million for depreciation of the equipment.

The value of animal manure for cooking fuel is more controversial. Dung cakes are the main source of household energy for millions of poor households in the developing world. It is often argued that using dung for fuel removes soil nutrients and therefore carries high opportunity costs. However nitrogen is the only major nutrient that is lost because the remaining ash is high in phosphorus and potassium.

**Table. 7.3. Amount and Value of Manure in Fertilizer Equivalents in Asia's Irrigated Areas**

| | Nitrogen | Phosphorus |
|---|---|---|
| Manure kg/ha | 5.7-9.8 | 7.9-11.7 |
| Fertilizer Equivalent (kg/ha) | 16.3-27.9 | 7.9-11.7 |
| Financial Value (US $/ha) | 6-10 | 2-3 |
| Total Economic Value (US $ mill) | 404-697 | 124-183 |

### *Biodiversity*

In mixed farming systems, livestock-environment interactions can be a key focal point. As human population pressures increase, some types of wildlife or plant diversity can be lost while other types of biodiversity may actually increase. Reid *et al.* demonstrate how the number of tree, bird and mammal species changes as human use of the resource base intensifies *(Figure 7.1)*.

These results are important for demonstrating the dynamic nature of ecological systems. They also show that man's agricultural activities must be balanced with the environment's capacity to sustain them.

An often overlooked component of biodiversity is soil micro-flora and fauna. Arthropods, with 90 per cent of all species, dominate biodiversity. For example, in a New York alfalfa 'ecosystem' Pimental *et al.*reported 600 species of above ground arthropods.

Livestock and manure have a beneficial effect on this biodiversity. For example, in mixed farms in Japan, the species diversity of the micro-fauna under grass more than doubled when manure was added to the land.

In forest and communal grasing areas, adjacent to mixed farming areas, plant and animal biodiversity is decreasing because of over-grasing. There are many examples quoted in the literature confirming this trend, for example, in Syria, Rajastan, and West Africa.

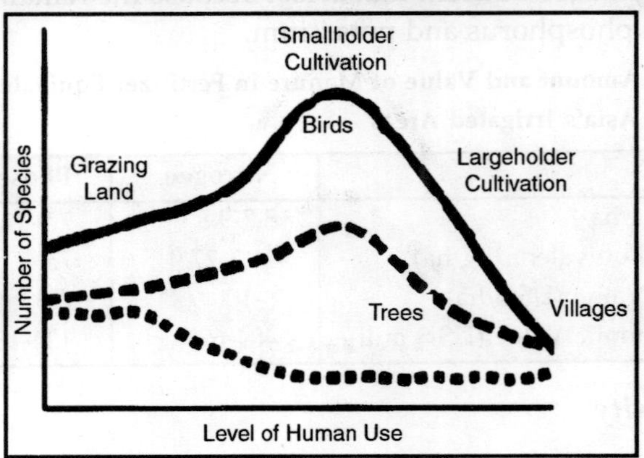


**Fig. 7.1. Changes in Biodiversity as Human use Intensifies**

It is not clear, though, whether these are irreversible, long term changes. For example, Thomas and Middleton report that no systematic pattern of vegetation change could be detected in a 27-year vegetation survey of 77 villages in the Sudan. However, wildlife biodiversity is disturbed if land is fragmented and river sides are cultivated. Finally, the mixed farming areas of the world contain the main centres of domestic animal genetic resources (local livestock breeds) of the world. Urgent steps to safeguard that future capital are proposed.

## DRIVING FORCES

### LAND

Human population pressure, poverty and infrastructure are, as in grasing systems, the most important fundamental driving forces affecting the environmental impact of mixed farming systems in the developing world. And in that respect, the mixed farming systems are entering a dynamic period of growth and change because they cover some of the countries with the highest birth rates in the world (*e.g.*, Uganda, the Sahelian countries, Ethiopia, Nepal, Bangladesh). Human population pressure affects soil fertility. In many parts of Africa and in the mountainous areas of Asia and Latin America, farmers attempt to maintain soil nutrient balance with, at best, small inputs from outside. Poverty and poor infrastructure usually prevent them from buying commercial feed and fertilizer. Nutrient balance depends, therefore, on the ratio between arable and non-arable land. This also varies widely according to the climatic conditions. For example, in West Africa, the ratio was about 10 to 40 hectares of dry season grasing and 3 to 10 hectares of wet season grasing to provide adequate nutrients for one hectare of millet cropland.

However, with increasing population pressure more and more grasing land is converted into cropland, the crop/grasing land ratio narrows, and the nutrient flow into cropland decreases. For example, cropland has increased in the Machakos area of Kenya from 35 per cent of the higher potential area in 1948 to 81 per cent.

In Northern Mali, the rate of increase of the arable cropping area was the same as the 2.6 per cent rate of annual population growth over the last twenty years. This trend can lead to increased competition for cropland and grasing on the open rangelands, which in turn, can lead to privatisation of crop residues and rangelands. For example, the common property lands in India, have decreased since, 1960 by 50 per cent, so that in 1992 they constituted only 15 per cent of the total area. Population pressure also causes farmers to push cultivation out into more resource limited areas, causing soil erosion. Mabbutt reports, for example, that in Niger millet fields are appearing 100 km north of the recommended limit to cultivation, increasing the risk of crop failure and leaving soil exposed and at risk of erosion. Livestock are moved to the most marginal areas.

Globally mixed farmers have a history of attempting to optimise manure use in an effort to maintain soil fertility. Such efforts, however, are dependent upon access to livestock, feed resources for livestock, and the ability to store and apply manure. The examples presented below detail how well such efforts work and the potential problems involved in attempting to balance soil nutrient levels.

In Nepal, farmers know livestock are essential for maintaining soil fertility. Quantities of 3 to 20 MT/ha of manure are applied, with irrigated fields receiving larger amounts. Yields of 1.6 and 1.3 MT/ha respectively for a crop of Maize followed by wheat can be sustained with 21 MT/ha of manure application.

In these areas total livestock densities range from 9.8 to 16.7 livestock units/ha of cultivated lands. Six livestock units are needed to provide sufficient farmyard manure for one year to grow one hectare of rice-Maize-wheat. This quantity of manure is presently not available, due to partial collection and inefficient storage. In Indonesia, upland farmers apply manure on vegetables, rice, Maize and cassava. Inorganic fertilizer applications are low. Maize and cassava grown on valley bottoms show a negative N, P, and K balance. The average density of cattle in upland Java is 2 head/ha which yields 2.5 MT/ha per year of dry farmyard manure.

In Kenya, a typical subsistence farm would havea negative nitrogen balance of about 50 kg nitrogen/ha and is about self-sufficient in phosphorus. A move towards commercial dairy production would increase the outflow. But with the cash generated from the dairy cattle a nutrient balance can be achieved through a combination of manure and commercial fertilizer. Nutrient balance studies (Ransom *et al.*, 1993) demonstrate how farmers strategically use commercial fertilizer on coffee and use manure on Maize fields to achieve a nutrient balanced system. On sampled farms manure application ranged from 3,000 to 13,000 kg/ha/year. Commercial fertilizer use was not consistent as manure was used alone in 5 out of 7 years.

Unless nutrients are replenished from outside sources, soil fertility continues to decline as the ratio between crop and grasing land declines. This is typically the case of many mixed farming systems in the tropics. Reported losses range from about 15 kg N/ha/year in Mali, to more than 100 kg N/ha/year in the highlands of Ethiopia.

Downward spirals of declining soil fertility, overgrasing, and increased erosion and losses in soil micro-flora and fauna are the result and will cause, ultimately, significant decreases in agricultural productivity and political stability. The Rwanda example clearly underscores the need for a balance between crop activities, animal inputs and human population pressure, to avoid the collapse of the farming systems, impoverishment and even civil war.

In irrigated mixed farming, grasing is more likely to be contained within the system although the source of feed supply is likely to shift increasingly from non-arable grasing to grasing of crop residues and the use of fallow land. Inorganic fertilizers are used to overcome soil nutrient deficiencies.

The main feature of the irrigated areas has been the dramatic intensification of crop production as a result of the Green Revolution. With the introduction of improved 'dwarf' varieties, the quality and quantity of crop residues decreased, but cereal production and total farm income increased. This has decreased the amount of feed available for ruminants, but increased the supply of cereals available for intensive production. Moreover, rising incomes as a result of the Green Revolution increased demand for livestock products. The two trends together promoted the development of intensive industrial units which, combined with the high fertilizer use in the Green Revolution areas, has led to increasing concerns about nutrient loading in regions such as the Punjab in India. In addition there are environmental concerns from the crop sector about salinisation of soils, increased erosion rates around irrigation areas and increased use of pesticides.

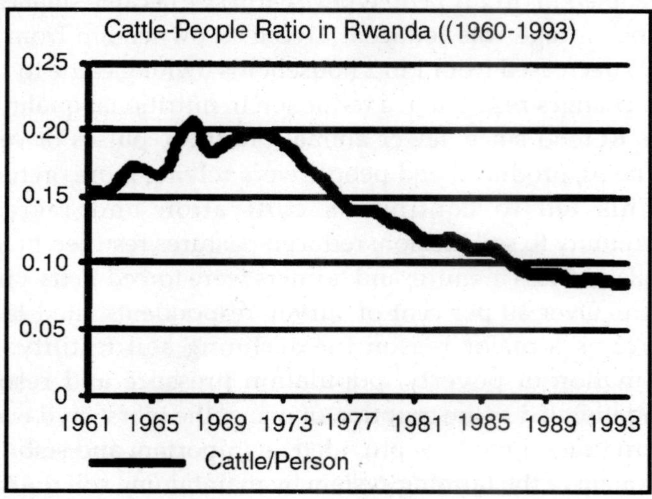


**Fig. 7.2.**

The Green Revolution has also had an effect upon the use of draught power, one of the other major links between crops and livestock. Off-farm employment increases labour costs and, if the time available to prepare land becomes shorter, tractorisation becomes more important, decreasing the use of buffalo and cattle for traction. For example, in India the number of bullocks used for animal power has decreased from 85 million in 1960 to 60 million while, over the same period, the number of tractors increased from 30,000 to 1.4 million. Only about 30 per cent of the total arable land in India is still cultivated by animal power.

## MIXED FARMING IN RWANDA

Prior to the colonial period, Tutsi and Hutu, the major ethnic groups of Rwanda, had a working relationship which balanced the nutrient flows in the farming system. This was accomplished by the Hutu herding Tutsi cattle in return for receiving excess male offspring, manure and milk. As a result the Hutu farmland maintained or increased in soil fertility.

In the 1940's human and animal populations started increasing, and land previously reserved for grasing was converted into cropping lands. For example, from 1948 to 1991, population density in the Gikongoro province increased from 100 people/km$^2$ to 287 people/km$^2$. Farm sise became smaller and livestock forage was reduced. Livestock ownership from 1967 to 1993 decreased from 1 in 2 households owning cattle to 1 in 4. These changes resulted in a reduction in nutritional quality and access to food since, fewer animal products, pulses or cereals were being produced and people were relying more on tubers.

This led to continuous cultivation and increased vulnerability to soil erosion; reduced pastures resulted in fewer animals and less manure; and farmers were forced to try buying manure. Over 40 per cent of survey respondents cited lack of manure as a major reason for declining soil fertility. This combination of poverty, population pressure and resource degradation led to the eruption of one of the worst civil wars in modern times. Livestock provided an important and stabilising component of the farming system by maintaining soil nutrients.

Their increasing absence contributed to the destabilisation of a previously balanced system. While it is certainly not clear whether this drama could have been avoided, one might assume from this analysis that improved incentives and technologies for smallholder development, including, for example the introduction of high yielding small ruminants, could have reduced the downward spiral in resource degradation.

## BIODIVERSITY

Increased pressure and intensification of livestock production can cause both positive and negative effects. When livestock are used to reduce dependence on chemical methods to control weeds and insect pests, biodiversity losses are reduced. On the other hand, excessive grasing pressure on communal areas adjacent to mixed farms has a negative effect, causing losses in biodiversity. There are many documented examples of the effect of livestock grasing on plant and animal biodiversity, especially on open access grasing areas. Overgrasing leads to a change in the composition of plant species. Fewer perennial varieties survive but annuals, of less nutritive value as fodder, become more abundant.

This can have a long term negative effect on the value of grasing land and may lead to soil erosion as well as loss of biodiversity. In addition, intensification of production, following increasing population pressure leads, especially in dairy production, to the replacement of local livestock breeds by a small number of exotic breeds. The significant increase in tractorisation, especially in Asia, has had the same effect, because the hardy, strong dual purpose traction/dairy breeds have been replaced with specialised dairy breeds.

Rubber production in South East Asia is practised both on plantations and smallholder farms (2 to 4 hectares in size). In both cases, weeds are controlled by spraying. Rubber producers in Malaysia and Indonesia spend approximately US$ 150 million and US$ 38.8 million, respectively, trying to control the weeds which compete with rubber tree growth. Researchers in both countries have found 60 to 70 per cent of the weeds that grow under rubber can be used to support profitable sheep enterprises.

Sheep provide much-needed cash to rubber producing smallholders. Environmentally, by combining sheep and rubber production, herbicide use is reduced by 18 to 38 per cent. Furthermore, by using sheep in this manner, fertilizer costs are also reduced.

Policies have often limited the beneficial impact of crop-livestock integration and exacerbated its negative environmental effects. These policies have been instigated in some countries by a desire to achieve self-sufficiency, especially in cereals, and in others by the desire to provide cheap food for urban areas. To achieve self-sufficiency, markets were protected and subsidies were provided on inputs such as fertilizer, feed, fuel, etc., in order to increase production.

This created disincentives for the use of on-farm products such as crop-residues, animal draught power and manure and contributed to a decline in mixed farming, with subsequent negative effects on the environment.

More specifically:

- Subsidising fertilizers, common in the oil-producing countries such as Nigeria, and many of the North African and Middle Eastern countries, hindered the integration of crops and livestock because it reduced the need for organic fertilizer;
- Subsidising mechanisation and fuel, again common in the Middle East, North Africa and Asia, reduced the need for animal traction and, as mentioned before, made possible the expansion of arable farming into marginal areas;
- Subsidising concentrate feed, common in the Middle East and, indirectly through differential import duties on feeds in the EU, leads to the excessive use of concentrate feeds. It also reduces the need for mixed farming. Globally, it contributes to a 'feed nutrient trade deficit' in the developing world; and
- Poor land tenure security, especially in the rainfed mixed farming systems of the developing world, has discouraged investment in long-term soil fertility improvements, such as the use of inorganic fertilizers

and the use of green manure and leguminous fodder crops within the crop rotation.

The policy of providing cheap food to urban centres has at the same time discouraged intensification, in some cases to the detriment of agricultural production as a whole and livestock in particular:

- Imposing high import duties to protect domestic cereal production, has had the effect of extending cropping into marginal areas and upsetting the equilibrium between crops and livestock;
- Overvalued exchange rates in sub-Saharan Africa and Latin America have favoured imports of cheap food from the industrialised world, thus competing against local production and providing no incentives for local producers to intensify into mixed crop/livestock systems nor to practise soil conservation.

## RESPONSE: TECHNOLOGY AND POLICY OPTIONS

A fundamental requirement to achieve environmental sustainability of the natural resource base is to accept change and flexibility in the respective production systems and overall landscape. Agriculture, and crop agriculture in particular, seeks to stabilise production and limit environmental change thereby reducing the flexibility of the eco-system. But any ecosystem which supports the production of food, can be enhanced by the integration of livestock as a mechanism to promote system flexibility.

Mixed farming, with careful attention to the nutrient balance, is therefore probably the most environmentally desirable system, and should be the prime focus of agricultural planners and decision makers. The challenge will be to identify the technologies and policies, which generate the sustained and accelerated growth needed to satisfy the world's booming demand for meat and milk. This challenge will be enormous. Past global growth of the meat and milk output of the mixed system has remained behind the increase in global demand. Will the growth in demand levels continue to rise beyond the capacity of mixed farm systems to meet national demands and therefore result in an immediate transition to highly intensive industrial systems? This study argues that, for environmental reasons, it is important to promote mixed farming in order to satisfy, as far as possible, global demand for meat and milk.

The Machakos case. Human pressure and intensification can also work positively. Tiffen *et al.*, showed clearly that despite a 500 per cent population growth over the last 60 years in the semi-arid Machakos district in Kenya, the natural resource base improved. The key factor leading to this success was dynamic market development making farming profitable, generating off-farm employment and supplying the capital for investmens in soil and water conservation. Horticulture and smallholder dairy production are the main activities generating the cash for resource conservation, such as terracing. The famine predicted in the 1930's for the Machakos district never occurred.

The key enabling factor seems to be access to inputs and attractive markets, as illustrated by the Machakos case study in Kenya. Here, a dynamic market and access to inputs has led to a fully sustainable development of a resource poor area, in which the population had quintupled over the last six decades*(Box 3.6)*. Use of livestock in such intensive situations includes a shift in species from cattle to sheep and/or goats. In such intensive situations, sheep and goats are kept where difficult access to markets and milk processing facilities make keeping cattle a less attractive option. Integrated crop-livestock systems have an immense potential to contribute to the required growth in productivity in the highland areas of Latin America and the semi-arid areas and highlands of sub-Saharan Africa where the population density is already high.

In spite of all the advantages of mixed farming, current trends point to specialisation in either crop or livestock production, whereby the rate of change in any particular situation will depend on existing infrastructure, relative price ratios between the different inputs and outputs, and economies of scale. The development path that has been followed in the developed world and east Asia confirms this trend.

## TECHNOLOGY

In mixed farming systems, there are exciting opportunities for technological change. Applied research and extension are of critical importance if the environmentally friendly factors of the system are to be maintained, although McIntire *et al.,* (1992) make the point that African farmers are well aware of the technologies involved. The challenge will be to convince farmers about the value of technology. In the nutrient deficient systems of the developing world, the emphasis should be on control of soil erosion and improving nutrient recycling. Some examples are:

*Improvement of soil* cover through the use of alternative crops for mulching, and introduction soil management techniques such as conservation tillage, bench terracing, strip cropping, contour farming, etc.;

*Improvement of feed production and quality* to reduce the pressure on grasing areas and improve internal nutrient transfers. Technologies to do so include:

- Introduction of fodder shrubs and trees to reduce soil erosion and improve soil fertility. Several mixed farming systems using fodder shrubs and trees have been developed. An example is the agroforestry system with three strata (grass, fodder shrubs, and tree crops, such as oil and coconut palms, cashew nuts, etc.) as successfully introduced in Indonesia;
- Improvement in feed quality, for example through urea treatment of feeds, as reportedly successfully used now by more than 5 million farmers in China (Li Biagen, pers. com.) and through increased efforts in plant breeding to correct the grain bias of the green revolution 'dwarf' varieties and raise nutrient quality of the crop residues; and
- Use of non-conventional feeds (sugarcane tops and sugar cane juice, fruit tree and bamboo leaves).

Reduction of nutrient losses from manure and improved efficiency of their application by:

- Promotion of stall feeding which doubles the effective availability of nitrogen and phosphorus; and

- Strategic supplementation for specific classes of animals (lactating animals) to improve the efficiency of limited amounts of available feed.

*Increased production efficiency,* and thereby farm income, resulting in improved purchasing power for soil improvement and conservation methods.

They include:

- Within breed improvement.
- Where appropriate, changing to small ruminant production or to optimal combination of ruminant and non-ruminant species.
- Strategic supplementation of lactating and growing animals.

**POLICY**

Clearly, for optimal development of mixed farm systems, a more open market economy is needed. In an open market there should be reduced subsidies for feed, fertilizer and mechanisation. Phasing out of subsidies will promote a closer integration of crop and livestock systems in many parts of the world. It will enhance the use of home grown feeds, organic fertilizer and animal traction. To capitalise on free market transitions, better extension, improved financial institutions, security of tenure and, above all, better infrastructure are required.

The greater reliance on market forces needs to be accompanied by policies which seek to provide, for the most densely populated areas, the highest priority for employment generation outside the sector. This can be accompanied by market development for intensive crop and livestock production, such as horticulture and, in livestock, in industrial pig and poultry and possibly small ruminant production. This will enable adequate flows of nutrients in to the system and a rebuilding of environmental sustainability.

For the less critical, but still densely populated areas, markets and infrastructure are still important. For those systems, closer crop-livestock integration will help to reduce eventual nutrient deficits, but markets will always be required to supply external inputs. Technology and market policies should encourage rotations that maintain soil fertility and find synergies between crop and livestock activities.

## NUTRIENT SURPLUSES

The mixed farming systems of the developed world cover about 17 per cent of the world's pasture land and half of its arable land. They contain about one-fifth of both the world's cattle and small ruminant population. These systems generally show a much slower growth than mixed farming systems in the developing world.

In some countries, mixed farming is contracting, reflecting the combination of stabilised demand in the OECD countries and the decline in the former Soviet Union and Eastern Europe, because of restructuring following the transition to a market economy.

## ENVIRONMENTAL CHALLENGES

With increasing population pressure, growing incomes and improved infrastructure and market opportunities, more intensive forms of crop and livestock production, including integrated systems evolve. These integrated systems come into dis-equilibrium in several regions of the world as a consequence of large nutrient imports from outside the region, causing an overloading of soil and water with pollutants.

The environmental challenge in the industrial countries, and to a large extent also in the fast growing economies of east Asia, is thus to identify, before it is too late, the point where land and aquatic eco-systems become overloaded. This is better than trying to identify technologies and policies which mitigate the negative effects of nutrient overloads once they have occured. In other words, 'prevention is better than cure'.

A further environmental challenge is to maintain biodiversity and an aesthetic landscape in heavily populated and developed mixed farming areas. Although opportunities to conserve biodiversity will not be able to mimic exactly the diversity associated with mixed farming in less developed areas, it should be possible to achieve some level of conservation. The challenge is to put in place technologies and policies which encourage farmers to retain a mixed farming system instead of specialising in the production of one or two crops only.

## STATE

In the developed world, the environmental effects of mixed farming systems may include a deterioration in land and water quality (through soil erosion and nutrient loading), and biodiversity loss, especially through habitat change.

*Soil erosion* in the temperate zones, with a loss rate of about 15 ton/ha/yr, is half that of the developing world. But even this lower erosion rate exceeds by far the average soil formation of about 1 ton/ha/yr.

## SOIL FERTILITY

Soils in north western Europe, in the eastern and midwestern USA and in the fertile and densely populated, and increasingly affluent, areas of east and south Asia, often reveal a surplus of nutrients. There are also widespread areas of central and eastern Europe where, as a result of very large livestock production units, there is a serious surplus of soil nutrients. While the total area with surplus nutrients is probably still very small (less than one per cent of global arable lands, through run-off its effect on water quality is much more widespread. Often such areas are near ports and/or large urban areas so that the transport costs associated with imported fertilizers, and the subsequent sale of milk and meat, are low.

The excess nitrogen and phosphorus 'leaks' through leaching or run-off in surface or groundwater, damage aquatic and land eco systems. In Pennsylvania about 40 per cent of the soil samples taken from dairy-crop farms revealed excessive phosphorus and potassium levels. Soils are saturated and surplus nutrients leach into surface water, pollute the environment, in this case the Chesapeake Bay. A similar situation is found in Brittany, France where all eight counties report nitrate levels of more than 40 mg/litre whereas, in the 1980s, only one county reported levels this high.

## BIODIVERSITY

The intensification of mixed farming and the subsequent shift in production towards regional specialisation puts pressure on plant and animal biodiversity. In addition, the move towards sown pastures coupled with high levels of organic and inorganic fertilizer use reduces the richness of flora and fauna. This problem can be exacerbated by the use of insecticides for the control of external parasites, especially in areas with high water tables.

In the Brittany region of France, farmers import at least 40 per cent of their animal feed requirements from other regions, with the result that, on average, 134 kg nitrogen is available per hectare from manure. In addition 93 kg is purchased in the form of inorganic fertilizer, against a crop uptake of only 146 kg N/ha. This results in an excess of about 80 kg N/ha, causing high nitrate levels in drinking water, and eutrophication of inland surface waters and marine ecosystems. Nitrate concentration typically exceeds 40 mg per litre, compared with 25 mg/l as a guide level in drinking water. Eutrophication of marine ecosystems causes algae growth creating problems for shellfish producers. In some parts (*Saint-Brieuc Bay*), shellfish have been contaminated with bacteria and sales have been banned

## DRIVING FORCES

Soil erosion is strongly influenced by grasing pressure and cropping intensity. Reynolds *et al.*reported how variable soil erosion can be observed under different grasing pressures. Soil loss on lands with a good grass ground over has been estimated at 1 ton per hectrare, this increased dramatically on overgrazed pastures to a level of 53 tons per hectare. If grasing pressure is in balance with the forage resource being produced, livestock's interaction can encourage more stable land use practices. Pimental *et al.*, discussed how, in the United States, in order to increase farm size, grass strips and shelter belts were removed, thus increasing the erosion rate. In the past, livestock provided a rationale for grass strips and shelter belts but, with the separation of crop and livestock systems in OECD countries, the rationale for using land resources in this way has weakened.

Nutrient surpluses are the main cause of deteriorating land and water quality. These surpluses come from a combination of inorganic and organic fertilizers. Inorganic fertilizer is used, in spite of the fact that the system could be balanced using the nutrients supplied by the manure produced within the farming system.

For example, in Brittany, organic manure produced by intensive industrial and mixed farms of the region could provide adequate nutrients but substantial surpluses emerge because of the additional import of large quantities (between 35 and 100 kg N/ha per year) of inorganic fertilizers. Inorganic fertilizer is said to be necessary because of the ready availability of its nutrients and its easy transport but, as in pure intensive grasing systems, lower inputs might be adequate and even more economical. The preparation of nutrient balances (inorganic and organic) on a regional basis is therefore a critical element in identifying land conservation and fertilizer policies.

Policies designed to protect domestic production of most animal products, especially beef and milk, against imports and a broad array of producer subsidies, especially on feed imports, have led to the wide use of feed concentrates and therefore to situations where nutrients are in surplus. Such situations occur most often on the many smallscale enterprises which tax advantages and quota systems usually favour and where regulations are more difficult to enforce. Smaller size enterprises tend to have more lenient standards and are able more easily to exploit loopholes in regulations designed to protect the environment. These intensive systems using concentrate feed demonstrate how policies designed for social objectives can misdirect resource use and technology development.

## RESPONSE: TECHNOLOGY AND POLICY OPTIONS

### Policy

In the developed world, regulations are being introduced to restrict the emission of nutrients in the case of point source pollution, and restrict stocking rate ('manure quota') in the case of non-point source polluters. A cross section of current legislation in some of the developed and developing world is provided in *Table*. Regulations include a variety of restrictions on stocking rate and use of fertilizer, manure storage and times and techniques of application, encouraged by government subsidies on manure processing and management.

- A variety of measures may be introduced to reduce nutrient surpluses. These include:
- Taxation of inorganic fertilizer, in order to discourage unnecessary use where a system is already in surplus;
- Maximum application limits and regulation of times of application in order to reduce leaching and volatilisation.
- Taxation on feed imports to reduce the significant transfer of nutrients from the already nutrient deficient developing world to the nutrient surplus areas of the industrialised world. Such taxation might be supplemented with, or used as, subsidies for a transfer of nutrients back to the developing world.
- Incentives to achieve a more balanced distribution of crop and livestock activities.

**Technology**

Of particular importance are the following technologies to reduce nutrient surpluses:

- Improved nutrient formulation in terms of incorporating optimum levels of nitrogen into feed and adding enzymes to improve the utilisation rate of plant phosphorus. Optimum nutrient ratio and composition management reduce loading the environment with these elements.
- Improved manure handling and storage are key requirements for more efficient use in nutrient deficient areas, and to prevent leaching and pollution of surface water where there is a nutrient surplus. It gives an overview of some of the most common factors which determinine whether the effect of manure is minimal, moderate or severe.

In addition, over the last decade, there has been considerable interest in promoting low-input mixed farming systems, as sustainable and environmentally friendly systems. In the USA, the Rodale Institute in Pennsylvania, and the LISA (Low Input Sustainable Agriculture) movement, strongly promoted by USDA have been in the forefront. In Europe, the ILEIA (Institute for Low External Input Agriculture) has been one of the prime movers. Mixed farming systems are often especially suitable for low-input production.

Some of the main technologies which can be used in the livestock sector are:

- Use of grass-legume mixtures as the basic feeding system for ruminants. The nitrogen fixation of legumes (such as clovers), can replace the nitrogen lost through milk and meat.
- Mixed species grasing (cattle and small ruminants), which increases grass yield, botanic composition and reduces the parasite load.
- Genetic improvement focusing on maximum capacity to digest roughage, rather than on concentrate feed consumption, and based on life-time production, rather than on short term lactation yield, to achieve optimum efficiency on the basis of renewable resources.
- Housing, which allows adequate movement and is based in the animal's natural social behaviour, produces high quality manure using large quantities of straw.
- Disease control based on good feeding and breeding practices, and preferably using organic medicines, to mimimise environmental contamination.

On the crop side, this has to be accompanied by environmentally friendly low-input techniques, such as zero tillage, manuring and composting, integrated pest management (IPM) etc.

Precise information about soil nutrient levels, coupled with economic incentives, not only helps to minimize production costs but also helps to maintain the soil nutrient balance as well as a landscape that is aesthetically pleasing. The National Research Council of the United States has provided some excellent guidelines for low-input agriculture.

**Table. 7.4. A Cross Section of Manure Management Regulations**

<table>
<tr><th>Country</th><th>N - Emissions</th><th>P - Emissions</th></tr>
<tr><td>European Union</td><td>Maximum stocking rate: 2.0 cows, equivalent to 170 kg N per year in manure<br><br>Nitrate level in drinking water: MAC* 50 mg $NO_3$/l</td><td>$P_2O_3$ in drinking water: 5,000 microgram/l.</td></tr>
<tr><td>Netherlands</td><td>Same water standards as EU. Reduction of $NH_3$ emission by 50-75 percent, through low ammonia emission techniques: injection, bans on autumn and winter applications, and covered manure storage. Cost sharing for manure drying and transport to manure deficient regions.</td><td>Max. amount of $P_2O_5$ in animal manure allowed to be added to the soil to decline as follows:<br><table><tr><td></td><td>1990</td><td>2000</td></tr><tr><td>Grassland</td><td>250</td><td>90</td></tr><tr><td>Maize</td><td>350</td><td>65</td></tr></table><br>with levies for every kg of phosphate produced per hectare of farm-owned land in excess of a tax-free amount of 55 kg P per ha. The tax of US $ 0.40 per kg of $P_2O_5$ is doubled for production over 87 kg. per ha.</td></tr>
<tr><td>Germany</td><td>Varies according to the State. Maximum fertilizer rate at 240 kg N per ha, and in some states maximum</td><td>Unlike Netherlands, most attention is on nitrogen</td></tr>
</table>

*(Contd...)*

| | | |
|---|---|---|
| | stocking rates of 3.5-4.5 cows (or manure equivalent) per ha. Manure application (winter) and storage restrictions. Mineral record keeping required. | |
| **USA** | Varies according to the State. Manure management plans required for all farms (with federal and state sharing cost in implementation) and permits required for concentrated animal feeding operations (CAFO's). Bans on the direct discharge on surface water.<br>* Maximum Allowable Concentration | |

Low-input farming can have a special attraction to consumers who like to buy 'environmentally safe' products under 'green' labels and to support eco-farming, organic farming, etc. As for any other food product 'green label', food must be subject to clear and strict quality standards (especially regarding residues) and be supervised by reliable quality control systems. Prices of such 'organic' food products are between 20 and 50 per cent higher than conventionally produced foods, mainly as a result of low volumes and stagnant market share (2 to 5 per cent of the EU market). Producers, who are therefore unable to practise economies of scale, nevertheless have to meet high distribution costs.

'Green label' eggs (free range production) are one of the most widespread products and now have a market share of 5 to 10 per cent in the EU. By and large, low-input production has, until now, only proved viable where consumers are ready to pay a premium for 'eco-products' and where there is market saturation.

**Table. 7.5. Some Parameters for the Assessment of Impact of Manure in Temperate Enviroments**

| Characteristic | Minimal impact | Moderate impact | Severe impact |
|---|---|---|---|
| Ratio of manure phosphate to crop phosphate | less than 0.9 | 0.9-1.1 | Over 1.1 |

(*Contd...*)

| | | | |
|---|---|---|---|
| Distribution of manure over farmland | Homogeneous | Medium | Heterogeneous |
| Exposure of stored manure to air and soil | Low | Medium | High |
| Time lapse between manure application and planting date | 1-7 days | 1-4 weeks | More than 1 month |
| Time lapse between manure application and working-in | 0-1 hr | 1-12 hr | More than 12 hours |
| Use of water with manure application | Much | Some | None |
| Organic matter saved from waste | Much | Some | None |
| N working coefficient | High | Medium | Low |

## LIVESTOCK SYSTEMS

Industrial production[1] of pork, poultry and (feedlot) beef and mutton is the fastest growing form of animal production. In 1996, it provided more than half the global pork and poultry meat (broiler) production and 10 per cent of the beef and mutton production. This represented 43 per cent of total global meat production, up from 37 per cent in 1991-93. Moreover, it provided more than two-thirds of the global egg supply. Geographically, the industrialised countries dominate intensive industrial pig and poultry production accounting for 52 per cent of the global industrial pork production and 58 per cent of the poultry production. Asia contributes 31 per cent of the world's pork production.

Industrial ruminant production is concentrated in Eastern Europe, the ex-Soviet Union and in the OECD countries (*Figure 7.3*). Typical examples are large-scale feedlots in the USA and in the former centrally planned economies. Industrial sheep feedlots are found in the Near East, North Africa and the USA.

The industrial production system is open both in physical and economic terms. It depends on outside supply of feed, energy and other inputs. Technology, capital and infrastructure requirements are based on large economies of scale and, because of this, production efficiency is high in terms of output per unit of feed or per man-hour, although less so when measured in terms of energy units. Yet, as the world's main provider of eggs, poultry meat and pork at competitive prices, it meets most of the escalating demands for low cost animal products in rapidly growing urban centres of the developing world.

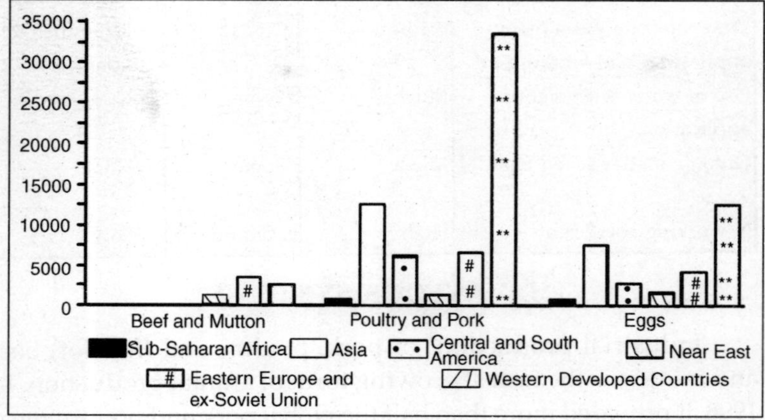


**Fig. 7.3. Industrial System Livestock Production by world Region ('1000 tons)**

## ENVIRONMENTAL CHALLENGES

Because of its open nature and many interfaces with the natural resource base, the industrial 'bio-industry' system signifies for many the epitome of what is wrong with animal production. The industrial scale implies large herd/flock sizes, large volumes of wastes, high animal health risks, and less attention to animal welfare. It has multiple opportunities to dump its waste products without accounting for the environmental costs. There are, however, solutions which could substantially reduce the negative environmental effects, although at a cost. The biggest challenge that the sector faces over the next decade is to identify technologies and establish policies that will internalise the environmental costs.

### State

The industrial system acts directly on land, water, air and biodiversity through the emission of animal waste, use of fossil fuels and substitution of animal genetic resources. In addition, it affects the global land base indirectly, through its effect on the arable land needed to satisfy its feed concentrate requirements. Ammonia emissions from manure storage and application lead to localised acid rain and ailing forests, for example in European countries.

Also, the industrial system requires the use of uniform animals of similar genetic composition. This contributes to within-breed erosion of domestic animal diversity. The effects of each of the direct agents are described below and the indirect environmental effects of feed concentrate production and the pressure on domestic animal diversity, are described.

**Land, Water and Air**

These are the environmental components mostly affected by the concentration of animals and waste production. Manure is the main agent having effect, mostly during storage and after application on the land. Pigs and poultry excrete some 65 and 70 per cent, respectively, of their nitrogen and phosphate intake. Nitrogen, under aerobic conditions, can evaporate in the form of ammonia with toxic, eutrophic and acidifying effects on ecosystems.

A greenhouse gas, nitrous oxide, is formed as part of the denitrification process with particularly harmful effects on the environment. Nitrates are leached into the groundwater posing human health hazards and run-off and leaching of nitrogen directly lead to eutrophication and bio-diversity loss of surface waters and connected ecosystems. Phosphorus, on the other hand, is rather stable in the soil, but, when P saturation is reached after long term high level application of manure, leaching occurs and this also causes eutrophication.

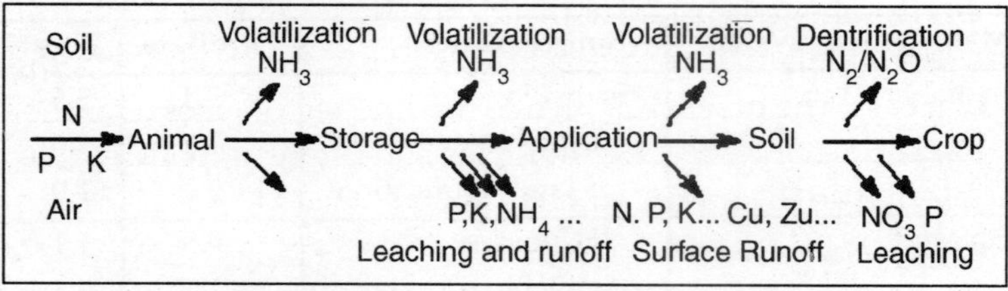


**Fig. 7.4. Possible Nutrient Losses from Manure between Excretion and Crop Uptake**

Ammonia and other nitrogenous gases result from the digestion of protein, part of which is lost in manure and urine. Growing pigs, for example, excrete 70 per cent of the protein in feed while beef cattle excrete 80 to 90 per cent and broiler chickens 55 per cent. Ammonia, in high concentrations in the air, can have a direct effect on plant growth, by damaging leaf absorption capacities but its indirect effect on soil chemistry is even more important.

Ammonia acidifies the soil, interferes with the absorption of other essential plant elements, particularly in nitrogen-poor ecosystems such as forests. Livestock production is a major source of ammonia emissions in the industrial world. For example, of the 208,000 tons of ammonia emitted in the Netherlands in 1993, 181,000 tons was estimated to come from manure.

This was about 55 per cent of the total acid deposits in the Netherlands, industry and traffic being other important contributors. In many developing countries, industrial pollution, especially from high sulphuric acid coal burning is the more important source of acid rains. Ammonia also constitutes a health threat for farm workers.

The various forms of nitrogen losses lead to much reduced levels available for crop nutrition. Plant uptake and use depend on a series of other factors such as species, climatic and soil conditions. According to Bos and de Wit, 20, 50 and 44 per cent of the nitrogen excreted by pigs, broilers and laying hens respectively are lost to the atmosphere as $NH_3$, as shown in *Table 7.6*. Because of its different chemical properties, phosphorus losses are insignificant because phosphorus mainly remains in the soil.

**Table. 7.6. Annual Global Nitrogen Production in Manure and Losses of Industrial Monogastric Systems (in Million Tons)**

| Management system | Source of loss | Broilers | Pigs |
|---|---|---|---|
| In stable | excreted | 3.4 | 3.5 |
| | various losses | 1.2 | 1.6 |
| | for land application | 2.2 | 1.9 |
| On land | $NH_3$ losses | 0.5 | 1.1 |
| | Available for crop nutrition | 1.7 | 0.8 |

The amount of N, P, K and other nutrients available to the crop within the soil determine the fertilizer value of manure. Further significant losses may occur depending on the type of stable and manure management system and thus define the direct environmental impact.

Substantial nitrogen and phosphorus losses also occur when manure is applied on the land. It gives an overview of key factors affecting the environmental effects of manure spreading. The spreading of manure directly on the land can lead to nitrogen leaching into the water as nitrates and contamination of surface waters. This in turn leads to high algae growth, eutrophication and hence, damages aquatic eco-systems. Not all soils are equally susceptible to nutrient loading and (ground) water contamination. Sandy soils with low cation exchange capacity, and therefore poor retention characteristics and high run-off, are particularly at risk.

**Table. 7.7. The Relative Importance of Different Manure Management Systems (Percentages for each Animal Type)**

| Animals | Lagoons | Liquid systems | Solid storage | Anaerobic digester | Burned for fuel | Deep pit stacks and litter | Directly discharged |
|---|---|---|---|---|---|---|---|
| Pigs | 10 | 71 | 10 | 1.5 | 1.5 | 5 | 1 |
| Broilers | | | | | | 100 | |
| Laying hens | 1 | 77 | <1 | | 1 | 20 | |
| Beef | | 6 | 88 | | | 6 | |

Because of feed's high energy content and, for example, the direct use of fossil energy to heat stables, significant amounts of $CO_2$ are emitted. Anaerobic decomposition of manure also releases large amounts of methane into the atmosphere when it is stored in liquid form.

## Heavy Metals

Copper and zinc, which are essential minerals for livestock diet, are deliberately added to concentrate feed whereas other heavy metals, in particular cadmium, are introduced involuntarily via feed phosphates. Only 5 to 15 per cent of metal additives are absorbed by animals, the rest is excreted. Soils, on which pig and poultry manure are continuously applied at high rates, accumulate heavy metals, jeopardising the good functioning of soil, contaminating crops and posing human health risks.

## Fossil Fuels

The industrial system is a poor converter of fossil energy. Fossil energy is a major input of intensive livestock production systems, mainly indirectly for the production of feed. For example, *Table* shows that feed accounts for 72 to 74 per cent of the total energy input, except for veal production where it is almost 90 per cent. Similar observations can be made for industrial pig and poultry production.

**Table. 7.8. Energy Input of some Types of Industrial Meat Production Systems (in Mega Joule (MJ) per kg of Liveweight)**

| Component | Beef | Veal | Mutton |
|---|---|---|---|
| Energy input feed[1)] | 11.5 | 41.7 | 14.0 |
| Energy input animals[2)] | 1.3 | 1.5 | 0.8 |
| Energy input fattening (buildings, equipment, fuel and other) | 2.7 | 3.6 | 4.5 |
| Total energy input | 15.5 | 46.8 | 19.3 |

*Note:* [1)] includes fossil energy requirements for production, transport and processing of feed

[2)] fossil energy for the production of the animals

Energy output for livestock products comprises food and non-food items. Southwell and Rothwell calculated output/input ratios of 0.38, 0.11 and 0.32 for pork, poultry meat and eggs respectively, while for milk it was 0.5. These calculations take into consideration fossil energy input only.

A large portion of non-food energy output is in the form of manure and the potential for recovery of this energy has greatly increased in recent years. Techniques for methane recovery are described.

The heavy concentration of animals in certain regions, particularly in the pig and poultry systems, has given rise to the development of large scale processing of manure for use elsewhere.

Manure processing and transport further increases fossil fuel consumption, particularly if drying is involved. This extra energy expenditure may offset the energy savings made by concentrating livestock production.

**Biodiversity**

The industrial system has a three fold effect on species wealth through:

- Its demand for concentrate feed, which changes land use and intensifies cropping. The production of feed grains, in particular, adds additional stress on biodiversity through habitat loss and damages in ecosystem functioning.
- Waste production and its effects on terrestrial and aquatic ecosystems. These effects are often geographically confined to areas of high livestock densities. Eutrophication and destruction of habitats is a common phenomena in parts of north-eastern Europe and the USA as well as in the densely populated areas of the developing world, in particular Asia and to a lesser extent, Latin America. Ammonia emissions lead to acidification of particularly fragile habitats and so causes losses in biodiversity.
- The requirement for extremely uniform animals of similar genetic composition. This contributes to within-breed erosion of domestic animal diversity, and is discussed.

**Table. 7.9. Energy Input for Pigs and Poultry Systems (in MJ per kg of Liveweight)**

| Component | Pork | | Poultry meat | | Eggs | |
|---|---|---|---|---|---|---|
| | Canada | Netherlands | Canada | Netherlands | Canada | Netherlands |
| Housing | | | | | | |
| - fuel, electricity | 3.0 | 3.0 | 8.2 | 3.5 | 5.4 | 1.2 |
| - building equipment | 0.4 | . | 1.0 | . | 0.5 | . |
| Total Housing | 3.4 | 3.0 | 9.2 | 3.5 | 5.9 | 1.2 |
| Feed | | | | | | |
| - transport | | 3.7 | | 2.4 | | 3.6 |
| - production, processing | . | 12.2 | . | 12.2 | . | 9.3 |
| Total feed | 20.5 | 15.9 | 13.6 | 14.6 | 18.9 | 14.1 |
| Total energy input | 23.9 | 18.9 | 22.9 | 18.1 | 24.8 | 14.1 |

## ENVIRONMENTAL BENEFITS OF INDUSTRIAL PRODUCTION SYSTEMS

First, the rapid development of 'modern' industrial pig and poultry systems helps to reduce total feed requirements of the global livestock sector to meet a given demand. It may therefore alleviate pressures for deforestation and degradation of rangelands, such as is happening in parts of Latin America and Asia, thus saving land and preserving biodiversity. Second, the feed-saving technologies developed for this system can be effective at any scale and therefore can be successfully transferred to mixed farming systems. The same holds true for waste prevention and treatment technologies which have been developed following regulations applied mainly to the industrial system. Therefore, the resource-saving and waste management technologies generated by the industrial systems bring benefits to the sector as a whole.

### Driving Forces

Population growth, rising income and urbanisation are the fundamental driving forces determining growth of industrial livestock production. Globally, industrial animal production is the fastest growing sector, with over 4 and 5 per cent growth per year in pork and broiler production, respectively. Annual growth for eggs is 3.8 per cent and for mutton and beef 2.5 per cent. Driven by rising incomes and rapid urbanisation (which in itself causes an increase in meat consumption), Asia experienced over the last decade a staggering growth of 9 per cent per year in industrial pig and poultry production, and this trend can be expected to accelerate. Sub-Saharan Africa shows good growth in all monogastric products, while Latin America continues to exhibit significant growth in poultry products. In Western Europe and the USA, growth is levelling off, while in the former Soviet Union, after the transition, all intensive meat and egg production is shrinking.

Industrial animal production has become concentrated in certain areas because of a number of factors which usually interact:

Transport costs and market opportunities are the main determinants. First, the industrial system, especially for pigs and poultry, is characterised by a significant, and often exclusive, use of feeds of high energy content (mainly cereals, oilseeds and their by-products). This high energy density allows movement of feeds over longer distances at substantially lower costs than perishable animal products, even though the quantities are larger. For example, sea transport costs of grains is one-tenth per unit weight that of frozen meat Cunningham. Thus, with an average feed conversion of 3:1 for pigs and 2:1 for poultry it is less costly to transport feed than meat. In addition, over short to medium distances, live animal transport costs are similar to those of grains. These relative costs encourage production, slaughter and meat processing facilities to be located near urban centres.

The large number of industrial units being established around Beijing, Shanghai, Mumbai and Calcutta demonstrate this incentive for close proximity to the consumer. Second, ruminants require fibrous feeds such as silage, hay or fresh chopped forages, in addition to concentrate feed, to maintain the rumen functions.

This requirement increases the transport costs for feed significantly and explains why industrial ruminant production is generally more connected to the landbase (and less to the consumer market) than pigs or poultry. In addition, feed conversion of concentrate feed per kg of beef or mutton is substantially poorer than with pigs and poultry. Intensive beef production is therefore only competitive where consumers can afford to pay a substantial premium for quality beef over chicken or pork. Third, in net grain importing developed countries, with abundant road and cooling infrastructure, large-scale industrial operations are located close to ports, such as pig operations in the Netherlands and northern Germany.

The Netherlands, France (Brittany) and Denmark depend, respectively, on 85, 40 and 20 per cent on feed imports for their intensive pig and poultry industry. As a result, large quantities of manure have to be transported over long distances (up to 100 km in the Netherlands) to 'manure deficit' areas. In Brittany, the distance over which manure is transported needs to cover, on average only 15 km, whereas in Denmark almost all manure can be applied in the immediate surrounding area.

Agrarian structure has favoured high livestock densities and the evolution of industrial-type systems where shrinking farm size forced farmers to engage in value-adding activities without significant land requirements, such as in some southern parts of Germany and the Netherlands, or to abandon agriculture altogether.

Different policy settings within a country or free-market zone through, for example, tax advantages, low energy costs or low environmental standards, may lead to concentration of the industrial system. An example is where intensive poultry, and more recently also pig production, moved from the corn belt of the USA to the southern States, and, in the EU, to Italy and Spain.

**Policies**

In the past, industrial and intensive mixed farming systems have benefited from policy distortions and the absence of regulations or their enforcement and, in many cases, this vacuum has given this system a competitive edge over land-based systems. Furthermore, some policies have misdirected resource use and encouraged the development of technologies which are inefficient outside the distorted context. For example:

In the EU, high domestic prices for beef, pork and milk, together with cheap imports of cereal-substitutes, such as cassava *(Box 4.2)*, have benefited industrial production. In addition, parts of the industrial ruminant system, for example, veal production, have greatly benefited from the subsidy policy on milk replacers. This policy originated from the surplus production of milk caused by milk quotas in excess of market requirements although these have also been reduced;

Differential import tariffs for cereals and cereal substitutes such as cassava and sweet potato meal, and improved feed formulation techniques strongly promoted the import of those cereal substitutes from the Far East, leading in the early '90s to an import of 7 million tons (15 per cent of the EU's total consumption of energy feeds, mostly in the Netherlands). This implies an annual import of about 40,000 tons of nitrogen and 7,000 tons of phosphorus, or about 15 kg of N per hectare per year agricultural land there, which, as it is not evenly distributed, constitutes a considerable environmental burden.

In WANA, small ruminant feedlots were (and still are) heavily dependent on subsidised feed, and this has encouraged inefficient feed use;

In the former centrally planned economies, the feedlot system was based on heavily subsidised feed grain and on subsidised fuel and transport; and

Many developing countries not only have direct subsidies on feed but also on energy. As energy is a major direct and indirect cost item in industrial production systems, economy wide policies often tend to favour industrial production over grasing systems and mixed farming.

Finally, in practically no country in the world, is the industrial system charged with the full environmental costs of production. It appears that societies prefer the cheap supply of animal products over the functions of concerned ecosystems. Self-sufficiency in animal products and supply of high-value food commodities to urban populations seem to be overriding policy objectives, particularly in developing countries.

## RESPONSE: TECHNOLOGY AND POLICY OPTIONS

In the developed world, stagnating demand and increasing human health concerns have, to some extent, alleviated the pressure. For example, growth of industrial beef feedlots in North America, is still only driven by population growth, because per capita consumption of beef has remained constant. The importance of feedlots in the European Community is likely to decline as production becomes more extensive in response to policies that reduce support to agriculture and promote environmentally friendlier production systems. With the shift to a market economy in Eastern Europe and the former Soviet Union, the importance of industrial ruminant production is declining and ruminant production is moving back to the land base and to smaller scales of operation.

In addition, and more importantly, the pollution of land, water and air has raised acute awareness in the developed world of the environmental problems associated with industrial production systems. This has, in many cases, triggered the establishment of policies and regulatory measures, removing many of the favouring factors, and inducing a series of technologies that are increasingly applied, wherever regulations are enforced. They are detailed below.

Point source pollution originates from a specific location and it is usually possible to determine how much of the pollution is entering the environment. Discharge of manure into surface waters, for example, is point source pollution. Non-point source pollution results from seepage of surface discharges, precipitation or atmospheric deposition. It spans a wide area of land, often depending on weather conditions, making both the occurrence and extent of pollution difficult to predict. Environmental damage through excess manure application to land is non-point source pollution.

**Policies and Regulations**

Regulatory instruments are imposed to control the distribution and concentration of livestock production and introduce technical control systems. Some of these regulations are relatively easy to enforce whereas others, for example the maximum permitted amount of manure per unit area, are more difficult. The regulatory approach is most efficient in situations of point source pollution and where there are strong enforcement institutions. In countries with weak institutions, the enforcement of regulations at reasonable social cost remains a major challenge and limits the validity of this approach. Compliance with regulations affects cost of production and may therefore influence regional distribution. Specific examples of regulations are given in*Table*. They include the limits on the number of animals in the EU, and most of the member states, taxes on surplus animals as in Belgium, taxes on surplus P (most EU countries), a ban on direct discharge of manure into surface waters (USA, Malaysia), and the establishment of nutrient management plans (Indonesia, the USA and a number of European countries). Guidelines on manure storage and application methods, timing, crops and quantities are available in practically all countries with high animal densities.

Between 1967 and 1987, the densely populated island state of Singapore went through a series of policy changes and technology adaptation and developments. Initially food security policies and consumer preference for fresh meat resulted in an upgrading of technologies, including least cost feed formulations, improved animal husbandry and veterinary health. In the 1970s, Singapore achieved self-sufficiency in eggs, poultry meat and pork. Starting in the late '70s Singapore started to establish a network of waste discharge measures including a 95 per cent reduction of Biological Oxygen Demand, BOD and a sludge of at least 20 per cent total solids content. Technologies for waste disposal were mainly imported from western developed countries and adapted to the specific conditions. In spite of having to incorporate a large part of the environmental costs in their prices, Singapore producers remained competitive *vis-á-vis* live animal imports. In 1984, environmental standards were raised, particularly with regard to odour control. In the same year, Singapore abandoned the national objective of self-sufficiency in monogastric products and pig farming was phased out in 1987.

Zoning can regulate regional distribution. Zoning is, and will remain, an important policy for controlling animal manure storage and processing, not only for environmental reasons but also for concerns of human health and rational regional development. Zoning has been important both in environmental and in regional development policies, as well as in successfully moving industrial production units away from urban centres in OECD countries. An important prerequisite for successful zoning is good infrastructure because animal products will have to be transported over larger distances. Marketing and processing infrastructure must therefore be taken into account when defining zones in order to make the best use of investment.

The creation of confined 'industrial parks', with prescribed and sometimes shared facilities for waste collection and treatment, offers opportunities to fully charge industrial production systems with environmental costs while still maintaining advantages of market access and economies of scale. Governments have frequently established guidelines for the siting of production units, particularly to protect urban settlements from obnoxious smells. Zoning, when done within a comprehensive area development plan, also allows for common waste collection and treatment facilities to be shared by a number of producers. The ultimate zoning strategy has been introduced by Singapore, which completely prohibits animal production.

A trend to rational zoning is not only fostered through environmental concerns but also by changes in overall policies, often triggered by the removal of government interventions and trade liberalisation. In the Near East, for example, industrial small ruminant systems have been kept viable through subsidies on grains and are increasingly under pressure because of the financial requirements to maintain these subsidies.

No systematic evaluation exists and data are scarce. Costs are very site-specific and rarely are full environmental costs actually covered. However, regulations for intensive production systems in some countries are so strict that practically all environmental costs, at least for waste, are absorbed by the producer.

Here are some examples:

- In Malaysia, for cultural reasons swine production is kept out of sight and no pig manure can be applied to land. In certain prescribed areas, industrial pig producers have to reduce BOD to less than 50 mg/l (95 per cent reduction), through screening and aerobic treatment. For a 500 animal pig unit, investment costs are around 10000 Ringgit Malaysia (RM) and operating costs are 24 RM per production place (Hassan, pers. com.). This implies an incremental production cost of 0.23 RM (approx. 9 US cents) per kilogram of liveweight produced, equivalent to a cost increase of around 6 per cent.
- In Singapore, in 1986, the large-scale Ponggol Pigwaste plant turned wastewater into recycled water (7 mg/l BOD5), essentially removing all waste-related environmental effects. Total average annual costs were calculated at US$ 14.39 (Taiganides, 1992) per porker marketed or between 8 and 9 per cent of total production costs.

- Australian beef feedlot regulations are the strictest in the world and contribute to construction costs of new feedlots being much higher than in the United States. Most feedlots are in the vicinity of grain producing areas. The regulatory frameworks differ between the States and costs of compliance with environmental regulations have been given at A$ 27 per head for feedlots in Queensland and A$ 41 for New South Wales or approximately 4 and 6 per cent respectively of total production costs. Investment costs related to compliance with environmental regulations are 6 per cent of total investment costs.

While it appears that overall impact on production costs, even in extreme cases, do not exceed 10 per cent incremental costs, investment requirements and effect on income can be prohibitive if such measures are applied unilaterally. Furthermore, unit costs for establishing and operating waste treatment facilities decrease with increasing size, so small producers are disadvantaged. However, the latter often face less severe regulations, such as dairies in the USA, or are exempted altogether.

The most efficient and direct financial instrument would be to internalise all environmental costs into the consumer price. This should certainly be the policy over the medium term. However, implementation of such policies is not easy. First, there is a lack of accurate economic evaluation of these costs, for example for biodiversity and some gaseous emissions and some indirect costs (soil erosion because of feed production, for example). Initial calculations point to an increase of 10-15 per cent in cost price. Second, unequal application of the inclusion of environmental costs in the product price puts some producers at a comparative disadvantage. A more global approach will therefore be required.

Current financial instruments therefore focus on reducing the emission of nitrogen and phosphates and other potential pollutants, particularly in susceptible and already burdened areas. The levies and taxes currently imposed on the intensive mixed and industrial systems in practically all developed countries fall into this category. This includes many of the measures listed above, such as levies on waste discharge, taxes on excess animals or phosphate-loads.

Others are:

- Removal of subsidies, or imposition of taxes on imported concentrates, to increase the cost of feed concentrate-intensive production and to favour land-based systems over the industrial system. This is the main cause that large-scale feedlots can no longer compete in the contracting market of the former centrally planned economies. Here, the general trend points to a more land-based livestock production, removing a large part of the waste problem in the medium term. In a more indirect way, removal of subsidies or taxes on fossil fuel may have a similar effect by raising the cost of feed. Government income from such sources could be used to alleviate environmental problems;
- Removal of import restrictions on materials and equipment that improve feed efficiency, such as amino-acids to improve protein, enzymes to improve phosphate digestion and feeding equipment that restricts intake. These technologies lead, indirectly, to lower waste loads through better feed conversion;
- Subsidies for investment or running costs to improve the adoption of emission control technologies. For example, subsidies for constructing manure storage facilities are given in many EU countries. In the USA, cost-sharing and state revolving funds have been established for manure storage sheds and dead bird composters; and
- A system of tradable manure emission quota to limit waste production and still create incentives for efficient resource use. Marketable permits and pollution trading would be based on the establishment of payment per unit of pollution or the use of pollution reduction credits.

## TECHNOLOGIES

As can be expected according to the theory of induced technology, these measures have led to the introduction of a wide range of new techniques. Because of the commercial and demand-driven nature of the industrial system, development and transfer of technologies are usually not a problem, although their impact can be expected to level off as high levels of technology are reached.

A whole range of technologies exists that could alleviate the environmental burden created by this system. The effectiveness of these technologies with regard to manure disposal can be measured with parameters. These technologies seek improvement in two areas:

### *Reduction of Nitrogen and Phosphate Excretion by Improving Feed Utilisation* can be Achieved Through

- Introduction of multi-phase feeding in order to match feed composition to the needs of the individual animal classes. By better adjusting the nutrient supply to the needs of animals, less waste is produced and therefore less nitrogen and phosphates are released in waste and into the environment.
- Improving the accuracy of determining nitrogen and phosphate requirements, followed by better balancing of feeds with these essential nutrients. In this respect, important gains have already been obtained in better balancing pig and poultry rations with essential amino-acids, the building blocks of feed proteins. For example, a combination of better balanced feed improved digestibility and the inclusion of synthetic amino acids, allows for a substantial reduction of the protein content in feed and, hence,, a reduction of nitrogen excretion by 20 to 40 per cent. Concentrate conversion rates range between 2.5 to 3 kg feed dry matter/kg liveweight gain in pigs, 2.0 to 2.5 kg feed/kg of liveweight gain in broilers, and even less for eggs. They have been reduced by at least 30-50 per cent since, the '60s; for example,

the average feed conversion of pigs in the Netherlands in 1957 was 3.5 kg feed per kg liveweight gain. Through selection and better feed formulation, there is considerable potential for further improvement. For ruminants, key production efficiency parameters are daily weight gains and feed conversion, which reflect the profitability of the use of capital for feed, lean animals and investments. Cattle weight gains are usually in the range of 1 to 1.5 kg/day and feed conversion rates are of about 8 to 10 kg of grains per kg of weight gain during their period in the feedlot. A more detailed discussion of concentrate to animal conversion. Other options include the use of growth hormones (somatropine) or other stimulants (clenbuterol), frequently used in the USA, but banned in most of Europe.

Indicators for manure management:

- Nutrient balance: manure P/crop P.
- Distribution of manure over available land.
- Exposure to air and contact with soil.
- Time lapse between application and planting.
- Time lapse between application and working-in.
- Use of water with liquid manure.
- Nitrogen losses.
- Organic matter losses.

Spectacular improvements have been obtained with the addition of an enzyme (phytase) for catalysing the digesting of phosphates in feed. The same enzyme might also increase the availability of zinc in feed, reducing the need for feed additives; and promoting feeding systems which reduce intake and stop the buffet-style, *ad libitum* feeding which was popular in the 1980s.

### *Reduction of the Emission from Manure Storage and During Application*

Possible technologies are:

- A reduction of nutrient losses from manure in stables and during storage through improved collection and storage techniques. In animal buildings, manure is stored either under a solid floor, under a slatted floor, or within a housing system with litter. A large part of ammonia emissions comes from the manure surface in storage, either under the slatted floor or in open tanks. The main focus has to be on reducing nitrogen losses, most of which are in the form of ammonia from the manure surface. Possibilities are:

*Solid storage systems,* which collect the faeces only for storage in bulk (often for extended periods), and have low gaseous emissions;

*Liquid or slurry systems* where animals are kept on slatted floors and the manure and urine are collected and stored in large tanks. This system is particularly common in pig production, and part of the energy may be recovered through the use of anaerobic digesters;

*Lagoon systems* consist of flushing systems using large amounts water. Nitrogen losses and methane emissions are high;

*Covered tanks and manure* kept under solid floors in stables. Minimal amounts of ammonia are emitted when manure is stored under solid floors. Reductions in emissions of 80 to 90 per cent can be achieved by covering storage tanks; and

*Reducing odour and ammonia* after emission from the source. In addition to natural or forced ventilation systems the air can be cleaned through bio-filters or bio-washers that absorb odours and ammonia from polluted air. This is done by oxidising ammonia into $NO_2$ and $NO_3$. Up to half of the ammonia can be eliminated through such air washing systems. However they are costly in investment and operation.

For the protection of water resources, Denmark has established regulations that allow manure to be applied only during the growing season. Consequently, the manure has to be stored for up to nine months, creating immense storage problems and costs. This induced an initiative in 1988 by which a number of farmers are served by *Joint Biogas Plants* which are large common storage facilities. This overcomes the problem of economies of scale which individual farmers would be unable to overcome. In 1994 nine plants delivered more than 2 million $m^3$ monthly to public utilities.

Methods that efficiently re-use energy and nutrients in manure in cases where manure is not used directly for agriculture. Biogas plants of all sizes and different levels of sophistication exist. They not only recover the energy contained in manure but also eliminate most of the animal and human health problems associated with micro-biological contamination of waste by micro-organisms.

Other methods of controlling the waste load are purifying and drying the manure:

- Reducing nutrient losses during and after application of manure on soils. Injection or sward application of manure into the subsoil and appropriate timing significantly reduces nitrogen losses as shown by the Netherlands' experience since, 1995. Nitrification inhibitors can be added to slurry to decrease leaching from the soil under wet conditions;
- Large-scale manure processing is possible where intensive production is concentrated in certain zones but that is often not viable economically. The efficient use of manure for feed and energy production requires high capital investment which often cannot be borne by individual farmers;
- Recycling manure by feeding it back to livestock, including fish is practised only on a limited scale. In addition to widespread reluctance to use manure as feed, mainly originating from fear of health hazards, most types of manure have a low nutritive value with the exception of poultry manure which is of reasonable quality, *i.e.*, 55-60 per cent Total Digestible Nutrients (TDN) and 20-30 per cent Crude Protein (CP). Consequently, in intensive production systems with large amounts of collectable manure, cheaper feeds are also available, while in production systems where utilisation of low quality feeds is common, high collection and opportunity costs (manure as fertilizer or fuel) prohibit the use of manure as feed. A recent overview of the possibilities is given by Sanchéz.

# 8

# Post-harvest Management of Food Crops

## CURING OF CEREALS

This is a common practice in the lower elevations of the state and has a scientific basis:

- The maize plant along with the stalk is harvested and tied into small bundles called *'Pahra'*. All bundles from different fields are collected at one place and stacked in an upright position. Upright stacking of maize bundles is called *'Thua'* or *'Zhumb'*. After a period of one and half month, the maize cobs are separated individually from the husk.

**Fig. 8.1. Maize Curing by Stacking**

Stacking of maize in the *Zhumb* for 30-45 days, ensures ripening and it also facilitates the easy separation of cobs from the husk. Curing results from heat and moisture equilisation in the grains in the *Zhumb*. It has also been observed that initially sweet grains, upon complete drying and curing, become tasteless which is attributable to the conversion of sugars to starch, a common phenomenon also observed in pea and maize grains.

- Harvested paddy is tied into small bundles. Each bundle is called *Pooli* or *Poola.* After drying under open condition for 3-4 days, all bundles are stacked at one place and allowed to remain there for few days. Each stack is called a *Kundli* (Fig. 8.2).
- Similarly, millet grains called *Mandal* or *Sonk* are allowed to ripen partially by stacking them in a heap and covering the heap with tarpoline. This procedure is locally termed *Garr Dena.*

The preparation of small bundles *Pahra, Pooli or Poola* help in easy handling and quick drying. Stacking bundles in heaps possibly aids heat and moisture regulation thereby resulting in uniform ripening. The creation of moist heat also leads to curing which eases the process of threshing the grains.

**Fig. 8.2. Sun drying of paddy in stack (Kundli)**

## CURING OF CHILGOZA (*PINUS GERARDIANA*)

In Kinnaur, chilgoza seeds are separated from the cones by collecting the harvested cones at one place and covering them with chilgoza pine needles, leaves and soil. After 15-20 days, the chilgoza cons are cut-open using a sharp edged axe (*Behla*), with a gentle strike the seeds are easily separated. The procedure of covering harvested cones with pine needles, leaves and soil possibly helps in maintaining desired temperature and humidity inside the heap, which results in the curing of cones.

## CLEANING OF GRAINS

- Winnowing of grain and pulses is a common practice in every home in Himachal. It is performed using a container made of tin, called *Stoop* or *Chhaj*. The grains are placed in the *Chhaj* and slow winnowing leads to separation of dirt and husk from the grain. Almost all types of dry grain like wheat, maize, paddy, pulses etc. can be cleaned in this manner.

**Fig. 8.3. Winnowing of Grains**

- Bulk cleaning of grain is done using a container made up of bamboo sticks called *Panaudi* (Fig. 8.4). The dry grain, placed in the *Panaudi,* are allowed to fall from a height of about 4-5 ft in a thin vertical flow in the path of a cross wind. The lighter dirt particles and husk are blown away and the heavier grain is thus separated as it falls straight to the ground. The use of a fan (mechanical or electrical) greatly accelerates this process of cleaning. This method of cleaning is based on the differences in density of the materials to be separated. The use of modern air separators/cyclone separators for grain cleaning is based on this principle.

**Fig. 8.4. Panaudi for Cleaning Grains as Well for Separating Husk from Grain**

## PACKAGING OF FOOD COMMODITIES

### FRESH PRODUCTS

Different types of containers are used for packaging food commodities. In lower areas of Himachal/containers made of bamboo sticks called *Ddalh* are used in the fields for packing grain, maize cobs, potato, ginger, turmeric etc. and also for carrying the material from the field to the house.

For packing clean grain, pulses and flour etc. the *Ddalh* is internally lined with cow dung. The *Ddalh* has a capacity to hold 25-30 kg material. A Similar container, small in size, is called *Tokroo.* In the higher regions of the state, such containers are called *Kiltas,* however, the shape of this container is different from that of the *Ddalh* and has a greater storage capacity Fig.

The *Ddalh* is carried on the head while *Kilta is* carried on the back and is also provided with two large ropes meant for securing it onto the shoulders much like a bagspack. Raw materials carried in *kiltas* includes fresh apples, pears, potatoes etc. and even farm yard manure (FYM). *Kiltas* are internally lined with gunny bags to provide a cushion so as to prevent injury to the fresh fruit. For transportation of culled apples, and vegetables like peas, beans, capsicum, potatoes, ginger etc. to distant places gunny bags are used as the packing material. Packaging of perishables/delicate crop, like tomatoes, is accomplished in bamboo boxes called *Tokra,* which are then covered with thin gunny bags on the top. The shape of the container *Ddalh, Kilta* or *Tokra* provides easy carriage of material on human head or back. The structure is easy to clean and dries soon even after washing it with water. The wide spread use of such containers was probably due to easy availability of bamboo and wood in these areas.

In some parts of Shimla district and Bharmour area of Chamba district, wooden boxes made up of very thick wood were used to pack and transport apples. The weight of the empty wooden boxes ranges from 20 to 25 kg *i.e.* the empty weight was invariably more than that of apples, it carried in it. The box was made sturdy to enable its carriage on mule backs to distant distribution points/centres.

## PACKING OF PICKLES

In lower parts of Himachal pickled mangoes, *galgal,* lime etc.) are packed in earthen pots. The earthen pots are sterilised using fumes generated from burning red chillies along with *Asafoetida* (Heeng) and a little mustard oil. The top of the container is covered with a lid made of wood. The antimicrobial properties of fumes of red chillies, mustard oil and *Asafoetida* not only sterilise the containers and result in increasing shelf life of its contents but also has potential for preservation which serves as a replacement to inorganic chemicals. An excess use of inorganic chemicals may pose health problems.

# STORAGE OF FOOD COMMODITIES

## FOOD GRAINS

Food grains like maize, wheat and paddy are stored in special structures made of bamboo called *Peri* or *Peru*.

Prior to use, these structures are plastered on the inside with a mixture of cow dung and clay. These containers are placed on the ground floor and grain is loaded into them from a hole made on the roof of the first floor called *Baurh.* To take out grains, as per need, a special opening is provided near the bottom of each *Peri.* Interestingly, these structures are invariably kept in a separate room called *Overi* and access to which is allowed only to very few persons.

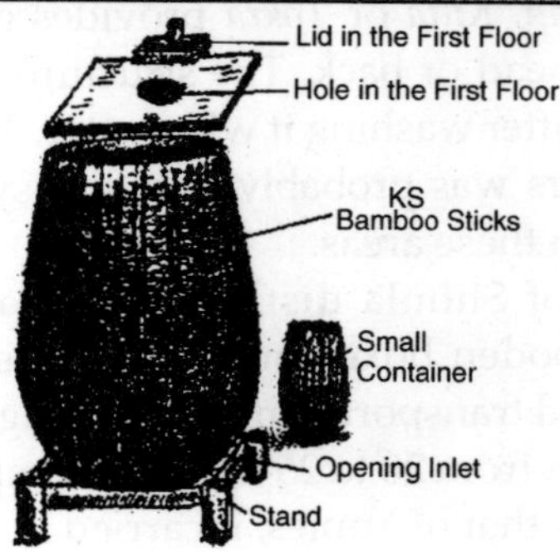


**Fig. 8.5. 'Peri' or 'Peru' for Gram Storage Made of Bamboo**

The use of bamboo containers allows the free exchange of gases inside the grain and keeping containers on the ground floor ensures cool temperature for storage. Loading from top and unloading from bottom offers easy material handling. Keeping storage structures away from main living room protects grain from fire etc.

In some parts of Sirmour, Solan, Shimla and Kinnaur districts grain is stored in wooden structures known as *Darauntha* and are kept away from *the* main living rooms. *Daraunthas* made of deodar wood are preferred as this wood checks the entry of insects/larvae. Wooden houses built away from living quarters check the entry of rodents etc. Windows with wire mesh, provide adequate ventilation. The size of the store house is proportional to the size of land holdings.

**Fig. 8.6. Grain Storage Structure Made of Cedar Wood (Darauntha)**

Grain storage in earthen rooms: In some parts of Lahaul and Spiti, special earthen rooms are constructed for storing cereal crops immediately after harvest. Storage in such rooms also provides a cool temperature so essential for the storage of grain.

**Fig. 8.7. Wooden Structure for Grain Storage**

Poor farmers in some parts of temperate Himalayas, have grain storage chambers made of bamboo. These are built out side in the safe vicinity of the farm house.

**Fig. 8.8. Traditional Green Storage Chamber made of Bamboo**

The logic behind constructing these storage houses/rooms at some distance from the family units was to save the food grains from the hazards such as fire, which was a common feature in the early days, as the entire structure of living rooms was fabricated from wood.

**Fig. 8.9. Inside-view**

## Use of *Neem* Leaves/Turmeric/Mustard Oil in Storage

The use of *Neem* as a pesticide is now well documented. Similarly Walnut, *Bhera* and Mint leaves also seem to possess certain antimicrobial or pesticidal properties, which help in grain storage. The antimicrobial substance in mustard is allyl isothidcyanate. The turmeric powder also appears to perform a similar function. Some of the uses to which these natural products are put are enlisted below:

Grain is mixed with leaves of Neem/Walnut/*Bhera*/Mint (*Pudina*) and then stored in bins.

For storing pulses, specially *Urad,* the grains are mixed with turmeric powder or smeared lightly with mustard oil and then sealed in air tight containers.

Storage of pulses after soaking in cow urine followed by drying is also practised in some parts of the Himachal.

However, the scientific basis for storing pulses after soaking them in cow urine is yet to be explained.

## STORAGE OF TUBER CROPS

In the tribal belt as well as in some other parts of Himachal, at the on-set of winter, root crops like potato, ginger, turmeric, colocasia (*arbi*) *etc. are* stored in under ground pits and the top is covered with thatch and soil. These products are consumed up to the next summer.

Storage of cabbage heads, meant for seed crop in done, in under ground pits dug in the fields. This is a common practice in Kinnaur. Apart from other storage benefits, the crop is also protected from the hazards of snow.

In Mandi district, a thin layer of grass is spread at the base of the pit to serve as a cushion, prior to storage of the root crops,*the* top of the pit (up to 6") is covered with grass and soil and is raised slightly above ground level to prevent entry of rain water into the pit In some areas, the top of the pit is plastered with cow dung.

Storage of ginger in pits for seed crops is stall prevalent in Sirmour and some part of Solan and Bilaspur districts. The pits in these areas are known as *Khatti*

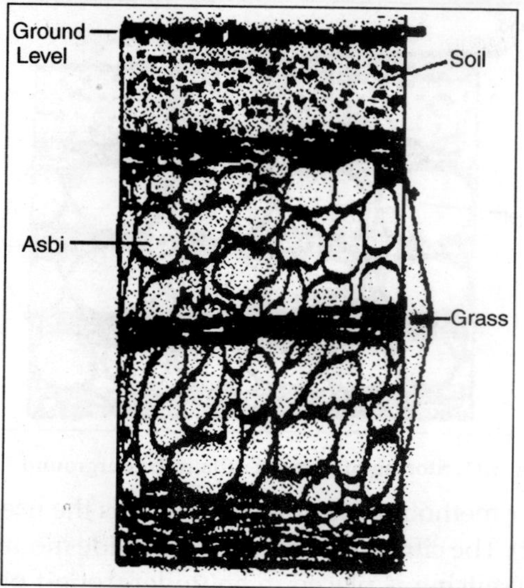


**Fig. 8.10. Storing of Colocasia, Ginger and Zamikand in the Underground pits ('Khatti')**

These methods of storage provide cool conditions for storage of these commodities, ensuring freshness for prolonged use.

However, it has been observed recently that storage of ginger in pits (*Khatties*) leads to spoilage of almost the entire crop, which might be attributed to a build up of pathogenic inoculum due to long and continuous use of same pits for the same crops. Therefore, digging of new pits is recommended and lighting a fire inside the pit, prior to storage. This is done for creating hygienic conditions inside the pit.

## STORAGE OF FRUIT CROPS

### *Citrus Fruits*

In Mandi district, ripe *galgal* fruit (*Citrus pseudolimon*) *is* stored in pits dug in the fields. At the base, a layer of ash is spread and then the fruits are placed in alternate layers of ash and fruit. The top of the pit is covered with ash and soil. Ash seems to possess antifungal properties, which help in checking spoilage. Storing in cool pits enhances the shelf life of this citrus fruit.

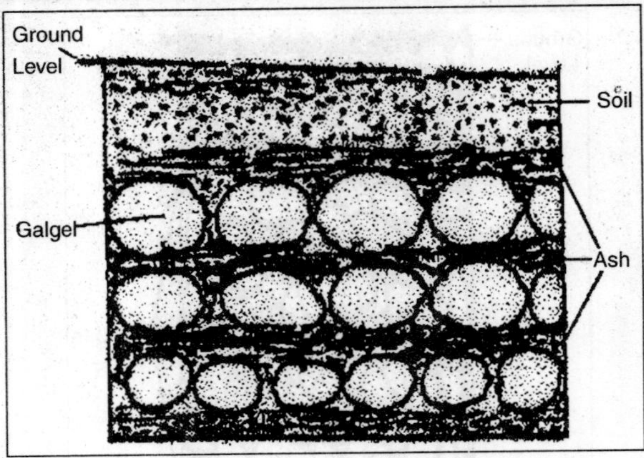


**Fig. 8.11. Storing of Citrus Fruits in Underground Pits**

Another method of storing citrus fruit is the use of a pitcher (earthen pot). The citrus fruit are placed in wide mouthed pitchers and then the pitcher is placed in an underground pit. The top is covered with about a 6" thick layer of soil. Using this technique, citrus fruit can be stored for 25-30 days without any spoilage. This practice is in vogue in the Nurpur (Kangra) area of the State.

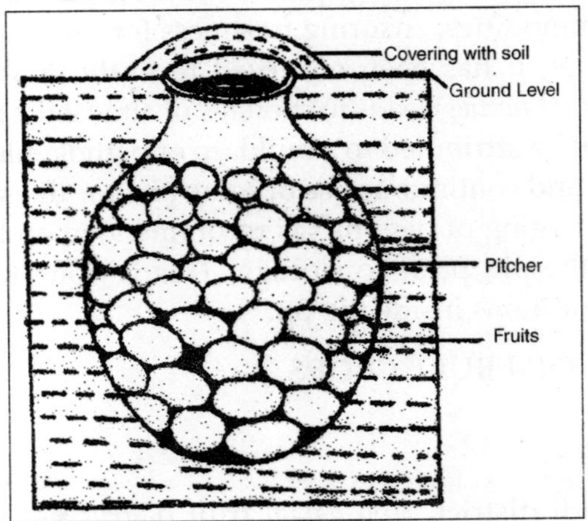


**Fig. 8.12. Pitcher for Citrus Storage**

## *Apple*

The apples are stored in the tribal areas of Lahaul-Spiti and Kinnaur districts in the underground pits, prior to the onset of winter. Apples are packed into wooden boxes which are then placed in underground pits and the mouth of pits is covered with thatch and soil. In this way, the apples can be stored up to summer time without any appreciable loss in quality.

The method appears to be a modification of the pit storage procedure described earlier, since here the direct contact of fruit and soil in the pit is prevented. A pitcher or wooden box placed in a pit creates a cool store. The development of the zero energy cool chamber (ZECC) appears to have its genesis in this technology.

***Banana***

Banana fruit wrapped in grass/cloth is also ripened in soil pit and also enhances its storage period.

The shelf life of fruit and vegetables is also enhanced by wrapping them in moist gunny bags through the cooling effect generated by evaporation.

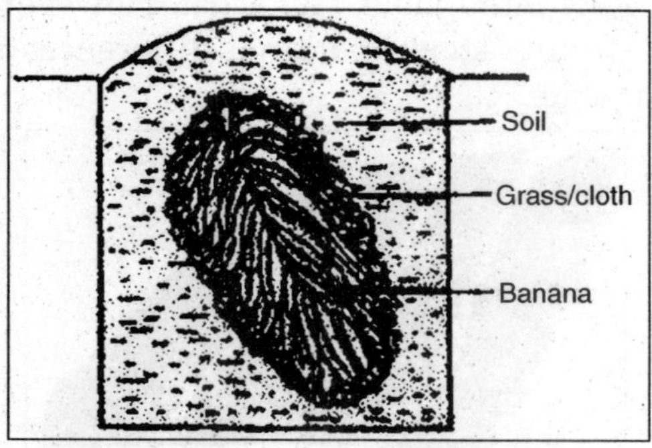


**Fig. 8.13. Patting Banana in Pit for Ripening**

## STORAGE OF GUR/SHAKKAR

In Hamirpur, Una, Bilaspur, parts of Kangra and Paonta Valley of Sirmour districts of the state, it is a common practice to store *gur/shakkar/jaggery* in large earthen pots commonly called *Rushans*. These *Rushans axe* supported by jute cords to ease under their handling. The top cover is made up of wood, though occasionally, earthen covers are also used. Another container for packing *Shakkar*, is made up of large sized leaves of the *Torr* tree.

Each leaf is held in place by using small bamboo sticks. Each container has a capacity to store about 30-40 kg *gur/shakkar*. Such containers are called *Purih or Purah.* Such containers, besides being economical, are also completely biodegradable. The exchange of air/gases, permitted in them, helps in the complete drying and best storage of the product.

**Storage of Pumpkin**

To prevent decay of pumpkin crop and to store it for prolonged periods cow dung is pasted around the stalk of each pumpkin. It is believed that this practice prevents decay and enhances shelf life. However, the true antimicrobial properties of cow dung are yet to be discovered.

## DRYING OF FOOD CROPS

Open sun drying of cereals, pukes, oil seed crops and fruit/vegetables is an age old practice used for storage of food grains for long periods throughout Himachal. However, the actual methods of drying, show marginal differences in different regions of the state.

**Fig. 8.14. Sun Drying of Cereal Crops**

## WHEAT IN CHHOTA BHANGAL

Wheat matures in this area during the rainy season when drying of grain proves to be problematic. The wheat and maize cobs are dried using the indirect heat of the hearth (*Chullah*); *fire.* In these areas, residential houses consist of three storeys. The ground floor is meant for sheltering animals while the floor is the residential portion. Directly above the kitchen, there is a store house where freshly harvested wheat grains are stored. The heat from the *Chullah* below provides the required temperature to dry the wheat grains.

Maize cobs are also dried by keeping them on the rooftop where both kitchen heat and sun facilitate the drying process.

**Fig. 8.15. Sun and Kitchen Heat Drying of Maize Cobs on Root-top**

The development of the kiln dryer for drying hops in Lahaul Valley and other food crops seems to have its origin from these practices.

## DRYING OF CEREAL/PULSES/OIL SEEDS

As mentioned earlier, cereals (wheat, paddy), pulses (gram, *wad, masoor,* etc.) and oil seeds (*sarson,* lentil etc.) are harvested when they are just ripe and then kept in the open sun in tile form of small bundles called *Pooli or Poola* for drying. On complete drying, the grain is separated by beating the small bundles against a stone. Due to complete drying, the seeds/grain are easily separated from the husk. However, in present times, threshers and shellers have replaced this practice for wheat and maize respectively. Since completely dry grain is prone to shattering, harvesting crops at the ripe stage, prevents this loss during handling and harvesting.

## DRYING OF FRUIT AND VEGETABLES

In the tribal areas and in some parts of Shim la, Sirmour, Kullu and Chamba districts of Himachal Pradesh, fruits such as the apricot, wild apricot (*chuli*), apple and local grapes (in Kinnaur) etc. are dried under the open sun by spreading them out on the roof tops. After 10-15 days of continuous drying, the fruit is collected and packed into gunny bags for subsequent use. Except for the uneven slicing of apples with iron sickles (*Drati* or *Drat*) no pretreatment is administered to any crop. Dried apricot is a commercial product of Kinnaur.

Open sun drying of vegetables like tomatoes, cabbage, turnip (stalk and leaves), mustard leaves is also practised in Kinnaur district and other adjoining areas. After making four incisions on the tomatoes (keeping the slices intact), slicing of turnip (stalks and leaves), cabbage and sarson leaves, these are placed in the open sun for drying. After 15-20 days of continuous drying, the dried products are collected and used during the lean season.

## DRYING OF UNRIPE MANGO SLICES

This is a common practice in the lower areas where *in situ* mango varieties are found in abundance. The mature but unripe mangoes are sliced and placed in bamboo baskets (*changer or Chharolu*) which are then kept in the open sun for drying. The dried product called Bukarian is stored in earthen pots and used as an acidulent.

## APRICOT-DRYING ON THE TREES

In the high altitude dry areas *e.g.* Malling, Nako, Pooh, etc. in Kinnaur district, apricots are not harvested fresh but allowed to dry on the tree itself. Due to very low relative humidity, the apricots dry rather well on the tree. The dried product is of excellent quality, not obtained even after adopting modem techniques of drying (*e.g.* checking, sulphuring and mechanical dehydration). The apricots dried on the trees are approximately two to three times more expensive than sun dried apricots.

The prevalence of low temperature and dry weather conditions help first in the accumulation of sugar in the fruits and then in the subsequent drying of the fruit to develop a rich colour and sweetness in the product. This is one example of low temperature drying under natural conditions.

## DRYING OF CUCUMBER AND PUMPKIN SEEDS

The drying of cucumber seeds, using ash is practised in Mandi district of the state. In this method, seeds are mixed with wood ash and then placed on a plate, (*Thali*) in the open sun. The procedure is considered to aid fast drying of seeds since wood ash probably absorbs excess water from the seeds and prevents them from sticking together. The segregation of each seed leads to increase the surface area which results in faster drying.

**Fig. 8.16. Sun Drying of Pumpkin Seed**

## DRYING AND PRESERVATION OF MEAT

In some parts of Shimla, Kinnaur, Lahaul and Spiti and Chamba districts, meat is dried for use during winters, by hanging strips of meat on stings tied across the room. Due to heavy snow, and the low temperature spoilage of the product is prevented. At low temperature and very low humidity, the meat dries very well and is hence preserved better for longer period.

In some places, salt is also sprinkled on the carcass prior to drying, which also assists in preservation.

In Nako and Malling areas of Kinnaur district, the meat is hung in the kitchen. The smoke from the hearth (*Chullah*) serves to smoke the meat, and hence preserves it.

In some parts of Mandi, Kullu and Chamba areas, meat is preserved by smearing it with a mixture of mustard oil and turmeric powder.

Low temperature checks the growth of micro-organisms. Reduction in water activity by drying and use of salt helps in preservation. Smoking is one of the oldest method of food preservation. Both mustard oil and turmeric powder are known to possess antimicrobial properties, and thus help in preserving meat.

**Dried Ginger (Sonth)**

In Shillai and Renuka areas of Sirmour district, ginger is also sun dried. Fresh ginger upon soaking in water is rubbed against a gunny bag or placed in bamboo baskets to remove the peel. The coarsely peeled ginger is then dipped in lime solution followed by warmth for faster and better fermentation.

## DISTILLED COUNTRY LIQUOR

Preparation of alcoholic beverages by distillation is common throughout the tribal belt of Himachal Pradesh. Government excise department too permits this practice, allowing each family to keep up to 24 bottles in this possession at any given time thereby acknowledging the socio-culture fabric of the region.

### FERMENTATION

The liquid is prepared from fruits like local grapes (coloured and seeded), apricot, wild apricot (*chuli*), pear, apple, wild almond (*bemi*), etc. In higher reaches of Kinnaur, however, millet is the main ingredient. Country liquor is a strong alcoholic drink obtained after distillation of fermented musk.

Fruits like apple or pear are cut into coarse pieces, grapes, *chuli* and *apricots* are either hand washed or washed by feet and then placed into large tanks (concrete or wooden). In the agricultural lean period, dried fruits like apple slices, grapes and*chuli* are also used for this purpose. Generally wooden drums are preferred for fermentation as they maintain suitable temperatures.

To obtain higher alcohol output, occasionally molasses are also added to the fermenting musk. Drums are then tightly sealed with wooden or heavy stone lids (Weather permitting, the fermentation continues for 15-20 days). The completion of fermentation is judged using different parameters like alcoholic or acetuous odour, small vapours appearing on the inside of the lid or non-sticky nature of the pulp, when pressed between the forefinger and the thumb. All these characteristics are indicative of complete fermentation. In some places the fermenting vat or bottle is placed in a cow dung pit (*Mahlash*). Generation of heat during decomposition of cow dung in the pit provides required warmth for faster and better fermentation.

### *Distillation*

The fermented musk is then distilled to obtain the liquor by different methods. The fermented liquid is boiled in a vessel called as *Baltoi.* At the base of which a temporary stand is made under place a Container to collect distilled liquor. Upon heating, the fermented liquid boils, and its vapours are cooled by striking the top of the container (holding cold water), the condensed vapours drop into the container, meant for collecting the liquor. Cold water is repeatedly replaced until the process is completed.

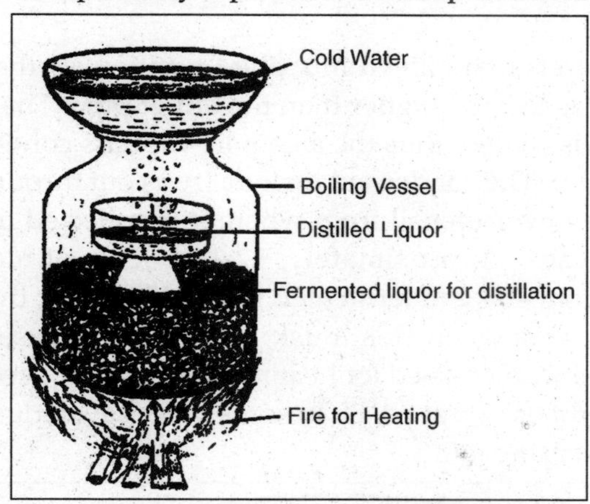


**Fig. 8.17. Distillation of Fermented Musk for Preparing Country Liquor ('Ghanti')**

In this manner, recovery is comparatively low since some vapours also fall back into the boiling liquid. Moreover, there is no provision for complete separation of its methyl alcohol content.

*In some places, this method has been further improved as under*:

Herein, an empty *ghee* tin (canister 15 kg capacity) is made slightly rounded, and at its base, is placed a temporary stand on which a pot is placed for collecting the condensed vapours. The pot is attached to a rubber pipe to receive the liquor in bottles/ plastic cans. This has a higher efficiency and it also allows the separation of the initial drops of the liquor which contain high levels of methanol.

As a further improvement in the distillation process, the fermented musk is placed in a metallic pitcher which is covered with a (stone) slate with a hole at its centre for the passing out vapours. The slate is used ostensibly to avoid the overflow of the material as it boils. Another metallic pan with a hole is kept on the slate and is attached to a side pipe where condensed alcoholic vapours are collected. To cool the vapours, this container is housed in a bigger metal pan which is cooled by continuously running tap water. Two rubber pipes *viz.* inlet and outlet aid the circulation of cold water and the release of warm water.

The pan is maintained in a tilted position, so that the inlet of the pipe is located higher than the outlet pipe. The bottom of the utensil is cooled, thus the alcoholic vapours condense on its lower surface. The condensed material runs out through the side pipe of the lower utensil from where it is collected into bottles or plastic cans. Approximately, 12-14 bottles of alcohols are collected from 40 kg of fermented musk. However, by using 5-6 kg of molasses/*gur* in this musk, the yield increases to 18-19 bottles. Fuel wood is used for heating. All joints are secured using barley, *phafra* or wheat paste. In some places even dung paste is used for securing joints.

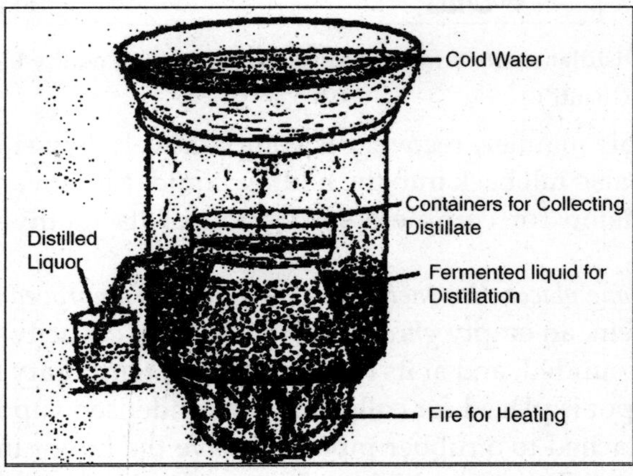


**Fig. 8.18. Ghanti' Liquor Distillation System Provide with Rubber Pipe**

The simplest method involves a rubber pipe being inserted through a hole in the slate lid, to collect the vapours. The vapours are cooled by maintaining a continuous flow of cold water from the tap. The condensed alcoholic vapours are received in the bottle.

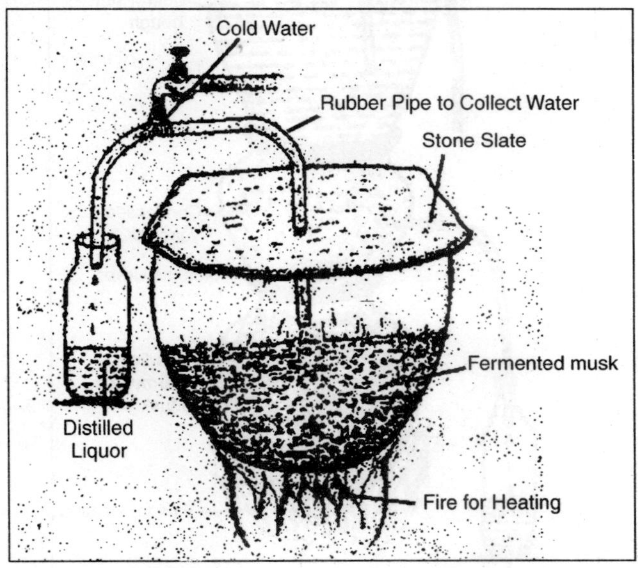


**Fig. 8.19. Traditional Method of Country Liquor Distillation**

## *Improved Method of Distilling Country Liquor*

In some areas of Himachal the above stated methods have been further improved by replacing the water trough by rubber pipe, to collect vapours from the boiling fermented liquor. In this method an empty *ghee* tin, *i.e.,* 15 kg capacity canister, is used for boiling the fermented liquid by heating it on fire. On the top opening of the canister, a rubber pipe is inserted to receive the alcoholic vapours, the pipe is paired through a water trough to condense the vapours. The alcoholic product is then collected in glass bottles or plastic cans.

In order to increase the alcohol yield Gur is sometimes added. In the agricultural lean period, dried grapes, apple and *chuli*etc. are used for preparing the fermented musk.

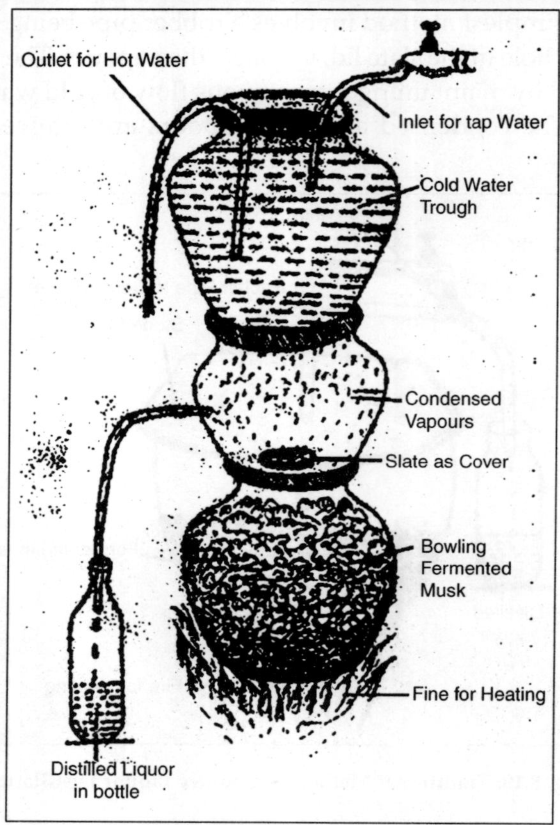


**Fig. 8.20. Traditional Continuous Distillation Method of Country Liquor**

The product prepared from grapes is called *Angoori.* Chhang is prepared using Millets and Ghanti is prepared from any other source. During initial distillation, first 1-2 bottles of liquor are called Moon and contain the maximum amount of alcohol while last distillate contains comparatively lower amounts of alcohol and is called *Rashi.* Costwise, Angoori is the costliest, followed by Moori and least expensive is *Rashi* often only ₹.10-20 per bottle (700 ml).

Due to extreme winters, the consumption of country liquor (*ghanti*) is extensive in the entire cold dessert regions for medicinal purposes. Besides social use the product is also used during rituals and religious occasions.

## TRADITIONAL APPLE PLUCKING

It is done by climbing an apple tree with putting by a small basket made, which is put around the neck of gunny bag cloth. This prevents the damage of fruits. Plucked apples, from the gunny bags are transferred to a bigger basket (Kilta) which is also provided with a rough cloth cushion. In this way, apples are carried to the store room for grading.

**Fig. 8.21. Traditional Apple Plucking**

## STEAM COOKING

A big special vessel made of brass is used for preparing steam cooked cake of maize or barley. This vessel is called Chalta in which at the bottom of the vessel water and rice straw is placed. Above this round cover, made from maize or barley flour is placed and cooked in steam.

**Fig. 8.22. Vessel for Steam Cooking of Cakes (Chalta)**

# 9

# Crop Evapotranspiration Under Standard Conditions

## INTRODUCTION

The evapotranspiration rate from a cropped surface can be directly measured by the mass transfer or the energy balance method. It can also be derived from studies of the soil water balance determined from cropped fields or from lysimeters.

Crop evapotranspiration can also be derived from meteorological and crop data by means of the Penman-Monteith equation. By adjusting the albedo and the aerodynamic and canopy surface resistances to the growing characteristics of the specific crop, the evapotranspiration rate can be directly estimated.

The albedo and resistances are, however, difficult to estimate accurately as they may vary continually during the growing season as climatic conditions change, as the crop develops, and with wetness of the soil surface. The canopy resistance will further be influenced by the soil water availability, and it increases strongly if the crop is subjected to water stress.

As there is still a considerable lack of consolidated information on the aerodynamic and canopy resistances for the various cropped surfaces, the FAO Penman-Monteith method is used in this handbook only for estimating $ET_o$, the evapotranspiration from a well-watered hypothetical grass surface having fixed crop height, albedo and surface resistance.

## CROP COEFFICIENT APPROACH

In the crop coefficient approach the crop evapotranspiration, $ET_c$, is calculated by multiplying the reference crop evapotranspiration, $ET_o$, by a crop coefficient, $K_c$:

$$ET_c = K_c \, ET_o$$

where,

$ET_c$ crop evapotranspiration [mm $d^{-1}$],

$K_c$ crop coefficient [dimensionless],

$ET_o$ reference crop evapotranspiration [mm $d^{-1}$].

Most of the effects of the various weather conditions are incorporated into the $ET_o$ estimate. Therefore, as $ET_o$ represents an index of climatic demand, $K_c$ varies predominately with the specific crop characteristics and only to a limited extent with climate. This enables the transfer of standard values for $K_c$ between locations and between climates. This has been a primary reason for the global acceptance and usefulness of the crop coefficient approach and the $K_c$ factors developed in past studies.

The reference $ET_o$ is defined and calculated using the FAO Penman-Monteith equation. The crop coefficient, $K_c$, is basically the ratio of the crop $ET_c$ to the reference $ET_o$, and it represents an integration of the effects of four primary characteristics that distinguish the crop from reference grass.

These characteristics are:

- *Crop height*: The crop height influences the aerodynamic resistance term, $r_a$, of the FAO Penman-Monteith equation and the turbulent transfer of vapour from the crop into the atmosphere. The $r_a$ tenu appears twice in me full form of the FAO Penman-Monteith equation.
- *Albedo (reflectance) of the crop-soil surface*: The albedo is affected by the fraction of ground covered by vegetation and by the soil surface wetness. The albedo of the crop-soil surface influences the net radiation of the surface, $R_n$, which is the primary source of the energy exchange for the evaporation process.
- *Canopy resistance*: The resistance of me crop to vapour transfer is affected by leaf area (number of stomata),

leaf age and condition, and the degree of stomatal control. The canopy resistance influences the surface resistance, $r_s$.

- Evaporation from soil, especially exposed soil.

The soil surface wetness and the fraction of ground covered by vegetation influence the surface resistance, $r_s$. Following soil wetting, the vapour transfer rate from the soil is high, especially for crops having incomplete ground cover. The combined surface resistance of the canopy and of the soil determines the (bulk) surface resistance, $r_s$.

The surface resistance term in the Penman-Monteith equation represents the resistance to vapour flow from within plant leaves and from beneath the soil surface.

The $K_c$ in Equation predicts $ET_c$ under standard conditions. This represents the upper envelope of crop evapotranspiration and represents conditions where no limitations are placed on crop growth or evapotranspiration due to water shortage, crop density, or disease, weed, insect or salinity pressures. The $ET_c$ predicted by $K_c$ is adjusted if necessary to non-standard conditions, $ET_{c\ adj}$, where any environmental condition or characteristic is known to have an impact on or to limit $ET_c$. Factors for correcting $ET_c$ to $ET_{c\ adj}$ are described in Part C.

## FACTORS DETERMINING THE CROP COEFFICIENT

The crop coefficient integrates the effect of characteristics that distinguish a typical field crop from the grass reference, which has a constant appearance and a complete ground cover. Consequently, different crops will have different $K_c$ coefficients. The changing characteristics of the crop over the growing season also affect the $K_c$ coefficient.

Finally, as evaporation is an integrated part of crop evapotranspiration, conditions affecting soil evaporation will also have an effect on $K_c$.

### Crop Type

Due to differences in albedo, crop height, aerodynamic properties, and leaf and stomata properties, the evapotranspiration from full grown, well-watered crops differs from $ET_o$.

The close spacings of plants and taller canopy height and roughness of many full grown agricultural crops cause these crops to have $K_c$ factors that are larger than 1. The $K_c$ factor is often 5-10 per cent higher than the reference (where $K_c$ = 1.0), and even 15-20 per cent greater for some tall crops such as maize, sorghum or sugar cane (Figure). Typical values for the crop coefficient for full grown crops ($K_{c\ mid}$) are listed in Table.

Crops such as pineapples, that close their stomata during the day, have very small crop coefficients. In most species, however, the stomata open as irradiance increases. In addition to the stomatal response to environment, the position and number of the stomata and the resistance of the cuticula to vapour transfer determine the water loss from the crop. Species with stomata on only the lower side of the leaf and/or large leaf resistances will have relatively smaller $K_c$ values. This is the case for citrus and most deciduous fruit trees. Transpiration control and spacing of the trees, providing only 70 per cent ground cover for mature trees, may cause the $K_c$ of those trees, if cultivated without a ground cover crop, to be smaller than one (Figure 9.1).

**Climate**

The $K_c$ values of Table are typical values expected for average $K_c$ under a standard climatic condition, which is defined as a sub-humid climate with average daytime minimum relative humidity ($RH_{min}$) » 45 per cent and having calm to moderate wind speeds averaging 2 m/s.

Variations in wind alter the aerodynamic resistance of the crops and hence, their crop coefficients, especially for those crops that are substantially taller than the hypothetical grass reference. The effect of the difference in aerodynamic properties between the grass reference surface and agricultural crops is not only crop specific.

It also varies with the climatic conditions and crop height. Because aerodynamic properties are greater for many agricultural crops as compared to the grass reference, the ratio of $ET_c$ to $ET_o$ (*i.e.*, $K_c$) for many crops increases as wind speed increases and as relative humidity decreases. More arid climates and conditions of greater wind speed will have higher values for $K_c$. More humid climates and conditions of lower wind speed will have lower values for $K_c$.

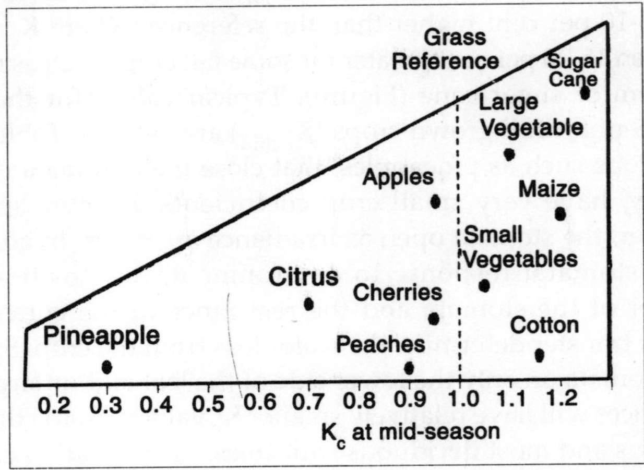


**Fig. 9.1. Typical $K_c$ for Different Types of Full Grown Crops**

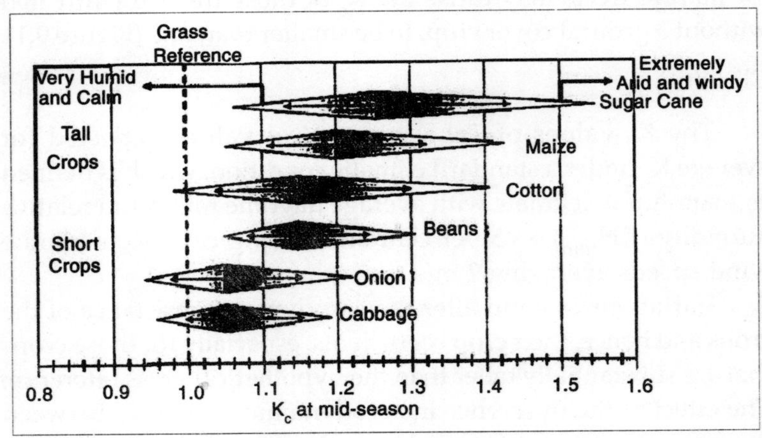


**Fig. 9.2. Extreme Ranges Expected in $K_c$ for Full Grown Cropsas Climate and Weather Change**

The relative impact of the climate on $K_c$ for full grown crops is illustrated in Figure 9.2. The upper bounds represent extremely arid and windy conditions, while the lower bounds are valid under very humid and calm weather conditions. The ranges expected in $K_c$ as climate and weather conditions change are quite small for short crops but are large for tall crops. Guidelines for the adjustment of $K_c$ to the climatic conditions as a function of crop height are given in Chapter.

Under humid and calm wind conditions, $K_c$ becomes less dependent on the differences between the aerodynamic components of $ET_c$ and $ET_o$ and the $K_c$ values for 'full-cover' agricultural crops do not exceed 1.0 by more than about 0.05. This is because full-cover agricultural crops and the reference crop of clipped grass both provide for nearly maximum absorption of shortwave radiation, which is the primary energy source for evaporation under humid and calm conditions.

Generally, the albedos, a, are similar over a wide range of full-cover agricultural crops, including the reference crop. Because the vapour pressure deficit ($e_s$ - $e_a$) is small under humid conditions, differences in ET caused by differences in aerodynamic resistance, $r_a$, between the agricultural crop and the reference crop are also small, especially with low to moderate wind speed.

Under arid conditions, the effect of differences in $r_a$ between the agricultural crop and the grass reference crop on $ET_c$ become more pronounced because the ($e_s$ - $e_a$) term may be relatively large.

The larger magnitudes of ($e_s$ - $e_a$) amplify differences in the aerodynamic term in the numerator of the Penman-Monteith equation (Equation) for both the crop and the reference crop. Hence, $K_c$ will be larger under arid conditions when the agricultural crop has a leaf area and roughness height that are greater than that of the grass reference.

Because the $1/r_a$ term in the numerator of the Penman-Monteith equation (Equation) is multiplied by the vapour pressure deficit ($e_s$ - $e_a$), the ET from tall crops increases proportionately more relative to $ET_o$ than does ET from short crops when relative humidity is low.

The $K_c$ for tall crops, such as those 2-3 m in height, can be as much as 30 per cent higher in a windy, arid climate as compared with a calm, humid climate. The increase in $K_c$ is due to the influence of the larger aerodynamic roughness of the tall crop relative to grass on the transport of water vapour from the surface.

## Soil Evaporation

Differences in soil evaporation and crop transpiration between field crops and the reference surface are integrated within the crop coefficient. The $K_c$ coefficient for full-cover crops primarily reflects differences in transpiration as the contribution of soil evaporation is relatively small.

After rainfall or irrigation, the effect of evaporation is predominant when the crop is small and scarcely shades the ground. For such low-cover conditions, the $K_c$ coefficient is determined largely by the frequency with which the soil surface is wetted.

Where the soil is wet for most of the time from irrigation or rain, the evaporation from the soil surface will be considerable and $K_c$ may exceed 1. On the other hand, where the soil surface is dry, evaporation is restricted and $K_c$ will be small and might even drop to as low as 0.1 (Figure 9.3).

Differences in soil evaporation between the field crop and the reference surface can be forecast more precisely by using a dual crop coefficient.

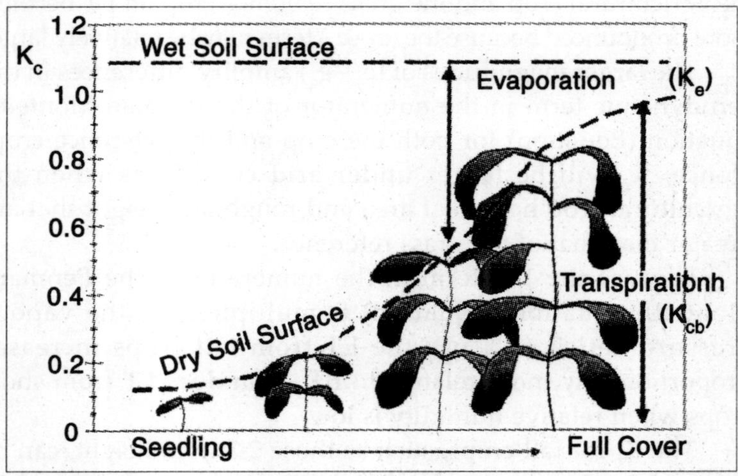


**Fig. 9.3. The Effect of Evaporation on $K_c$. The Horizontal line Represents $K_c$ when the Soil Surface is kept continuously wet. The Curved line corresponds to $K_c$ when the Soil Surface is kept dry but the Crop Receives Sufficient water to Sustain full Transpiration**

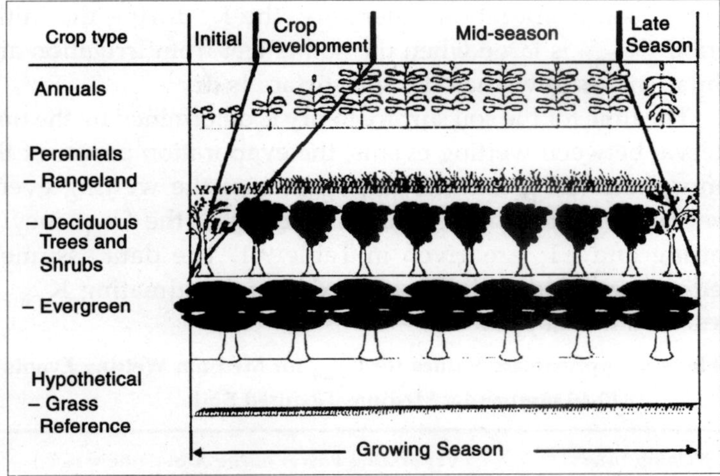


**Fig. 9.4. Crop Growth Stages for Different Types of Crops**

## CROP GROWTH STAGES

As the crop develops, the ground cover, crop height and the leaf area change. Due to differences in evapotranspiration during the various growth stages, the $K_c$ for a given crop will vary over the growing period. The growing period can be divided into four distinct growth stages: initial, crop development, mid-season and late season. Figure 9.4 illustrates the general sequence and proportion of these stages for different types of crops.

### *Initial Stage*

The initial stage runs from planting date to approximately 10 per cent ground cover. The length of the initial period is highly dependent on the crop, the crop variety, the planting date and the climate. The end of the initial period is determined as the time when approximately 10 per cent of the ground surface is covered by green vegetation. For perennial crops, the planting date is replaced by the 'greenup' date, *i.e.*, the time when the initiation of new leaves occurs. During the initial period, the leaf area is small, and evapotranspiration is predominately in the form of soil evaporation. Therefore, the $K_c$ during the initial period ($K_{c\ ini}$) is large when the soil is wet from irrigation and rainfall and is low when the soil surface is dry.

The time for the soil surface to dry is determined by the time interval between wetting events, the evaporation power of the atmosphere ($ET_o$) and the importance of the wetting event. General estimates for $K_{c\ ini}$ as a function of the frequency of wetting and $ET_o$ are given in Table 9.1. The data assume a medium textured soil. The procedure for estimating $K_{c\ ini}$ is presented in Chapter.

**Table. 9.1. Approximate Values for $K_{c\ ini}$ for Medium Wetting Events (10-40 mm) and a Medium Textured Soil**

| Wetting Interval | Evaporating Power of the Atmosphere ($ET_o$) | | | |
|---|---|---|---|---|
| | Low 1-3 mm/day | Moderate 3-5 mm/day | High 5-7 mm/day | Very High > 7 mm/day |
| less than Weekly | 1. 2- 0.8 | 1.1 - 0.6 | 1.0 - 0.4 | 0.9 - 0.3 |
| Weekly | 0.8 | 0.6 | 0.4 | 0.3 |
| Longer than once Per week | 0.7 - 0.4 | 0.4 - 0.2* | 0.3 - 0.2* | 0.2*- 0.1* |

Values derived from Figures.

*Note*: (*) Note that irrigation intervals may be too large to sustain full transpiration for some young annual crops.

### *Crop Development Stage*

The crop development stage runs from 10 per cent ground cover to effective full cover. Effective full cover for many crops occurs at the initiation of flowering. For row crops where rows commonly interlock leaves such as beans, sugar beets, potatoes and corn, effective cover can be defined as the time when some leaves of plants in adjacent rows begin to intermingle so that soil shading becomes nearly complete, or when plants reach nearly full size if no intermingling occurs. For some crops, especially those taller than 0.5 m, the average fraction of the ground surface covered by vegetation ($f_c$) at the start of effective full cover is about 0.7-0.8. Fractions of sunlit and shaded soil and leaves do not change significantly with further growth of the crop beyond $f_c$ » 0.7 to 0.8. It is understood that the crop or plant can continue to grow in both height and leaf area after the time of effective full cover. Because it is difficult to visually determine when densely sown vegetation such as winter and spring cereals and some grasses reach effective full cover, the more easily detectable stage of heading (flowering) is generally used for these types of crops.

For dense grasses, effective full cover may occur at about 0.10-0.15 m height. For thin stands of grass (dry rangeland), grass height may approach 0.3-0.5 m before effective full cover is reached. Densely planted forages such as alfalfa and clover reach effective full cover at about 0.3-0.4 m.

Another way to estimate the occurrence of effective full cover is when the leaf area index (LAI) reaches three. LAI is defined as the average total area of leaves (one side) per unit area of ground surface.

As the crop develops and shades more and more of the ground, evaporation becomes more restricted and transpiration gradually becomes the major process. During the crop development stage, the $K_c$ value corresponds to amounts of ground cover and plant development. Typically, if the soil surface is dry, $K_c = 0.5$ corresponds to about 25-40 per cent of the ground surface covered by vegetation due to the effects of shading and due to microscale transport of sensible heat from the soil into the vegetation. A $K_c = 0.7$ often corresponds to about 40-60 per cent ground cover. These values will vary, depending on the crop, frequency of wetting and whether the crop uses more water than the reference crop at full ground cover (e.g., depending on its canopy architecture and crop height relative to clipped grass).

## MID-SEASON STAGE

The mid-season stage runs from effective full cover to the start of maturity. The start of maturity is often indicated by the beginning of the ageing, yellowing or senescence of leaves, leaf drop, or the browning of fruit to the degree that the crop evapotranspiration is reduced relative to the reference $ET_o$. The mid-season stage is the longest stage for perennials and for many annuals, but it may be relatively short for vegetable crops that are harvested fresh for their green vegetation.

At the mid-season stage the $K_c$ reaches its maximum value. The value for $K_c$ ($K_{c\,mid}$) is relatively constant for most growing and cultural conditions. Deviation of the $K_{c\,mid}$ from the reference value '1' is primarily due to differences in crop height and resistance between the grass reference surface and the agricultural crop and weather conditions.

## LATE SEASON STAGE

The late season stage runs from the start of maturity to harvest or full senescence. The calculation for $K_c$ and $ET_c$ is presumed to end when the crop is harvested, dries out naturally, reaches full senescence, or experiences leaf drop. For some perennial vegetation in frost free climates, crops may grow year round so that the date of termination may be taken as the same as the date of 'planting'.

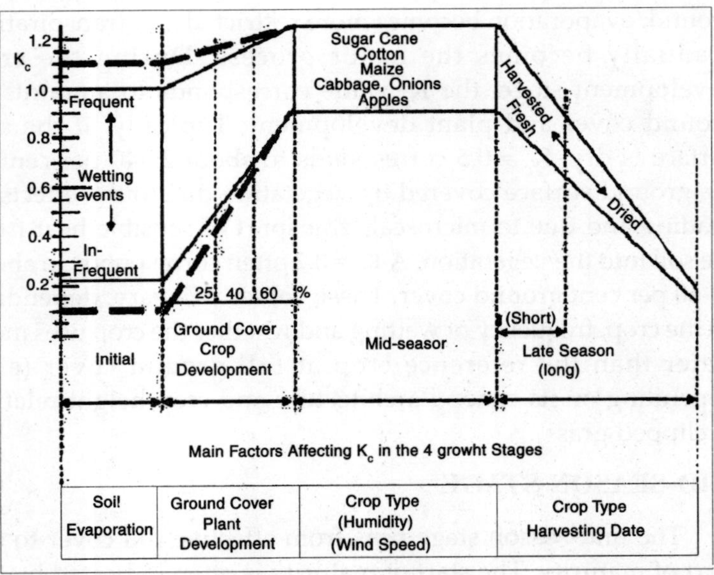


**Fig. 9.5. Typical Ranges Expected in $K_c$ for the Four Growth Stages**

The $K_c$ value at the end of the late season stage ($K_{c\ end}$) reflects crop and water management practices. The $K_{c\ end}$ value is high if the crop is frequently irrigated until harvested fresh. If the crop is allowed to senesce and to dry out in the field before harvest, the $K_{c\ end}$ value will be small. Senescence is usually associated with less efficient stomatal conductance of leaf surfaces due to the effects of ageing, thereby causing a reduction in $K_c$. Figure 9.5 illustrates the variation in $K_c$ for different crops as influenced by weather factors and crop development.

## CROP EVAPOTRANSPIRATION ($ET_c$)

Crop evapotranspiration is calculated by multiplying $ET_o$ by $K_c$, a coefficient expressing the difference in evapotranspiration between the cropped and reference grass surface. The difference can be combined into one single coefficient, or it can be split into two factors describing separately the differences in evaporation and transpiration between both surfaces.

**Table. 9.2. General Selection Criteria for the Single and Dual Cfficient Approaches**

| | Single Crop Coefficient $K_c$ | Dual Crop Coefficient $K_{cb} + K_e$ |
|---|---|---|
| **Purpose of Calculation** | Irrigation planning and design<br>Irrigation management<br>Basic irrigation schedules<br>Real time irrigation scheduling for non-frequent water applications (surface and sprinkler irrigation) | Research<br>Real time irrigation scheduling<br>Irrigation scheduling for high frequency Water application (microirrigation and automated sprinkler irrigation)<br>Supplemental irrigation<br>Detailed soil and hydrologic water balance studies |
| **Time Step** | Daily, 10-day, Monthly (data and Calculation) | Daily (Data and Calculation) |
| **Solution Method** | Graphical Pocket Calculator<br>Computer | Computer |

The selection of the approach depends on the purpose of the calculation, the accuracy required, the climatic data available and the time step with which the calculations are executed. Table 9.2 presents the general selection criteria.

## SINGLE AND DUAL CROP COEFFICIENT APPROACHES

## SINGLE CROP COEFFICIENT APPROACH ($K_C$)

In the single crop coefficient approach, the effect of crop transpiration and soil evaporation are combined into a single $K_c$coefficient. The coefficient integrates differences in the soil evaporation and crop transpiration rate between the crop and the grass reference surface. As soil evaporation may fluctuate daily as a result of rainfall or irrigation, the single crop coefficient expresses only the time-averaged (multi-day) effects of crop evapotranspiration.

As the single $K_c$ coefficient averages soil evaporation and transpiration, the approach is used to compute $ET_c$ for weekly or longer time periods, although calculations may proceed on a daily time step.

The time-averaged single $K_c$ is used for planning studies and irrigation system design where the averaged effects of soil wetting are acceptable and relevant. This is the case for surface irrigation and set sprinkler systems where the time interval between successive irrigation is of several days, often ten days or more. For typical irrigation management, the time-averaged single $K_c$ is valid.

## DUAL CROP COEFFICIENT APPROACH ($K_{CB}$ + $K_E$)

In the dual crop coefficient approach, the effects of crop transpiration and soil evaporation are determined separately. Two coefficients are used: the basal crop coefficient ($K_{cb}$) to describe plant transpiration, and the soil water evaporation coefficient ($K_e$) to describe evaporation from the soil surface. The single $K_c$ coefficient is replaced by:

$K_c = K_{cb} + K_e$ (57)

where,

$K_{cb}$ basal crop coefficient,

$K_e$ soil water evaporation coefficient.

The basal crop coefficient, $K_{cb}$, is defined as the ratio of $ET_c$ to $ET_o$ when the soil surface layer is dry but where the average soil water content of the root zone is adequate to sustain full plant transpiration. The $K_{cb}$ represents the baseline potential $K_c$ in the absence of the additional effects of soil wetting by irrigation or precipitation. The soil evaporation coefficient, $K_e$, describes the evaporation component from the soil surface. If the soil is wet following rain or irrigation, $K_e$ may be large. However, the sum of $K_{cb}$ and $K_e$ can never exceed a maximum value, $K_{c\ max}$, determined by the energy available for evapotranspiration at the soil surface. As the soil surface becomes drier, $K_e$ becomes smaller and falls to zero when no water is left for evaporation. The estimation of $K_e$ requires a daily water balance computation for the calculation of the soil water content remaining in the upper topsoil.

The dual coefficient approach requires more numerical calculations than the procedure using the single time-averaged $K_c$ coefficient. The dual procedure is best for real time irrigation scheduling, for soil water balance computations, and for research studies where effects of day-to-day variations in soil surface wetness and the resulting impacts on daily $ET_c$, the soil water profile, and deep percolation fluxes are important. This is the case for high frequency irrigation with microirrigation systems or lateral move systems such as centre pivots and linear move systems.

## CROP COEFFICIENT CURVE

After the selection of the calculation approach, the determination of the lengths for the crop growth stages and the corresponding crop coefficients, a crop coefficient curve can be constructed. The curve represents the changes in the crop coefficient over the length of the growing season. The shape of the curve represents the changes in the vegetation and ground cover during plant development and maturation that affect the ratio of $ET_c$ to $ET_o$. From the curve, the $K_c$ factor and hence $ET_c$ can be derived for any period within the growing season.

## Single Crop Coefficient

The generalised crop coefficient curve is shown in Figure 25. Shortly after the planting of annuals or shortly after the initiation of new leaves for perennials, the value for $K_c$ is small, often less than 0.4. The $K_c$ begins to increase from the initial $K_c$ value, $K_{c\ ini}$, at the beginning of rapid plant development and reaches a maximum value, $K_{c\ mid}$, at the time of maximum or near maximum plant development. During the late season period, as leaves begin to age and senesce due to natural or cultural practices, the $K_c$ begins to decrease until it reaches a lower value at the end of the growing period equal to $K_{c\ end}$.

## Dual Crop Coefficient

The single 'time-averaged' $K_c$ curve in Figure 25 incorporates averaged wetting effects into the $K_c$ factor. The value for $K_{c\ mid}$ is relatively constant for most growing and cultural conditions. However, the values for $K_{c\ ini}$ and $K_{c\ end}$ can vary considerably on a daily basis, depending on the frequency of wetting by irrigation and rainfall. The dual crop coefficient approach calculates the actual increases in $K_c$ for each day as a function of plant development and the wetness of the soil surface.

As the single $K_c$ coefficient includes averaged effects of evaporation from the soil, the basal crop coefficient, $K_{cb}$ describing only plant transpiration, lies below the $K_c$ value (Figure). The largest difference between $K_c$ and $K_{cb}$ is found in the initial growth stage where evapotranspiration is predominantly in the form of soil evaporation and crop transpiration is still small.

Because crop canopies are near or at full ground cover during the mid-season stage, soil evaporation beneath the canopy has less effect on crop evapotranspiration and the value for $K_{cb}$ in the mid-season stage will be nearly the same as $K_c$. Depending on the ground cover, the basal crop coefficient during the mid-season may be only 0.05-0.10 lower than the $K_c$ value. Depending on the frequency with which the crop is irrigated during the late season stage, $K_{cb}$ will be similar to (if infrequently irrigated) or less than the $K_c$ value.

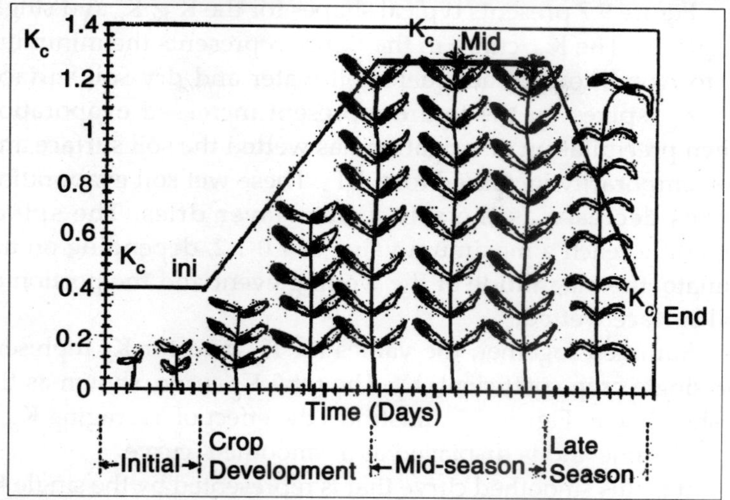


**Fig. 9.6. Generalised Crop Coefficient Curve for the Single Crop Coefficient Approach**

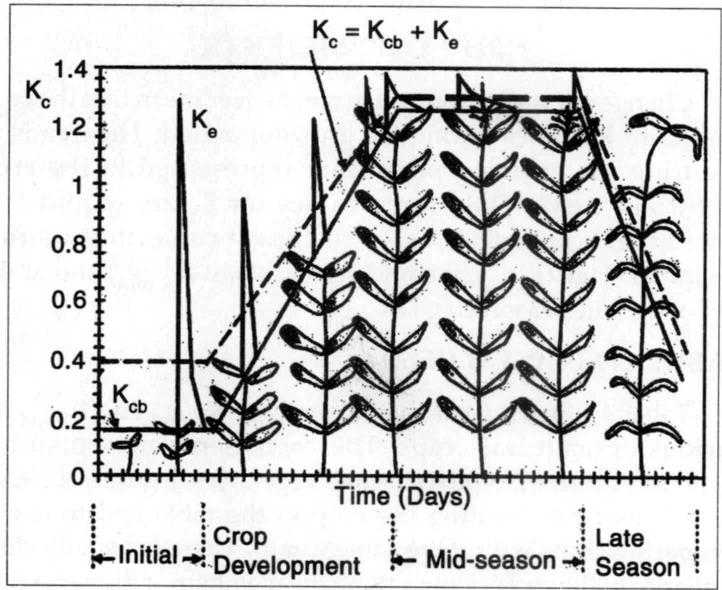


**Fig. 9.7. Crop Coefficient Curves showing the Basal $K_{cb}$ (Thick Line), Soil Evaporation $K_e$ (Thin Line) and the Corresponding Single $K_c = K_{cb} + K_e$ Curve (Dashed Line)**

Figure 9.7 presents typical shapes for the $K_{cb}$, $K_e$ and single $K_c$ curves. The $K_{cb}$ curve in the figure represents the minimum $K_c$ for conditions of adequate soil water and dry soil surface. The $K_e$ 'spikes' in the figure represent increased evaporation when precipitation or irrigation has wetted the soil surface and has temporarily increased total $ET_c$. These wet soil evaporation spikes decrease as the soil surface layer dries. The spikes generally reach a maximum value of 1.0-1.2, depending on the climate, the magnitude of the wetting event and the portion of soil surface wetted.

Summed together, the values for $K_{cb}$ and for $K_e$ represent the single crop coefficient, $K_c$. The total $K_c$ curve, shown as the dashed line in Figure 9.7, illustrates the effect of averaging $K_{cb}$ + $K_e$ over time and is displayed as a 'smoothed' curve.

It is this smoothed curve that is represented by the single $K_c$ calculation procedure. The $K_c$ curve lies above the $K_{cb}$ curve, with potentially large differences during the initial and development stages, depending on the frequency of soil wetting.

## CROP COEFFICIENTS

Changes in vegetation and ground cover mean that the crop coefficient $K_c$ varies during the growing period. The trends in $K_c$ during the growing period are represented in the crop coefficient curve. Only three values for $K_c$ are required to describe and construct the crop coefficient curve: those during the initial stage ($K_{c\ ini}$), the mid-season stage ($K_{c\ mid}$) and at the end of the late season stage ($K_{c\ end}$).

### TABULATED $K_C$ VALUES

Table 9.3 lists typical values for $K_{c\ ini}$, $Kc_{\ mid}$ and $K_{c\ end}$ for various agricultural crops. The coefficients presented are organised by group type (i.e., small vegetables, legumes, cereals, etc.,) to assist in locating the crop in the table and to aid in comparing crops within the same group. There is usually close similarity in the coefficients among the members of the same crop group, as the plant height, leaf area, ground coverage and water management are normally similar.

The coefficients in Table integrate the effects of both transpiration and evaporation over time. The effects of the integration over time represent an average wetting frequency for a 'standard' crop under typical growing conditions in an irrigated setting.

The values for $K_c$ during the initial and crop development stages are subject to the effects of large variations in wetting frequencies and therefore refinements to the value used for $K_{c\ ini}$ should always be made. For frequent wettings such as with high frequency sprinkler irrigation or rainfall, the values for $K_{c\ ini}$ may increase substantially.

**Table. 9.3. Single (Time-averaged) Crop Coefficients, $K_c$, and Mean Maximum Plant Heights for Non Stressed, Well-managed Crops in Subhumid Climates ($RH_{min}$ ≈ 45 Per cent, $u_2$ ≈ 2 m/s) for Use with the FAO Penman-Monteith $ET_o$**

| Crop | $K_{c\,ini}$[1] | $K_{c\,mid}$ | $K_{c\,end}$ | Maximum Crop Height (h) (m) |
|---|---|---|---|---|
| **a. Small Vegetables** | **0.7** | **1.05** | **0.95** | |
| Broccoli | | 1.05 | 0.95 | 0.3 |
| Brussel Sprouts | | 1.05 | 0.95 | 0.4 |
| Cabbage | | 1.05 | 0.95 | 0.4 |
| Carrots | | 1.05 | 0.95 | 0.3 |
| Cauliflower | | 1.05 | 0.95 | 0.4 |
| Celery | | 1.05 | 1.00 | 0.6 |
| Garlic | | 1.00 | 0.70 | 0.3 |
| Lettuce | | 1.00 | 0.95 | 0.3 |
| Onions | | | | |
| - dry | | 1.05 | 0.75 | 0.4 |
| - green | | 1.00 | 1.00 | 0.3 |
| - seed | | 1.05 | 0.80 | 0.5 |
| Spinach | | 1.00 | 0.95 | 0.3 |
| Radish | | 0.90 | 0.85 | 0.3 |
| **b. Vegetables - Solanum Family *(Solanaceae)*** | **0.6** | **1.15** | **0.80** | |
| Egg Plant | | 1.05 | 0.90 | 0.8 |
| Sweet Peppers (bell) | | 1.05[2] | 0.90 | 0.7 |

| | | | | |
|---|---|---|---|---|
| Tomato | | 1.15[2] | 0.70-0.90 | 0.6 |
| **c. Vegetables - Cucumber Family *(Cucurbitaceae)*** | **0.5** | **1.00** | **0.80** | |
| Cantaloupe | 0.5 | 0.85 | 0.60 | 0.3 |
| Cucumber | | | | |
| - Fresh Market | 0.6 | 1.00[2] | 0.75 | 0.3 |
| - Machine harvest | 0.5 | 1.00 | 0.90 | 0.3 |
| Pumpkin, Winter Squash | | 1.00 | 0.80 | 0.4 |
| Squash, Zucchini | | 0.95 | 0.75 | 0.3 |
| Sweet Melons | | 1.05 | 0.75 | 0.4 |
| Watermelon | 0.4 | 1.00 | 0.75 | 0.4 |
| **d. Roots and Tubers** | **0.5** | **1.10** | **0.95** | |
| Beets, table | | 1.05 | 0.95 | 0.4 |
| Cassava | | | | |
| - year 1 | 0.3 | 0.80[3] | 0.30 | 1.0 |
| - year 2 | 0.3 | 1.10 | 0.50 | 1.5 |
| Parsnip | 0.5 | 1.05 | 0.95 | 0.4 |
| Potato | | 1.15 | 0.75[4] | 0.6 |
| Sweet Potato | | 1.15 | 0.65 | 0.4 |
| Turnip (and Rutabaga) | | 1.10 | 0.95 | 0.6 |
| Sugar Beet | 0.35 | 1.20 | 0.70[5] | 0.5 |
| **e. Legumes *(Leguminosae)*** | **0.4** | **1.15** | **0.55** | |
| Beans, green | 0.5 | 1.05[2] | 0.90 | 0.4 |
| Beans, dry and Pulses | 0.4 | 1.15[2] | 0.35 | 0.4 |
| Chick pea | | 1.00 | 0.35 | 0.4 |
| Fababean (broad bean) | | | | |
| - Fresh | 0.5 | 1.15[2] | 1.10 | 0.8 |
| - Dry/Seed | 0.5 | 1.15[2] | 0.30 | 0.8 |
| Grabanzo | 0.4 | 1.15 | 0.35 | 0.8 |
| Green Gram and Cowpeas | | 1.05 | 0.60-0.35[6] | 0.4 |
| Groundnut (Peanut) | | 1.15 | 0.60 | 0.4 |
| Lentil | | 1.10 | 0.30 | 0.5 |
| Peas | | | | |
| - Fresh | 0.5 | 1.15[2] | 1.10 | 0.5 |
| - Dry/Seed | | 1.15 | 0.30 | 0.5 |
| Soybeans | | 1.15 | 0.50 | 0.5-1.0 |

| | | | | |
|---|---|---|---|---|
| **f. Perennial Vegetables (with winter dormancy and initially bare or mulched soil)** | **0.5** | **1.00** | **0.80** | |
| Artichokes | 0.5 | 1.00 | 0.95 | 0.7 |
| Asparagus | 0.5 | 0.95[7] | 0.30 | 0.2-0.8 |
| Mint | 0.60 | 1.15 | 1.10 | 0.6-0.8 |
| Strawberries | 0.40 | 0.85 | 0.75 | 0.2 |
| **g. Fibre Crops** | **0.35** | | | |
| Cotton | | 1.15-1.20 | 0.70-0.50 | 1.2-1.5 |
| Flax | | 1.10 | 0.25 | 1.2 |
| Sisal [8] | | 0.4-0.7 | 0.4-0.7 | 1.5 |
| **h. Oil Crops** | **0.35** | **1.15** | **0.35** | |
| Castorbean (*Ricinus*) | | 1.15 | 0.55 | 0.3 |
| Rapeseed, Canola | | 1.0-1.15[9] | 0.35 | 0.6 |
| Safflower | | 1.0-1.15[9] | 0.25 | 0.8 |
| Sesame | | 1.10 | 0.25 | 1.0 |
| Sunflower | | 1.0-1.15[9] | 0.35 | 2.0 |
| **i. Cereals** | **0.3** | **1.15** | **0.4** | |
| Barley | | 1.15 | 0.25 | 1 |
| Oats | | 1.15 | 0.25 | 1 |
| Spring Wheat | | 1.15 | 0.25-0.4[10] | 1 |
| Winter Wheat | | | | |
| - with frozen soils | 0.4 | 1.15 | 0.25-0.4[10] | 1 |
| - with non-frozen soils | 0.7 | 1.15 | 0.25-0.4[10] | |
| Maize, Field (grain) (*field corn)* | | 1.20 | 0.60-0.35[11] | 2 |
| Maize, Sweet (*sweet corn*) | | 1.15 | 1.05[12] | 1.5 |
| Millet | | 1.00 | 0.30 | 1.5 |
| Sorghum | | | | |
| - grain | | 1.00-1.10 | 0.55 | 1-2 |

| | | | | |
|---|---|---|---|---|
| - sweet | | 1.20 | 1.05 | 2-4 |
| Rice | 1.05 | 1.20 | 0.90-0.60 | 1 |
| **j. Forages** | | | | |
| Alfalfa Hay | | | | |
| - averaged cutting effects | 0.40 | 0.95[13] | 0.90 | 0.7 |
| - individual cutting periods | 0.40[14] | 1.20[14] | 1.15[14] | 0.7 |
| - for seed | 0.40 | 0.50 | 0.50 | 0.7 |
| Bermuda hay | | | | |
| - averaged cutting effects | 0.55 | 1.00[13] | 0.85 | 0.35 |
| - Spring crop for seed | 0.35 | 0.90 | 0.65 | 0.4 |
| Clover hay, Berseem | | | | |
| - averaged cutting effects | 0.40 | 0.90[13] | 0.85 | 0.6 |
| - individual cutting periods | 0.40[14] | 1.15[14] | 1.10[14] | 0.6 |
| Rye Grass hay | | | | |
| - averaged cutting effects | 0.95 | 1.05 | 1.00 | 0.3 |
| Sudan Grass hay (annual) | | | | |
| - averaged cutting effects | 0.50 | 0.90[14] | 0.85 | 1.2 |
| - individual cutting periods | 0.50[14] | 1.15[14] | 1.10[14] | 1.2 |
| Grazing Pasture | | | | |
| - Rotated Grazing | 0.40 | 0.85-1.05 | 0.85 | 0.15-0.30 |
| - Extensive Grazing | 0.30 | 0.75 | 0.75 | 0.10 |
| Turf grass | | | | |
| - cool season [15] | 0.90 | 0.95 | 0.95 | 0.10 |
| - warm season [15] | 0.80 | 0.85 | 0.85 | 0.10 |
| **k. Sugar Cane** | **0.40** | **1.25** | **0.75** | **3** |
| **l. Tropical Fruits and Trees** | | | | |
| Banana | | | | |
| - 1st year | 0.50 | 1.10 | 1.00 | 3 |
| - 2nd year | 1.00 | 1.20 | 1.10 | 4 |

| | | | | |
|---|---|---|---|---|
| Cacao | 1.00 | 1.05 | 1.05 | 3 |
| Coffee | | | | |
| - bare ground cover | 0.90 | 0.95 | 0.95 | 2-3 |
| - with weeds | 1.05 | 1.10 | 1.10 | 2-3 |
| Date Palms | 0.90 | 0.95 | 0.95 | 8 |
| Palm Trees | 0.95 | 1.00 | 1.00 | 8 |
| Pineapple [16] | | | | |
| - bare soil | 0.50 | 0.30 | 0.30 | 0.6-1.2 |
| - with grass cover | 0.50 | 0.50 | 0.50 | 0.6-1.2 |
| Rubber Trees | 0.95 | 1.00 | 1.00 | 10 |
| Tea | | | | |
| - non-shaded | 0.95 | 1.00 | 1.00 | 1.5 |
| - shaded [17] | 1.10 | 1.15 | 1.15 | 2 |
| **m. Grapes and Berries** | | | | |
| Berries (bushes) | 0.30 | 1.05 | 0.50 | 1.5 |
| Grapes | | | | |
| - Table or Raisin | 0.30 | 0.85 | 0.45 | 2 |
| - Wine | 0.30 | 0.70 | 0.45 | 1.5-2 |
| Hops | 0.3 | 1.05 | 0.85 | 5 |
| **n. Fruit Trees** | | | | |
| Almonds, no ground cover | 0.40 | 0.90 | 0.65[18] | 5 |
| Apples, Cherries, Pears [19] | | | | |
| - no ground cover, killing frost | 0.45 | 0.95 | 0.70[18] | 4 |
| - no ground cover, no frosts | 0.60 | 0.95 | 0.75[18] | 4 |
| - active ground cover, killing frost | 0.50 | 1.20 | 0.95[18] | 4 |
| - active ground cover, no frosts | 0.80 | 1.20 | 0.85[18] | 4 |
| Apricots, Peaches, Stone Fruit [19, 20] | | | | |
| - no ground cover, killing frost | 0.45 | 0.90 | 0.65[18] | 3 |
| - no ground cover, no frosts | 0.55 | 0.90 | 0.65[18] | 3 |
| - active ground cover, killing frost | 0.50 | 1.15 | 0.90[18] | 3 |

| | | | | |
|---|---|---|---|---|
| - active ground cover, no frosts | 0.80 | 1.15 | 0.85[18] | 3 |
| Avocado, no ground cover | 0.60 | 0.85 | 0.75 | 3 |
| Citrus, no ground cover [21] | | | | |
| - 70% canopy | 0.70 | 0.65 | 0.70 | 4 |
| - 50% canopy | 0.65 | 0.60 | 0.65 | 3 |
| - 20% canopy | 0.50 | 0.45 | 0.55 | 2 |
| Citrus, with active ground cover or weeds [22] | | | | |
| - 70% canopy | 0.75 | 0.70 | 0.75 | 4 |
| - 50% canopy | 0.80 | 0.80 | 0.80 | 3 |
| - 20% canopy | 0.85 | 0.85 | 0.85 | 2 |
| Conifer Trees [23] | 1.00 | 1.00 | 1.00 | 10 |
| Kiwi | 0.40 | 1.05 | 1.05 | 3 |
| Olives (40 to 60% ground coverage by canopy) [24] | 0.65 | 0.70 | 0.70 | 3-5 |
| Pistachios, no ground cover | 0.40 | 1.10 | 0.45 | 3-5 |
| Walnut Orchard [19] | 0.50 | 1.10 | 0.6518 | 4-5 |
| **o. Wetlands - temperate climate** | | | | |
| Cattails, Bulrushes, killing frost | 0.30 | 1.20 | 0.30 | 2 |
| Cattails, Bulrushes, no frost | 0.60 | 1.20 | 0.60 | 2 |
| Short Veg., no frost | 1.05 | 1.10 | 1.10 | 0.3 |
| Reed Swamp, standing water | 1.00 | 1.20 | 1.00 | 1-3 |
| Reed Swamp, moist soil | 0.90 | 1.20 | 0.70 | 1-3 |
| **p. Special** | | | | |
| Open Water, < 2 m depth or in subhumid climates or tropics | | 1.05 | 1.05 | |
| Open Water, > 5 m depth, clear of turbidity, temperate climate | | 0.6525 | 1.2525 | |

*Note*: [1] These are general values for $K_{c\ ini}$ under typical irrigation management and soil wetting. For frequent wettings such as with high frequency sprinkle irrigation or daily rainfall, these values may increase substantially and may approach 1.0 to 1.2. $K_{c\ ini}$ is a function of wetting interval and potential evaporation rate during the initial and development periods and is more accurately estimated using Figures 29 and 30, or Equation 7-3 in Annex 7, or using the dual $K_{cb\ ini} + K_e$.

[2] Beans, Peas, Legumes, Tomatoes, Peppers and Cucumbers are sometimes grown on stalks reaching 1.5 to 2 meters in height. In such cases, increased $K_c$ values need to be taken. For green beans, peppers and cucumbers, 1.15 can be taken, and for tomatoes, dry beans and peas, 1.20. Under these conditions h should be increased also.

[3] The midseason values for cassava assume non-stressed conditions during or following the rainy season. The $K_{c\ end}$ values account for dormancy during the dry season.

[4] The $K_{c\ end}$ value for potatoes is about 0.40 for long season potatoes with vine kill.

[5] This $K_{c\ end}$ value is for no irrigation during the last month of the growing season. The $K_{c\ end}$ value for sugar beets is higher, up to 1.0, when irrigation or significant rain occurs during the last month.

[6] The first $K_{c\ end}$ is for harvested fresh. The second value is for harvested dry.

[7] The $K_c$ for asparagus usually remains at $K_{c\ ini}$ during harvest of the spears, due to sparse ground cover. The $K_{c\ mid}$ value is for following regrowth of plant vegetation following termination of harvest of spears.

[8] $K_c$ for sisal depends on the planting density and water management (e.g., intentional moisture stress).

[9] The lower values are for rainfed crops having less dense plant populations.

[10] The higher value is for hand-harvested crops.

[11] The first $K_{c\ end}$ value is for harvest at high grain moisture. The second $K_{c\ end}$ value is for harvest after complete field drying of the grain (to about 18% moisture, wet mass basis).

[12] If harvested fresh for human consumption. Use $K_{c\ end}$ for field maize if the sweet maize is allowed to mature and dry in the field.

[13] This $K_{c\ mid}$ coefficient for hay crops is an overall average $K_{c\ mid}$ coefficient that averages $K_c$ for both before and following

cuttings. It is applied to the period following the first development period until the beginning of the last late season period of the growing season.

[14] These $K_c$ coefficients for hay crops represent immediately following cutting; at full cover; and immediately before cutting, respectively. The growing season is described as a series of individual cutting periods (Figure 35).

[15] Cool season grass varieties include dense stands of bluegrass, ryegrass, and fescue. Warm season varieties include bermuda grass and St. Augustine grass. The 0.95 values for cool season grass represent a 0.06 to 0.08 m mowing height under general turf conditions. Where careful water management is practiced and rapid growth is not required, $K_c$'s for turf can be reduced by 0.10.

[16] The pineapple plant has very low transpiration because it closes its stomates during the day and opens them during the night. Therefore, the majority of $ET_c$ from pineapple is evaporation from the soil. The $K_{c\ mid} < K_{c\ ini}$ since $K_{c\ mid}$ occurs during full ground cover so that soil evaporation is less. Values given assume that 50 per cent of the ground surface is covered by black plastic mulch and that irrigation is by sprinkler. For drip irrigation beneath the plastic mulch, $K_c$'s given can be reduced by 0.10.

[17] Includes the water requirements of the shade trees.

[18] These $K_{c\ end}$ values represent $K_c$ prior to leaf drop. After leaf drop, $K_{c\ end}$ » 0.20 for bare, dry soil or dead ground cover and $K_{c\ end}$ » 0.50 to 0.80 for actively growing ground cover (consult Chapter 11).

[19] Refer to Eq. 94, 97 or 98 and footnotes 21 and 22 for estimating $K_c$ for immature stands.

[20] Stone fruit category applies to peaches, apricots, pears, plums and pecans.

[21] These $K_c$ values can be calculated from Eq. 98 for $K_{c\ min} = 0.15$ and $K_{c\ full} = 0.75$, 0.70 and 0.75 for the initial, mid season and end of season periods, and $f_{c\ eff} = f_c$ where $f_c$ = fraction of ground covered by tree canopy (e.g., the sun is presumed to be directly overhead). The values listed correspond with those in Doorenbos and Pruitt (1977) and with more recent measurements. The

midseason value is lower than initial and ending values due to the effects of stomatal closure during periods of peak ET. For humid and subhumid climates where there is less stomatal control by citrus, values for $K_{c\ ini}$, $K_{c\ mid}$, and $K_{c\ end}$ can be increased by 0.1 - 0.2, following Rogers et al. (1983).

[22] These $K_c$ values can be calculated as $K_c = f_c\ K_{c\ ngc} + (1 - f_c)\ K_{c\ cover}$ where $K_{c\ ngc}$ is the $K_c$ of citrus with no active ground cover (calculated as in footnote 21), $K_{c\ cover}$ is the $K_c$, for the active ground cover (0.95), and $f_c$ is defined in footnote 21. The values listed correspond with those in Doorenbos and Pruitt and with more recent measurements. Alternatively, $K_c$ for citrus with active ground cover can be estimated directly from Eq. 98 by setting $K_{c\ min} = K_{c\ cover}$. For humid and subhumid climates where there is less stomatal control by citrus, values for $K_{c\ ini}$, $K_{c\ mid}$, and $K_{c\ end}$ can be increased by 0.1 - 0.2, following Rogers et al.. For non-active or only moderately active ground cover (active indicates green and growing ground cover with LAI > about 2 to 3), $K_c$ should be weighted between $K_c$ for no ground cover and $K_c$ for active ground cover, with the weighting based on the 'greenness' and approximate leaf area of the ground cover.

[23] Confers exhibit substantial stomatal control due to reduced aerodynamic resistance. The $K_c$, can easily reduce below the values presented, which represent well-watered conditions for large forests

[24] These coefficients represent about 40 to 60 per cent ground cover. Refer to Eq. 98 and footnotes 21 and 22 for estimating $K_c$ for immature stands. In Spain, Pastor and Orgaz (1994) have found the following monthly $K_c$'s for olive orchards having 60 per cent ground cover: 0.50, 0.50, 0.65, 0.60, 0.55, 0.50, 0.45, 0.45, 0.55, 0.60, 0.65, 0.50 for months January through December. These coefficients can be invoked by using $K_{c\ ini} = 0.65$, $K_{c\ mid} = 0.45$, and $K_{c\ end} = 0.65$, with stage lengths = 30, 90, 60 and 90 days, respectively for initial, development, midseason and late season periods, and using $K_c$ during the winter ('off season') in December to February = 0.50.

[25] These $K_c$'s are for deep water in temperate latitudes where large temperature changes in the water body occur during the year, and initial and peak period evaporation is low as radiation

energy is absorbed into the deep water body. During fall and winter periods ($K_{c\ end}$), heat is released from the water body that increases the evaporation above that for grass. Therefore, $K_{c\ mid}$ corresponds to the period when the water body is gaining thermal energy and $K_{c\ end}$ when releasing thermal energy. These $K_c$'s should be used with caution.

The values for $K_{c\ mid}$ and $K_{c\ end}$ in Table 12 represent those for a sub-humid climate with an average daytime minimum relative humidity ($RH_{min}$) of about 45 per cent and with calm to moderate wind speeds averaging 2 m/s. For more humid or arid conditions, or for more or less windy conditions, the $K_c$ coefficients for the mid-season and end of late season stage should be modified as described in this chapter.

The values for $K_c$ in Table are values for non-stressed crops cultivated under excellent agronomic and water management conditions and achieving maximum crop yield (standard conditions). Where stand density, height or leaf area are less than that attained under such conditions, the value for $K_{c\ mid}$ and, for most crops, for $K_{c\ end}$ will need to be modified.

## CROP COEFFICIENT FOR THE INITIAL STAGE ($K_{C\ INI}$)

### Calculation Procedure

The values for $K_{c\ ini}$ in Table 9.3 are only approximations and should only be used for estimating $ET_c$ during preliminary or planning studies. For several group types only one value for $K_{c\ ini}$ is listed and it is considered to be representative of the whole group for a typical irrigation water management. More accurate estimates of $K_{c\ ini}$ can be obtained by considering:

#### *Time Interval between Wetting Events*

Evapotranspiration during the initial stage for annual crops is predominately in the form of evaporation. Therefore, accurate estimates for $K_{c\ ini}$ should consider the frequency with which the soil surface is wetted during the initial period. Where the soil is frequently wet from irrigation or rain, the evaporation from the soil surface can be considerable and $K_{c\ ini}$ will be large. On the other hand, where the soil surface is dry, evaporation is restricted and the $K_{c\ ini}$ will be small.

***Evaporation Power of the Atmosphere***

The value of $K_{c\ ini}$ is affected by the evaporating power of the atmosphere, i.e., $ET_o$. The higher the evaporation power of the atmosphere, the quicker the soil will dry between water applications and the smaller the time-averaged $K_c$ will be for any particular period.

***Magnitude of the Wetting Event***

As the amount of water available in the topsoil for evaporation and hence, the time for the soil surface to dry is a function of the magnitude of the wetting event, $K_{c\ ini}$ will be smaller for light wetting events than for large wettings.

Depending on the time interval between wetting events, the magnitude of the wetting event, and the evaporation power of the atmosphere, $K_{c\ ini}$ can vary between 0.1 and 1.15. A numerical procedure to compute $K_{c\ ini}$ is provided in Annex 7.

**Time Interval between Wetting Events**

In general, the mean time interval between wetting events is estimated by counting all rainfall and irrigation events occurring during the initial period that are greater than a few millimetres. Wetting events occurring on adjacent days can be counted as one event. The mean wetting interval is estimated by dividing the length of the initial period by the number of events.

Where only monthly rainfall values are available without any information on the number of rainy days, the number of events within the month can be estimated by dividing the monthly rainfall depth by the depth of a typical rain event. The typical depth, if it exists, can vary widely from climate to climate, region to region and from season to season. Table 9.4 presents some information on the range of rainfall depths. After deciding what rainfall is typical for the region and time of the year, the number of rainy days and the mean wetting interval can be estimated.

**Table. 9.4. Classification of Rainfall Depths**

| Rain Event | Depth |
|---|---|
| Very light (drizzle) | ≤ 3 mm |
| Light (light showers) | 5 mm |
| Medium (showers) | $^{3}$ 10 mm |
| Heavy (rainstorms) | $^{3}$ 40 mm |

Where rainfall is insufficient, irrigation is needed to keep the crop well watered. Even where irrigation is not yet developed, the mean interval between the future irrigations should be estimated to obtain the required frequency of wetting necessary to keep the crop stress free. The interval might be as small as a few days for small vegetables, but up to a week or longer for cereals depending on the climatic conditions. Where no estimate of the interval can be made, the user may refer to the values for $K_{c\ ini}$ of Table.

### Estimation of Interval between Wetting Events

Estimate, from mean monthly rainfall data, the interval between rains during the rainy season for a station in a temperate climate (Paris, France: 50 mm/month), dry climate (Gafsa, Tunisia: 20 mm/month) and tropical climate (Calcutta, India: 300 mm/month).

**Table. 9.5**

| Station | Monthly Rain (mm/month) | Typical Rainfall (mm) | Number of Rainy Days | Interval between Rains |
|---|---|---|---|---|
| Paris | 50 | 3 | 17 | ~ 2 days |
| Gafsa | 20 | 5 | 4 | weekly |
| Calcutta | 300 | 20 | 15 | ~ 2 days |

### Determination of $K_{c\ ini}$

The crop coefficient for the initial growth stage can be derived from Figures which provide estimates for $K_{c\ ini}$ as a function of the average interval between wetting events, the evaporation power $ET_o$, and the importance of the wetting event.

*Light wetting events (infiltration depths of 10 mm or less): rainfall and high frequency irrigation systems*

Figure is used for all soil types when wetting events are light. When wetting during the initial period is only by precipitation, one will usually use Figure to determine $K_{c\ ini}$. The graph can also be used when irrigation is by high frequency systems such as microirrigation and centre pivot and light applications of about 10 mm or less per wetting event are applied.

## Graphical Determination of $K_{c\ ini}$

A silt loam soil receives irrigation every two days during the initial growth stage via a centre pivot irrigation system. The average depth applied by the centre pivot system is about 12 mm per event and the average $ET_o$ during the initial stage is 4 mm/day. Estimate the crop evapotranspiration during that stage.

From Figure using the 2-day interval curve:

$K_{c\ ini}$ = 0.85 -

$ET_c = K_c\ ET_o$ = 0.85 (4.0) = 3.4 mm/day

The average crop evapotranspiration during the initial growth stage is 3.4 mm/day.

Heavy wetting events (infiltration depths of 40 mm or more): surface and sprinkler irrigation.

Figure 9.8 is used for heavy wetting events when infiltration depths are greater than 40 mm, such as for when wetting is primarily by periodic irrigation such as by sprinkler or surface irrigation. Following a wetting event, the amount of water available in the topsoil for evaporation is considerable, and the time for the soil surface to dry might be significantly increased.

Consequently, the average $K_c$ factor is larger than for light wetting events. As the time for the soil surface to dry is, apart from the evaporation power and the frequency of wetting, also determined by the water storage capacity of the topsoil, a distinction is made between soil types.

Figure 9.9 is used for coarse textured soils and Figure 9.10 is used for fine and medium textured soils. Coarse textured soils include sands and loamy sand textured soils. Medium textured soils include sandy loam, loam, silt loam and silt textured soils. Pine textured soils include silty clay loam, silty clay and clay textured soils.

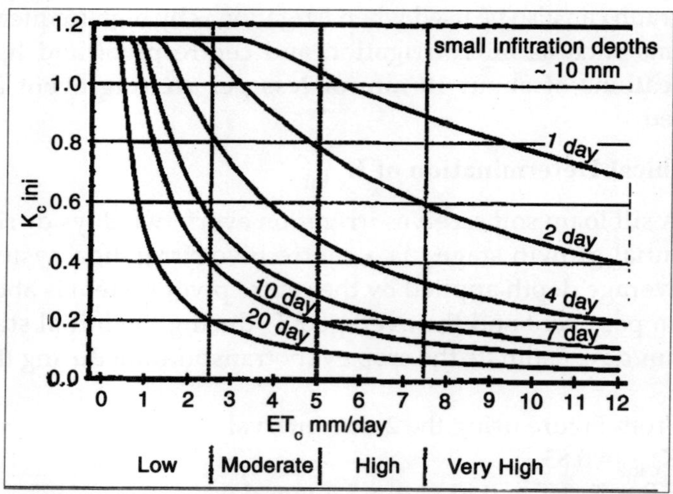


**Fig. 9.8. Average $K_{c\ ini}$ as Related to the Level of ETo and the Interval between Irrigations and/or Significant Rain During the Initial Growth Stage for All Soil Types when Wetting Events are Light to Medium (3-10 mm Per Event)**

Average wetting events (infiltration depths between 10 and 40 mm):

Where average infiltration depths are between 10 and 40 mm, the value for Kc ini can be estimated from Figure 9.10.

$$K_{cini} = K_{cini}(Fig) + \frac{(1-10)}{(40-10)}\left[K_{cin}(Fig) - K_{cini}(Fig)\right]$$

where

$K_{c\ ini}$ value for $K_{c\ ini}$ from Figure,
$K_{c\ ini}$ value for $K_{c\ ini}$ from Figure ,
I average infiltration depth [mm].

The values 10 and 40 in Equation are the average depths of infiltration (millimetres) upon which Figures based.

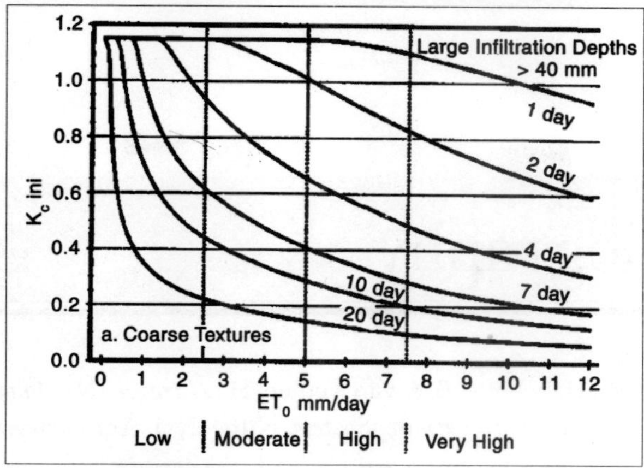


**Fig. 9.9. Average $K_{c\ ini}$ as Related to the Level of ETo and the Interval between Irrigations Greater than or Equal to 40 mm Per Wetting Event, During the Initial Growth Stage for Coarse Textured Soils**

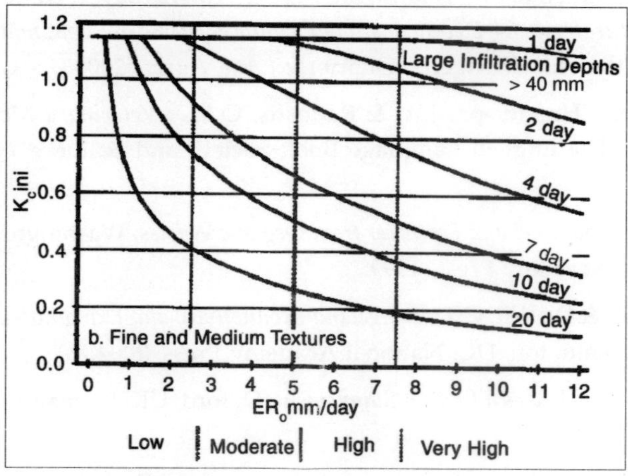


Fig. 9.10

Example. Interpolation between light and heavy wetting events.

Small vegetables cultivated in a dry area on a coarse textured soil receive 20 mm of water twice a week by means of a sprinkler irrigation system. The average ETo during the initial stage is 5 mm/day. Estimate the crop evapotranspiration during that stage.

# Bibliography


Aarts, H.F.M., Habekotte, B. & van Keulen, H.: *Nitrogen (N) Management in the 'De Marke' Dairy Farming System*, Nutr. Cycl. Agroecosyst, 2000.

Andreson, N. *The Foraging Pig. Resource Utilisation, Interaction, Performance and Behaviour of Pigs in Cropping Systems*, Sweden: Swedish University of Agricultural Sciences, Uppsala, 2000.

Bayer, W., Sulieman, R., Kaufmann, R.V. & Waters- Bayer, A.: *Resource Use and Strategies for Development of Pastoral Systems in Subhumid*, West Africa - the case of Nigeria: Quarterly J. Int. Agric., 2000.

Blood, D.C., Henderson, J.A. & Radostis, O.M. : *Veterinary Medicine*, London: The English Language Book Society and Bailliere Tindall, 2001.

BOSTID.: *Food, Fuel and Fertilizer from Organic Wastes*, Washington, DC: National Academy Press, 1999.

Breman, H. & De Wit, C.T.: *Rangeland Productivity and Exploitation in the Sahel*. Washington, DC: National Academy Press, 2004.

Briggs, M.H.: *Urea as a Protein Supplement*, Oxford, UK: Permagon Press, 2002.

Campbell, C.A.: *In* A. Budelman, *Agricultural R&D at the Crossroads: Merging Systems Research and Social Actor Approaches*, Amsterdam: Royal Tropical Institute, 1998.

Centro Mesoamericano de Estudios sobre Tecnología Apropiada (CEMAT).: *Memorias, Primer Seminario-taller Nacional Sobre Letrinas Aboneras Secas Familiares*, Oxford, UK: Permagon Press, 2002.

Chen, H.: *Integrated Systems of Animal Production in the Asian Region*, Animal Science Congress, Chiba, Japan: AAAP and FAO, Rome, 1999.

CIRAN/NUFFIC.: *Indigenous Knowledge and Development Monitor,* (CIRAN/NUFFIC), Netherlands: The Netherlands Press, 2001.

Conway, G.R. & Barbier, E.B.: *After the Green Revolution, Sustainable Agriculture for Development,* London, Earthscan Publications, 2003.

Coppock, D.L., Ellis, J.E. & Swift, D.M.: *Livestock Feeding Ecology and Resource Utilization in a Nomadic Pastoral Ecosystem,* Oxford, UK: Permagon Press, 2002.

Crotty, R.: *Cattle, Economics and Development,* UK: Commonwealth Agricultural Bureaux, 2003.

Defoer, T., Budelman, A., Toulmin, C. & Carter, S.E.: *Building Common Knowledge: Participatory Learning and Action Research,* Royal Tropical Institute: Amsterdam, 2003.

De Haan, C., Steinfeld, H. & Blackburn, H.: *Livestock and the Environment: Finding a Balance,* Fressingfield, Eye, Suffolk, UK, WREN Media, 2003.

De Jong, R.: *Dairy Stock Development and Milk Production with Smallholders,* Netherlands: Wageningen Agricultural University, 2004.

Dembele, I., Kone, D., Soumare, A., Coulibaly, D., Kone, Y., Ly, B. & Kater, L.: *Fallows and Field Systems in Dryland Mali*: London, IIED Press, 2004.

# Index

## F



## G



## H



## I



## K



## L



## M



## P



## R



## S



## T



## W